About Writing

A Rhetoric for Advanced Writers

Kristin R. Woolever
Northeastern University

Wadsworth Publishing Company
Belmont, California
A Division of Wadsworth, Inc.

English Editor: Angela Gantner
Editorial Assistant: Julie Johnson
Production Editor: Angela Mann
Print Buyer: Barbara Britton
Permissions Editor: Jeanne Bosschart
Designer: Kaelin Chappell
Copy Editor: Melissa Andrews
Technical Illustrator: G&S Typesetters, Inc.
Compositor: G&S Typesetters, Inc.
Cover: Bay Graphics Design, Inc.
Signing Representative: John Moroney

Printed in the United States of America   49

2 3 4 5 6 7 8 9 10—95 94 93 92 91

Library of Congress Cataloging-in-Publication Data

Woolever, Kristin R.
About writing : a rhetoric for advanced writers / Kristin R. Woolever.
    p.   cm.
Includes index.
ISBN 0-534-14640-6
    1. Authorship.   2. English language—Rhetoric.   I. Title.
PN145.W56   1991   90-43213
808'.042—dc20

Contents

Preface

Writing is a deeply personal process, full of mystery and surprise. No two people go about it in exactly the same way. We all have little devices to get us started, or to keep us going, or to remind us of what we think we want to say, and what works for one person may not work for anyone else. The main thing is to get something written—to get the words out of our heads. There is no "right" method. Any method that will do the job is the right method for you.

It helps to remember that writing is hard. Most nonwriters don't know this; they think that writing is a natural function, like breathing, that ought to come easy, and they're puzzled when it doesn't. If you find that writing is hard, it's because it *is* hard. It's one of the hardest things that people do.

—*William Zinsser, "The Act of Writing: One Man's Method"*

All communication has the potential for mystery and surprise, no matter whether the communication is oral, written, or even non-verbal. But the process of writing seems to be the most mysterious of all, especially to the writers themselves. It is often terrifying to face a blank sheet of paper or a blank computer screen and wonder how you can fill it with words that will express the right meaning. When this happens, some writers develop private incantations or rituals they perform to encourage inspiration; some writers search for writing formulas they can depend on to guide them through the process; and some plunge directly into composing, having faith that whatever they put on the page will eventually turn out well.

When people sit down to write, they struggle as much with these psychological concerns as they do with grammar and mechanics, sometimes even more so. This book begins with sympathy for those concerns and with the premise that writing is intensely psychological and should be represented as such from the outset. Before beginning the writing task, the writer should understand that the art of writing creates a delicate set of relationships: between the writer and the reader, between the meaning intended and the meaning expressed, and even between the writer's impatience and the patience needed to write well. These relationships all need to be kept balanced and tended as you write, which is no easy task. As William Zinsser says, writing is not as easy as breathing; it *is* hard. But understanding the nature of the composing process, from the initial stages to the finished product, makes writing easier. And knowing that there is no one absolutely right way to think about writing or to go about writing relieves some of the tension.

Writing is a creative act that can be easily stifled when the writer is force-fed absolute forms and modes for composing. Nonetheless, writers need to be aware of the many options available to them, and it sometimes helps to know how other writers have solved similar problems and what tools they have used successfully to craft their prose. As you read this text, you will find examples from writers in many circumstances, all wrestling with the same problems and needing advice about the nature of writing. Academic writers, engineers, lawyers, journalists, scientists, and many others find themselves in the same uncomfortable situation: sitting in front of that blank page trying to think of what to say. This book is designed to help anyone who has suffered similar difficulty. It does not suggest that one method alone is the "right" way to get words down on paper, but it does offer practical tips to make writing easier.

Another assumption underlying these chapters is that writing is not limited to the expository essay. Many textbooks and writing classes deal primarily with the essay form, although that form is only remotely related to most of the writing people do in their daily lives. Writing is communication—from everyday prose to the sophisticated essay—and the fears and frustrations writers experience as they try to express themselves are not unique to any one kind of discourse. Instead of concentrating on particular prose forms or particular disciplines, *About Writing: A Rhetoric for Advanced Writers* explores the common concerns all writers share:

- how to approach the writing task
- how to find something to say
- how to organize
- how to find the right voice
- how to revise effectively
- how to have more confidence in what you say
- how to know if your writing works

As this list suggests, *About Writing* focuses on writing as process, from invention to final revisions, but unlike many writer's guides, this one does not throw novices into the water and hope they learn how to swim. Instead, it discusses the possible methods writers can use and explains when they work and when they do not. Also unlike many process-oriented texts, this book does not require you to read it all the way through before beginning to write. Each chapter has specific writing suggestions and encourages writers to test various techniques by collaborating in writing groups.

By the time you finish the book, many of these techniques will be a permanent part of your writing tool kit, and you will be well equipped to handle even the most difficult writing assignments. Then the mysteries and surprises you encounter as you write may be welcome challenges, not insurmountable obstacles.

Acknowledgments

Like every other writer, I am indebted to more people than I can hope to thank for making this book a reality. The following people deserve special acknowledgment:

Douglas Atkins, University of Kansas; John Boe, University of California, Davis; Paula R. Buck, Florida Southern College; Christine Hult, Utah State University; Kate Kiefer, Colorado State University; Laura Knight, Mercer County Community College; L. Bensel Meyers, University of Tennessee; Walter S. Minot, Gannon University; Marie Nelson, University of Florida; Randall Popken, Tarleton University; John Price, California State University, Sacramento; Duane H. Roen, University of Arizona; Jeanne Simpson, Eastern Illinois University; Bill Smith, Virginia Commonwealth University; and William B. Stone, Indiana University Northwest, who reviewed drafts of this manuscript and provided valuable advice.

Thanks, too, to Steve Rutter, Angie Gantner, Angela Mann, and all the fine people at Wadsworth who worked on this project.

And finally, a very special thank-you to Chris Shipley and Molly, who understand that writing is hard and yet were still willing to put up with me during the process.

Chapter 1

The Writing Process

Perfect prose rarely, if ever, leaps fully formed from the author's head onto the page, ready for publication. In the process of composing, even the best writers struggle through a series of steps that often seem interminable and frustrating. The difference between novice writers and experienced ones is the realization that these frustrations are part of the writing process. Inevitably, words seem to slip and slide around on the page, refusing to behave, as you patiently work to corral them into effective prose. Writing well takes patience and a willingness to move forward and backward through the composing stages, crafting and recrafting the prose.

The Stages of Writing

The following stages are common to most writers and writing tasks. Understanding these stages will alert you to the length of the writing process and the patience required to produce effective prose.

Evaluating the Rhetorical Situation

One of the first things writers should do is to step back and look at the basic elements that play a part in the particular rhetorical (communication) situation they face. The writer begins by examining the writing task. What *is* the task? What purpose will the piece of writing serve? Who is the audience? What do readers need to know? What "voice" (or prose personality) will best communicate to that audience? In other words, this stage is an exploration of the known quantities. If writers can identify clearly these specific components before they begin to write, they can build the rest of the text on a definite foundation. It is a good idea to write down answers to some of these questions. Listing these "knowns" is also a good way to overcome the initial nervousness everyone has about starting to write. This is writing to get warmed up to write.

Invention Strategies

Once writers have determined the rhetorical situation, they turn their attention to the creative possibilities. There are no tricks to make this stage easy. Too many ideas may come flooding into your mind all at once, or perhaps you won't be able to think of a good idea when you need one. Since classical times and probably before, rhetoricians have considered this stage the most difficult in the composing process. They have, however, developed various heuristics (strategies for developing ideas) to inspire their creative muses. Instead of depending on flashes of inspiration, most writers carefully and systematically mine the many possibilities, making sure that they consider all related ideas before finally settling on the best ones.

Writing from Sources

All ideas, of course, do not have to come directly out of your own head. They can come to you from what you read and what you listen to. Writers doing research collect a lot of information from a variety of sources. How should they evaluate these sources? And once they have determined their value, how do they effectively incorporate these sources into the prose? Is it possible to research something fully and then write about it with original thoughts? How do writers document the sources they choose to include?

These and other research-related questions create problems for many writers as they track down sources and attempt to integrate them into the text. For many writers who do extensive research, the problem becomes one of using the sources properly and not allowing the external authorities to overshadow the writer's voice.

Arrangement

In simple terms, arrangement means organizing. Writers put the ideas they have generated and garnered from their reading and listening experience into an order that will best communicate to the audience. The problem here is again one of choice. Different organizations produce vastly different effects on the audience. The question is what effect you want. Attorneys who want to prove a client innocent put their facts together in an order that will lead their audience, a judge and jury, to believe that the client is indeed innocent. Medical research specialists who want to inform people about their latest findings decide how much they have to tell and what order of telling will lead to a reader's understanding. For the research to become meaningful, the researcher has to make well-thought-out decisions about what comes first, what comes next, and what comes last.

Beginnings, Middles, and Endings

Having decided what must be said in what order, the writer can turn from large-scale organization to arranging the paragraphs that make up the text itself. During this part of the process, the primary ideas become more and more defined as the writer organizes them within the larger pattern of the overall text. Instead of worrying about the direction of the whole paper, writers focus now on honing the subsections into well-crafted parts that fit together perfectly. By this time in the writing process, most writers have confidence in the major design of the text and are working on the finer details, such as sequences of paragraphs. In this stage, the writer shapes each part so that it accomplishes a purpose in the overall scheme of the paper.

Issues of Voice and Style

After they know what they want to say and in what order they want to say it, writers then need to focus on the way their words sound. At this point, they should be concerned with sentence rhythms and the sound of words. Sensitive writers pay attention to these things all the way through the composing process, but it is a good idea at this stage to review the prose with a specific intention to *listen* to it.

Read the text aloud—even professional documents—to hear the prose voice. Does it communicate, or is it a tangle of abstract, dense terms comprehensible only to the writer? If you need to, rearrange sentence lengths and structures and change words. The mark of an excellent writer is the willingness to hear the words and fine-tune them so that they communicate clearly and gracefully.

Revising

If your writing looks messy during its early stages, if it has words and sentences crossed out and others written in, that is probably a good sign. Writing is a recursive process, meaning that writers constantly circle back through the various writing stages, discovering new ideas and revising their work continually. Nonetheless, you should allow enough time at the end for substantial revision. Put the completed text aside for at least twenty-four hours if possible and then return to it with fresh eyes. Taking these "revision breaks" will cut your total working time significantly. Otherwise, you may reach the end of the text and realize that you need to do a major overhaul but are too tired and have too little time left to do it. Of course, this process depends on planning ahead and not procrastinating until the last minute. In spite of many people's claims that they write best under deadline pressure, last-minute prose is often substandard and rarely more than adequate. If you feel that you can only write under deadline pressure, give yourself an early deadline, and then take time to revise before the final deadline.

Proofreading

Proofreading the text to check for mechanical errors is the last stage in the writing process. Unfortunately, this last step comes at a time when most writers are tired and feel that they are already finished with the writing task. They must, however, make the extra effort to perfect their composition. Readers base their opinion on the finished product rather than on the composing effort. If the product they read is sloppy, this will undermine the writer's ideas, regardless of the time and care spent on the writing. Make time to proof your writing and to have someone else proof it as well. Then the product will not only look professional but will actually reflect your careful process.

PRACTICE EXERCISE 1·1

Write a brief (two to three pages) essay answering this question: What was the most significant learning experience in your life? As you write, keep a journal of the writing stages you move through as you work on this project. Include information on both your emotional state and your actual writing process.

When you have finished the essay and the journal entries, re-read pages 1–4 to compare your own experience with the general model. Which stages were easiest for you? Which were hardest? Did you find you repeated some of the steps as you went along? Do you think you should add any stages?

The second part of this exercise is intended to help you get in touch with your own creative process. Writing requires a delicate balance between discovering ideas and expressing them to others, a balance between attention to your own creative process and attention to the reader. In the early stages of writing it is important to focus on your creative process.

Writing as Discovery

When writers begin composing, their first attempts are usually the "discovery" part of the process, where the focus is definitely inward, not outward. Even though you may have taken all the preliminary steps of evaluating the rhetorical situation and determining generally what you want to say, the act of putting words on paper forces you to commit to specific ideas and organizing principles. You may discover that the direction in which you thought you wanted to go is not the best direction at all. Therefore, your first few pages—or even the entire first draft—are a type of throat clearing, an attempt to gather your thoughts into a coherent pattern before you communicate. During this part of the writing process, the focus is primarily turned inward on you as writer: what *you* think and how *you* feel about the subject. Full attention to your audience comes later.

There are several kinds of discovery processes. When you write, you may begin to understand more about how ideas relate to each other. Noting these relationships may cause you to see connections you had not recognized or had not thought important before. Another kind of discovery occurs when you revise your attitude about a subject in the process of writing about it. Perhaps you took the material for granted prior to looking at it more closely. Or perhaps the act of writing reaffirmed your viewpoint, increasing your confidence in what you have to say.

No matter how experienced you are in the art of writing, you can expect to make at least one "discovery" in these early composing stages. Do not be dismayed if this discovery causes a change in writing plans. Remember that the discovery process allows you to explore possibilities. At this stage of writing, the focus is on exploration of your thoughts and ideas.

False starts are the rule at the discovery stage. Most writers begin a draft, scratch out the first sentence at least twice, write a few paragraphs, scratch them out, and so on. Regardless of the type of writing you are doing, composing those initial paragraphs forces you to discover what you really mean to say and how to say it clearly. The following paragraphs illustrate how writers struggle in the "discovery draft" to bring the meaning into focus. These are the first lines written by a group of university faculty asked to write about their most significant learning or teaching experience. Notice how the paragraphs lack polish and give the sense of searching for the right words.

1. *A math professor writes:*

   "A student of mine got an 'F.' He then showed up and asked me to give him a chance to change his grade. I firmly said 'No,' because it would have been unfair to other students to whom I would not give such a chance. He persisted. He told me that he had special circumstances. That he was sick. That he had a death in his family. That he had a car accident."

2. *An engineering professor writes:*

   "My classroom presentations are typical of those in many engineering classes. Large expanses of blackboard are covered not only by an outline summarizing the fundamentals, but by sketches intended to convey important information for illustrative problems. Examinations are typed but they also utilize figures to convey essential data."

3. *A history professor writes:*

   "You ask me whether I am enjoying teaching after being a learner all my life, and I've been reflecting on what teaching is. From my own experience, what has been most mind-expanding and exhilarating has been finding 'connections.' Just as in life experience it has been gratifying to see *outcomes,* and patterns which have made meaningful the events and impressions of the past. Academia has—even if only now and then—offered the intellectual pleasure of finding overlaps and areas where the boundaries merge between fields of knowledge. As a nonscientist, it has been most exciting for me to read or hear about new research which jolts my memories of undergraduate physics and earth science, for example, and presents a beautiful, if still dim, picture of common cosmic forces which I labored over as taxonomic tables and equations."

As these paragraphs illustrate, the writers are not yet clear about what they mean to communicate. In the first example, the story is interesting enough, but it has no apparent point. This is also true for the second example. These beginning drafts are typical of what happens when writers first tackle a subject. The text begins wherever the writer's thoughts take hold, with no attention to readers' needs. Although each of these writers has a general idea of what to say, they must now focus their thoughts better to communicate them to an audience.

In the third example, the author begins much too generally and seems to switch the focus in the last few sentences from "connections" in teaching to dim memories of the past. This paragraph, more so than the other two, resembles a kind of "freewriting" the writer is using to find a subject and a voice. It is hard to grasp the major emphasis here or to understand where she is going with these ideas. Why is it important to mention that she is a nonscientist, for instance, and what are the "common cosmic forces"? This paragraph shows what happens when the relationships among the ideas are unclear, which is especially ironic in a piece about connections.

The second drafts of these paragraphs reflect a clearer concept of what each writer has discovered in those first false starts. These versions show more of a focus and suggest that the authors have more control of the subject. Note that in each case the writers begin with a context statement that cues the reader about the paragraph's main focus. Once the writers have discovered their principle ideas, they become confident enough to indicate them right away.

1. *The math professor writes:*
   "I don't know whether this story shows me from my good side or from my bad side, and I don't even know whether I learned a lesson from it. But I have no doubt that this is the most significant teaching/learning experience of my life.

   I gave one of my students an 'F' on the final exam. He showed up the next day and asked me to give him a chance to change his grade. I firmly said 'No,' because it would have been unfair to the other students. But he persisted and told me that he had special circumstances. That he was sick. That he had a death in the family. That he had a car accident. I still said 'No.' I was not exactly a novice at this game. By that time I had been at the university three years and had heard all these excuses before. I said 'No.' That night I got a phone call at home. . . ."

2. *The engineering professor writes:*

"My most significant teaching experience began the day a blind graduate student appeared in my graduate engineering course. Jane was doomed to failure. My classroom presentations were typical of those in many engineering classes. Large expanses of blackboard were covered, not only by an outline summarizing the fundamentals, but by sketches intended to convey important information for illustrative problems. Examinations were typed but also included figures for essential data. How could Jane hope to compete?"

3. *The history professor writes:*

"When I think about what's significant in my teaching experience—what I really *enjoy* about it—I realize that I've been more of learner than a teacher. True, I teach history which, according to students, is the most amorphous catch-all of information without even a basic theory they can learn to apply to particular sets of circumstances. But there's the challenge. And it's exciting for me to share with them all I'm learning about 'connections,' the patterns which have made meaningful the events and impressions of the past. Academia has—even if only now and then—offered the intellectual pleasure of finding overlaps and areas where the boundaries merge between fields of knowledge."

As these examples point out, writers use the first draft to explore ideas and to experiment with various methods of expressing them. Most writers have not thought through their ideas completely when they begin to write, and the discovery process may take several pages or drafts before the main point becomes clear even to the author. For many people, committing ideas to print is a risky business because they worry that the written ideas are open for attack. As a result of this fear, writers often spend the first page or two of the draft hiding behind a lot of introductory and often irrelevant material. Experienced writers realize that these explorations inevitably bog down the beginning of the writing process, and they allow enough time to sift through these preliminary meanderings, separating the irrelevant ideas from the relevant ones. These "discovery" pages should be edited out of the final version; the reader has no need to witness the writer's focusing process.

When writers are so rushed for time that they don't allow a discovery draft, the final product may be unfocused. For example, this section of a legal memorandum is little more than a full paragraph of throat clearning. The attorney who wrote the paragraph did not develop important points but rather strung together a series of "prefab" phrases. Unfortunately, this paragraph slipped through to the final version because the writer was too rushed to revise or even think about the words she was writing.

> One of the most unfortunate developments of the last decade has been the steady increase in the number of people who have no home. Providing shelter and other basic necessities for this steadily increasing population has become a substantial drain on state resources, particularly since during the same time period federal funding for programs to aid the indigent has markedly declined. Two of the few programs that have escaped major federal cut backs are Social Security and SSI benefits. Roughly one third of the estimated homeless have a history of hospitalization for a mental illness. Another roughly one third have histories of drug or alcohol abuse. Most of these individuals have no cash income other than Home Relief, which is funded totally by the state.

What is this paragraph about? The homeless? The state's responsibility? Statistics? Does it develop a point clearly? The information contained in this paragraph could have been written crisply and with more focus. With empty phrases such as "one of the most unfortunate developments of the last decade," the unthinking repetition of "steadily increasing," and the numerous extra words ("of the few," "markedly," "particularly since during"), the paragraph makes no impact at all, nor does the writer seem to have any conviction about the ideas. Further evidence of this lack of attention to the prose is the mid-paragraph change of subject. With the sentence beginning "Roughly one third . . ." the attorney changes the subject without warning and moves in an entirely new direction, leaving the reader lost somewhere between federal cutbacks and mental illness. As this example illustrates, it is essential for writers to focus on their own thoughts before they attempt to communicate them.

PRACTICE EXERCISE 1·2

Writers use a variety of techniques to aid in the discovery of ideas. One such technique is "freewriting." In a freewriting exercise, the writer sets a short time limit and writes continuously without editing until the time is up. This practice eliminates the critical editorial eye, thereby permitting ideas to flow more freely and in nonprescribed directions.

For this exercise, try your hand at freewriting to help you find something meaningful to say about a topic. (You decide on the topic, or use this exercise as a heuristic to get started in an assigned writing project.)

- Write continuously on the topic for five minutes, never lifting your pen or pencil from the paper or stopping to think. If you are using a keyboard, keep typing no matter how many errors you make. If you can't write complete sentences, use fragments or phrases.

If done well, this technique should help you find a focus for your thoughts, or, at the least, it should spark a lot of new ideas on the topic.

Writing as Problem Solving

Although discovery helps writers to focus on what they want to say, writing usually has a greater purpose than that. In writing done for business and industry, writers attempt to communicate solutions to problems. How much will it cost to remove the hazardous waste? Why should this project receive an NSF grant? Is the plaintiff entitled to summary judgment? Other types of writing are equally concerned with problem solving. The function of critical analyses in any discipline is to suggest plausible solutions to the problems in question. What is the nature of Greek comedy? What are the probabilities for a recession? Who is a better basketball player, Larry Bird or Magic Johnson?

Just as the discovery process has several parts, so does the problem-solving aspect of writing. In fact, the discovery draft's exploration of possibilities is an essential part of the search for a solution: such preliminary writing clarifies thinking about any subject. Once the writers have begun to focus their thoughts, they are on their way to effective, even persuasive, communication. The concern now becomes how to write about the subject so that the reader comes away with an *understanding* of the writer's perspective and sees the justification of the opinion. The attention shifts from the writer's viewpoint to that of the audience.

After being so immersed in the discovery stage, you may find that shifting gears in this way is hard to do. Discovering ideas may take so much effort that by the time you have determined what you are going to say and are ready to write, you are exhausted. Getting your own thoughts in order, however, is just the important beginning. Even though you are so closely involved with your subject, it is a mistake to assume that your audience will share that involvement. After you spend so much time clarifying ideas in your own mind, it may seem redundant to repeat the process in writing for an audience. Many writers put off this task until the last minute and then stay up all night writing. The finished product—which may seem inspired at 3:00 A.M.—may say what you intended to say but may not say it so that your reader, who, after all, was not in on the creative process, can understand it.

In any writing situation, relegating the actual writing to a last-minute activity is a common problem. For instance, an engineer may spend a month collecting data and evaluating the results but relegate writing the field report to the last minute. As long as all the pertinent information is in the report, the quality of the writing may seem secondary. Similarly, an attorney who has lived in the library researching cases may allow little time to write the legal brief presenting the results of her research. If the legal analysis is sound, why worry about its written presentation?

Mature writers realize that the expression of meaning is as important as the meaning itself. Therefore, once you know what you want to say, regard the writing itself as a second stage in problem solving. When readers read something to find an answer to a problem (What are the best options for removing the hazardous waste? Who is the better basketball player, Bird or Johnson?), they also want the answer to be stated clearly. The writing task is as much a form of problem solving as the analysis you do prior to writing. They demand equal attention. The problem-solving aspect of writing involves the following steps:

1. Determine what you want to say.
2. Use your expertise in writing to communicate your point.

The best way to show the need for integrating these levels of problem solving is to use an actual writing task from the professional world. The following letter, written by an engineer, does a poor job of communicating to the intended audience. It is a long letter and contains precise technical information obtained from the engineer's professional analysis of the situation. Although he has solved the engineering problem (the "content problem"), the writer has not organized his letter so that the solution is clearly and efficiently communicated. As a result, the town council may waste a lot of valuable time trying to decipher what Peter Olsen meant to say. Read the document and think about better ways to solve this writing problem.

February 4, 1991

Mr. Paul Smith, Chairman
Town Council
Town Hall
Carver, PA 01234

Dear Mr. Smith:

As a result of your request, the Kirby Company has analyzed a series of interim modifications to the West Grand Avenue Pump Station that would increase its flow potential. Thirteen options were reviewed but, in general, they are minor modifications to four options. These are:

1. Modifications of an existing pump and associated piping.

2. Replacement of an existing pump with a larger unit.

3. Installation of a booster pump in an ancillary structure.

4. Construction of a supplemental force main.

Cost estimates of three of the thirteen options were completed to indicate the magnitude of costs for the options. These three options varied in cost from $25,000 to $135,000 and the increase in pump station capacity ranged from 24 to 77 percent.

The Kirby Company met with the treatment plant staff, the Town Manager, and the Council Chairman to present the options and their associated costs. All options were reviewed in detail with the following considerations: (1) the increased station capacity; (2) the construction cost; and (3) the equipment and modifications that would be usable under the improvements that have been deferred temporarily.

The option of replacing one of the existing pumps with a new, larger pump was chosen, and the Kirby Company was directed by the town to perform the detailed design for the modifications to the West Grand Avenue Pump Station. This design will incorporate a series of internal piping modifications and will include variable speed pump operation. The need to have this capacity in place by the end of the year has been stressed. This option will increase the pump station capacity by approximately 77 percent and yields a peaking factor of about 2.0 for the average daily flow estimated in the 1989 report.

The Kirby Company was also requested to review the capabilities of the Main Street Extension Pump Station, assuming the construction of an 18-inch diameter force main. A review of the system hydraulics indicates that the capacity of the Main Street

Extension Pump Station will double with both of the existing pumps operating at high speed. This capacity increase provides a 3.0 peaking factor for the average daily flow estimated in the 1984 report.

With construction of the new force main and the West Grand Avenue Pump Station, the surges within the town's sewer system noted at present should be relieved. The pump station modifications recommended in the 1989 system study previously designed that have been deferred temporarily must be constructed at some point in the future. These modifications are necessary to provide additional flow capacity, but more important, the existing pump stations should be upgraded to provide better control, operation, and monitoring of these pump stations.

Should questions arise on review of this information or if additional details are desired, please contact me at 1-800-629-2121.

Sincerely,

The Kirby Company
Peter Olsen
Project Engineer

Although Olsen has used his expertise to solve the engineering problem, he has not sufficiently analyzed the writing problem. One of the major weaknesses of this letter is that Olsen is not always mindful that the reader is primarily looking for an answer. In this instance, the town council primarily wants to know whether the interim modifications on their pump station are sufficient. Note that Olsen has buried that point near the end of the letter, making it seem almost unimportant. The cardinal rule of writing as problem solving is to define the problem clearly and then state the solution in clear terms. In many instances, it is even a good idea to organize deductively by giving the answer first and then specifying the method for reaching that conclusion. But no matter how you decide to organize your material, it is essential to remember that the reader wants a definite answer to a specific problem. If you lose sight of that problem or fail to guide the reader logically to the conclusion, you have not done your job. In fact, you have probably added to the reader's confusion.

PRACTICE EXERCISE 1·3

Reread Olsen's letter. What does he need to do to solve the writing problem and make the text better express his professional evaluation of the town's dilemma?

1. Make a list of the things the audience needs to know. Put the list in priority order as you think the town council would want them.

2. Make a list of what Olsen needs to do. What things has he left out? What things should be in a different order? What things should be deemphasized?

3. Revise the letter so that it communicates well.

Writing to communicate precise opinions or information means that you need to pay special attention to organization, to format, and to the other techniques that enable the reader to grasp the meaning quickly and firmly. You have to be aware of all the aspects of the specific problem and the context in which it must be solved. Further, you need to investigate a variety of possible solutions and then explain why yours is the best one. Style, organization, evidence, and professionalism are all considerations as you try to present your material in a convincing fashion. At this point, the reader's response is all-important.

Writer-Based Versus Reader-Based Prose

The interaction between writer and reader is worth special attention. Discovery drafts are writer based, and problem-solving drafts are reader based.

When you prepare to write about something, you probably talk to yourself more than to a reader. Questions like "What do I mean here?" and "Do I believe that statement?" are common to this part of the composing process. As you gradually gain confidence in what you want to say, you begin thinking more about how to say it to a reader. The questions change to "How can I convince her that this is true?" or "Does this answer the question he has about the issue?" It is important at this stage to direct the prose toward the reader in order to communicate your meaning. If the prose remains writer based, the reader will have to spend more time than necessary decoding the meaning.

To experience for yourself the frustrations readers feel when confronted with writer-based texts, try to decipher these paragraphs.

1. The following is from an employee's handbook:

> The Department shall be obligated to pay the Grantee only for the expenditures made and noncancellable obligations incurred by the Grantee until such time as notice of termination from the Department is received by the Grantee.

Comment: This first paragraph shows what happens when the writer relies on professional jargon. In this sentence, the words plod along, lacking any recognizable action or clear message for a reader. The writer has internalized the jargon heard at the office and has regurgitated it onto the page, not realizing that the reader may not even know what a "grantee" is.

2. The following is from an essay on the connections among historical periods:

Then there is the common world view of alchemists and astrologers in the High Middle Ages—11th through 13th centuries. We used to snicker at the pseudo-science of these specialists, but the idea of the Great Chain of Being is still part of the culture of some societies. The bridges among the literati of various peoples in the ecumene break down of course in the 15th and 16th centuries, but in the 19th I can get into full swing again with the overarching developments of industrialization, imperialism, nationalism, and so on.

Comment: This is a classic example of writing by someone who is carried away with a line of thinking. The author is so involved in these musings that she has totally forgotten about the reader; in fact, the reader has become an eavesdropper on a private conversation the writer is having with herself.

3. The following is from the State Department of Social Services:

The two methods for shifting the financial burden of the state's homeless population to the Federal government are: (1) securing Federal funds to provide advocacy assistance to homeless individuals in preparing their social security and/or supplemental security income applications, and (2) ensuring favorable adjudication of the claims of the approximately 80% of the homeless population who have clinically recognizable mental disorders by directing the State Disability Determination Service, which processes the disability portion of Social Security and supplemental security income claims for the Social Security Administration, to adjudicate claims in a manner more consistent with the extant medical literature on the correlation between homelessness and mental illness.

Comment: This passage combines both of the above problems and adds yet another one. As in the first example, the writer unthinkingly overuses professional jargon. And as in the second example, he gets so carried away with all the information that he talks to himself, effectively shutting out the reader. The whole paragraph is one unreadable sentence.

As these passages illustrate, it is easy for writers to talk to themselves, to dump all the information into a paragraph and assume that it is readable, or to leave out information that readers need to follow the train of thought.

Writers should make allies of their readers. To preserve that friendly relationship, make it easy for readers to understand what you mean; their efforts should be to engage your ideas—not to decipher your prose. In fact, it is probably fair to say that readers who must struggle to understand prose like that of the third example will not even bother to try to find your ideas.

This chapter has focused on the psychology of the writing process, giving an overview of what writers can expect as they write and providing some warnings about possible pitfalls. The rest of the book zeros in on the details of the writing process. Keep in mind that none of the advice is offered as a formula for composition because writing is not static and cannot be programmed. If it could be, certainly computers would be doing all the writing in this age of high technology. But *people* write and write differently. Beyond basic grammar, there are no "rules" that govern writing. That freedom is what is so frightening about the writing process; that is also the beauty of it.

FOCUS ON

Your Writing Project

Write a short essay that answers a specific question. To do this, first generate a question worth writing about, and then think about various ways your essay can provide a worthwhile answer. When you have clear ideas about these things, begin writing. As you write, try to be conscious of how you move back and forth among the parts of the writing process. Turn in your observations about your own writing process along with the completed essay.

The Writing Group

"Brainstorming" is a discovery technique that writers use to find solutions to problems. Like freewriting, brainstorming uses an uncritical approach to promote the free flow of ideas. In a brainstorming session, writers jot down every idea offered by the whole group—even those remotely relevant to the issue at hand—hoping to see a pattern that will solve the problem. To see how this works to help you generate and sort through thoughts, put a group to work on a topic you have chosen to write about.

- Get together with a group of three or more people and toss out ideas on the topic. On a blackboard or a large sheet of paper, note all the thoughts, even those that seem irrelevant at the time. When the group has exhausted all possibilities, try to organize the notes into related categories. Those ideas that do not fit can go into a category of their own or be dropped from consideration.

- By the time you have finished, you should have a fairly good sense of the topic and many possible approaches to it. Sort through the categories the group has developed and try to put them into a logical order. Some of them you may decide to put aside for the present so that you can concentrate on others.

- Write a rough outline of areas to explore further based on the results of the brainstorming session.

Chapter 2

Evaluating the Rhetorical Situation

Thinking and finding ideas and analyzing the rhetorical situation are part of the work of writing.

The first thing every writer needs to do before starting to write is to analyze the specific situation. Although it often is hard to resist immediately starting a draft, you save yourself significant time if you are patient at the beginning of the process and take time to explore the components of the writing task. Every writing situation is different, requiring writers to arrange the prose in order to communicate effectively in the specific instance. What worked the last time may not work in this situation because all of the components are different. The audience may have changed, the subject matter is not the same, and even you have changed—you may not think about things the same way now as in the previous writing circumstance.

Although writing is a creative process, it helps to be somewhat systematic about these preliminary explorations. If you become thoroughly familiar with all the components of the writing situation before you write, your muses won't lead you down unnecessary side roads in search of inspiration. To avoid such side trips, learn as much as possible about the rhetorical elements of the particular writing task in front of you: the purpose, the audience, and the voice of the text itself.

The Rhetorical Triangle

Any form of communication is inherently dramatic. Whether oral or written, verbal communication involves dramatic elements similar to those used on the stage. Kenneth Burke, one of the most celebrated modern rhetoricians, claims that "An essay is an attenuated play," and many other rhetorical theorists agree with his view. Burke's comparison of the act of writing to what actors do when they play a part emphasizes the writer's role in creating prose that effectively appeals to an audience.

As an actor prepares a part, he concentrates on three major areas. First, he thinks about his own perspective on the role and what he would like to express in his performance. How should he interpret the character to achieve this artistic purpose? Second, the actor shifts attention to the probable audience for the play. How will they react to his artistic decisions? Is the audience sophisticated enough to catch the subtleties of gesture, or will he need to broaden the delivery? Does he want to keep them sympathetic to his character, or does he want to maintain a cool distance? Finally, with the answers to these questions in mind, he turns to the role itself and thinks about how he will play it to its best advantage. Now the actor is ready to begin rehearsals.

The same is true for the writer; the analogy of writing to drama is invaluable in its insistence on the relationship among the three components: actor/audience/role. In the world of writing, these dramatic elements change to writer/reader/text, but the relationship among them is very much the same.

As you prepare to write, you concentrate first on your own thoughts and purpose for writing: What do I want to say here? What purpose am I trying to achieve with this prose? Next, you turn your attention to the readers' probable response to the text: How will the readers react to this message? What do they need to know to best gain from the text? Do they have built-in biases that may color their response? And last, you focus on the design of the prose so that it smoothly connects writer to reader, thereby communicating effectively. That is the essence of the "rhetorical triangle": *writer* and *reader* connected by the *text,* in many ways parallel to the dramatic situation of actor and audience connected by the role.

Rhetorical theorists have expressed this concept in a variety of ways, but most maintain the three-part triangle form, emphasizing the integral connections among the parts. The writer cannot connect with the reader except through the text, just as the reader looks to the text to understand the writer's message. In his book, *A Theory of Discourse,* James Kinneavy takes the idea even further by suggesting that discourse is defined by its aims, and these aims depend on which of the triangle's points is primarily important. His version of the communication triangle looks like this:

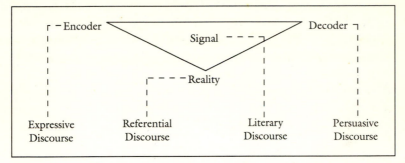

Reprinted by permission of James Kinneavy and W. W. Norton Co.

In this version (which makes the triangle more universal by using linguistic terminology rather than terms limited to composition studies), the writer becomes the "encoder," the reader is the "decoder," and the text is the "signal." Along the bottom of the triangle, Kinneavy has arranged the various types of discourse, showing by dotted lines which part of the triangle is the primary focus for each: expressive texts focus mainly on the encoder, referential texts focus mainly on reality, and so forth.

Kinneavy's model defines discourse as expressive if its aim is to emphasize the writer's view, as in journals, personal letters, and so on, and defines discourse as persuasive if its emphasis is on reader response. Other kinds of writing fall in between reader-directed and writer-directed prose as they emphasize other parts of the triangle. Applying this model to your own writing may help you to understand the nature of your prose—its aims and its components—and enable you to create texts that more clearly achieve their intended purposes.

No matter how the rhetorical triangle is labeled, the principle behind it is that communication is a naturally dramatic process involving the interplay between writer and reader, much the same as drama depends on the connection between actor and audience. When writers realize this interconnection, they can see beyond the narrowness of their own view—their own point on the triangle—and can try to get as many perspectives as possible on the writing task. This broader view allows writers to transform their prose from private monologues into real communication with an audience.

Looking at the writing task from all points of the triangle makes you aware of essential elements in the rhetorical situation. Composing effective prose means more than simply knowing the subject matter and the intended audience. Rather, you must understand your own purpose for writing, then consider the reader's expectations and needs, and finally compose text that fulfills both set of requirements. Unless you think of your prose in these multidimensional terms, you can easily get lost in your own thoughts and private monologues.

PRACTICE EXERCISE 2·1

This exercise asks you to do two things:

1. Find three short pieces of writing that vary in their aims. Analyze these aims by using Kinneavy's communication triangle. Discuss how the model applies to each example.

   Expressive Discourse: the primary focus is on the writer.
   Referential Discourse: the primary focus is on an aspect of reality.
   Literary Discourse: the primary focus in on the text.
   Persuasive Discourse: the primary focus is on the reader.

2. Determine the primary aim of a piece of your own writing. How does the text indicate this focus (in its organization, its style, its subject, and so forth)?

Purpose

The first step in evaluating the rhetorical situation is for writers to think about why they are writing. Nonfiction prose always has a definite purpose to it, a purpose writers should be clear about before they begin to write. As Linda Flower puts it in her book, *Problem-Solving Strategies for Writers,* "Why write? One of the most basic reasons for writing, which students, academic writers, journalists, and business people share, is to discuss and deal with problems." For example, an engineer writes to explain a technical solution, or an attorney writes to persuade a judge, or a banker writes to inform a customer. In each of these instances, the purpose for writing is functional—to have the reader do something or think in a particular way.

Such functional writing is the hallmark of writing in the professional world where people write to get things done, to solve specific real-world problems. Other kinds of writing also fall in this category, although the writers often do not realize the similarity. Academic writing is functional in that its purpose is to offer a solution to an intellectual problem or an opinion about a text. You want the reader to agree with your view. In both the business and the university communities, writers write for the same purpose: to solve problems. The nature of the problems differ, but the general reason for writing is similar.

You need to think in problem-solving terms as you approach the writing task. What precisely do you want to have happen as a result of your writing? Do you want the reader to take some action? To feel a certain way? To buy a product or an idea? Knowing your purpose allows you to write more to the point.

The following two cases, one from the university and one from industry, illustrate how important knowing the exact purpose of the prose is to the success of the document. In the first case, a graduate student attempts to explain how T. S. Eliot uses musical rhythms to enhance the poetic meaning. Her problem is to make the professor understand her view of the poem and to support that view with an explanation of how the poem conveys meaning.

Case 1: Analysis of a Poem

T.S. Eliot's poem "New Hampshire" depends more on musical rhythm and patterns of sound than on the actual meaning of the words. Notice how the poet creates the music within the poem:

New Hampshire

Children's voices in the orchard
Between the blossom- and the fruit-time:
Golden head, crimson head,
Between the green tip and the root.
Black wing, brown wing, hover over;
Twenty years and the spring is over;
To-day grieves, tomorrow grieves,
Cover me over, light-in-leaves;
Golden head, black wing,
Cling, swing,
Spring, sing,
Swing up into the apple-tree.

"New Hampshire" from Collected Poems, 1909–1962 *by T. S. Eliot, copyright 1936 by Harcourt Brace Jovanovich, Inc., copyright © 1964, 1963 by T. S. Eliot, reprinted by permission of the publisher.*

The poet's theme is the inevitable swift movement of Time. This can be seen by the series of rhyming syllables tumbling over one another in fast progression, by the juxtaposition of a few non-rhyming lines with the majority of rhyming lines giving the impression of an attempt to stop the incessant movement, and by the repetition of sounds creating almost a circular motion to the poem as the rhythm slowly rolls "o-ver" and then rushes down with the "ing." By the end of the poem, the reader expects that any slow upward movement anticipates an ultimate rush downward, so the last lines gain an implicit musical meaning. The "swing up into the apple-tree" gains only a temporary motionlessness prior to the inevitable tumble down.

In this literary analysis, the writer's purpose, in part, is to argue that Eliot's poem depends on musical rhythms. Although she does point out several of the poem's musical qualities—the rhymes and the repetition of sounds—the discussion falls short of convincing the reader because the writer did not determine the purpose of the writing task before she began to write. She wants not only to express what she thinks is true but also to explain *how* it is true. In her haste to get her thoughts down on paper, she gives little attention to supporting any of her assertions. She assumes that it is enough to state her opinion, and the reader will automatically agree. In a rhetorical situation such as this one, the writer not only must show the reader the end product of her thinking about the poem but also must illustrate how she came to that conclusion, so that the reader can follow the process. If she had clearly understood the dual nature of her purpose before writing—to assert and *support*—she might have been more persuasive. Note the difference in this excerpt from a revised draft:

STATEMENT OF MAIN POINT

The loss of childhood innocence theme in T. S. Eliot's poem "New Hampshire" is expressed as much by the poem's musical rhythm and patterns of sound as by the actual meaning of the words. . . .

ASSERTION

The structural arrangement of the lines parallels and emphasizes the inevitable motion of Time's pendulum. The series of rhyming

SPECIFIC SUPPORT ASSERTION

syllables and repeated words in the early part of the poem ("head," "wing," "hover," "over," "grieves," "leaves," and so on) establish a slow cadence at first, but the rhythm picks up speed in the poem's second half. Even the lines are shorter and move more quickly near the end as the rhyming single syllables tumble over each other, rush-

SPECIFIC SUPPORT

ing in faster and faster progression. ("Cling, swing,/Spring, sing,/ Swing . . . .") The rhythm creates, too, the actual sensation of

ASSERTION

swinging in a tree swing, the slow leg-pumping at the beginning with the double-syllable words "hover," "over," and "cover," mov-

ECIFIC
pPORT
{ ing faster into monosyllables until the swing reaches the highest point of its arc—"Swing up into the apple-tree." At this high point, the attentive reader sits poised with the child on the swing for a brief motionless moment, anticipating the inevitable rush downward.

In this second version, the author has addressed both of the goals the writing situation requires: to make the reader aware of the musical rhythms in Eliot's poem and to illustrate how they work. She was able to write an effective analysis only after she fully determined her purpose for writing.

The same principle works in the business world, as this next case illustrates. In this situation, the system support manager writes an internal memorandum to one of the company's assistant vice presidents. Read the first draft and notice the difficulty he has explaining his purpose for writing.

Case 2: Business Memorandum

August 15, 1991

TO: Mr. George Honeyman
        Assistant Vice President
        Product Operations

FROM: H. L. Porter
        Regional System Support Manager

RE: System Outage

As you know, we experienced a major system outage on Tuesday, August 13, from 9:30 A.M. to 1:30 P.M. due to a Central Processor failure. This outage was preventable due to a major feature built into this XYZ product line. The feature is the ability to dynamically split the system by releasing the failing unit along with basic components to allow the following:

   A. Continual system operation with minimal user community impact or visibility.

   B. Immediate availability of the failing unit to Service Engineers for diagnosis and repair.

The present procedure is to release the failing unit and to repair it on weekends or on off-hours during the week. Oftentimes the failing box is out of service for several days. I have reviewed your extra maintenance billing year-to-date July. It amounts to $89,731. I'm sure a major part of this billing was to effect corrective maintenance outside of your contracted service hours.

Splitting the system offers two advantages:

   High Systems Availability and Cost Effectiveness.

XYZ Company would be more than willing to discuss this with you and to train the people you select for this very important feature.

Mr. Honeyman probably had to read all the way through this memo before he understood the main point. H. L. Porter gives several false signals concerning the memo's purpose. For example, the indented blocks of text draw the reader's eyes to them immediately, falsely suggesting that the indented material is of primary importance. The first paragraph, which should establish the purpose of the memo, instead describes the system outage without a clear reason for doing so. Consequently, the reader must wade through apparently irrelevant details until the meaning is made clear at the end. The writer's obvious lack of attention to the real purpose for writing has resulted in an inefficient memorandum that wastes the reader's valuable time.

By clearly determining why he is writing to George Honeyman and what he wants Honeyman to do after reading this letter, Porter could write more effectively. Consider this second version in relationship to the first.

August 15, 1991

TO: George Honeyman
      Assistance Vice President
      Product Operations

FROM: H. L. Porter
        Regional System Support Manager

RE: Splitting the XYZ Computer System

DEFINITE SUBJECT ALERTS READER TO THE MEMO'S MAIN POINT

MAIN POINT PRESENTED FIRST

XYZ Company has offered to provide a training session for our people on how to split our XYZ computer system. If we had been able to split the system last Tuesday, we could have prevented the four-hour system outage that resulted from a Central Processor failure.

RATIONALE

The splitting feature, already built into the XYZ product line, releases the failing unit and basic components, allowing the system to continue operating while Service Engineers have access to the failing unit for diagnosis and repair. The present procedure is to release the failing unit and to repair it on weekends or off-hours during the week. Often, this means the failing box is out of service for several days.

RATIONALE

I have reviewed your extra maintenance billing, year-to-date July. It amounts to $89,731. I'm sure a major part of this billing results from corrective maintenance outside of your contracted hours.

REFERENCE AGAIN TO MAIN POINT

Splitting the system offers the advantages of cutting these costs and increasing system availability.

CLOSING REFERS TO MAIN POINT AND SUGGESTS FOLLOW-UP STEP

XYZ Company is more than willing to discuss this feature with you and to train the people you select to implement it. I'll call you next Thursday to get your reactions to this plan.

In this revision, the main idea is established in the beginning: Honeyman knows immediately that Porter is offering him a solution to the system failure problem. To help clarify this main point, Porter has followed it with supportive background details. First, he encourages Honeyman to buy the training session from XYZ Company, and then he explains why the session is worth the money. Whereas Honeyman could easily deny Porter's request as it is presented in the original memo, the organization of the revision makes it difficult to argue with the logic. The clear sense of purpose in the revision creates an emphatic structure to the prose, an emphasis totally missing in the original. (For a more detailed discussion of organizing for emphasis, see Chapter 5.)

Understanding and communicating the purpose for writing makes a major difference in your prose. But you should ask more than just "Why am I writing?" You also should consider "What do I want the reader to do or to think as a result of this prose?" As is evident from the previous two examples, it is not enough for writers to know that their task is to write a letter or an essay. They need to look beyond the general situation of writing to determine its real point:

to communicate information?

to persuade?

to explain?

to encourage action?

to instruct?

If you ask these questions about your prose, you can better focus it to achieve these goals.

Audience

> Whatever other purposes rhetoric may serve, it is, fundamentally, a means for achieving social cooperation: The writer's goal is to engage in some sort of cooperative activity with the reader.
> —*Richard Young, Alton Becker, Kenneth Pike*

> The whole duty of a writer is to please and satisfy himself, and the true writer always plays to an audience of one.
> —*William Strunk, Jr. and E. B. White*

Not everyone agrees on the role of the audience in the writing process. For some, attention to the audience is a form of "selling out" to commercial concerns. They are afraid that writers compromise the integrity of their art when they pay undue attention to the audience. They believe that by so doing, writing becomes selling instead of true expression. On the other hand, many believe that defining who the audience is and writing specifically for that audience's needs is a more efficient method of communication. Both views are correct to some extent.

As the previous section notes, writers usually have a definite purpose in mind as they write. Obviously, it is to your advantage to anticipate in the composing stages the reader's probable response to your prose. Otherwise, you risk seriously compromising your message by the way you express it. For example, consider the likely reaction of the judge who receives this paragraph as part of a legal brief:

> A practical matter that might make the Court hesitant to find for Vivian Casterbank is the problem of distinguishing and proving embarrassment, humiliation, and other nondisabling mental injuries within the head of a woman diagnosed by her own doctors as an obsessive compulsive neurotic schizophrenic with a well-developed obsessional component and reactive depression secondary to job loss. Read the "certified nut." A judge may well cringe in his robe at the thought of the potential parade of frauds and Freuds in his courtroom, especially given the defendant's connections in the health care field.

Any attorney who believes that such emotionally packed prose will have a positive effect on the judge is probably not long for the profession. Although the paragraph is humorous, such humor at the expense both of the defendant and of the judge's time is definitely inappropriate. Had the attorney thought more about her audience, she would have realized that she was doing her case more harm than good in presenting it in this flippant manner.

However, if you pay so much attention to the audience that you inhibit your self-expression, audience analysis has gone too far. A classic example of this is when students freeze while writing term papers because they are afraid of instructor criticism and simply recycle class notes instead of producing original work:

> Macbeth deserves his tragic fate because his bounding ambition has corrupted him totally. As we learned in class, "power corrupts, and absolute power corrupts absolutely." After all, violence to another is violence to the self—a lesson Macbeth learns too late to save himself. This play is built on the essentiality of social order and

without social bonds man becomes a beast, as the character of Macbeth illustrates.

This uninspired prose goes on, building cliché on cliché without really saying anything. The writing lacks conviction or any sense of original thought. If fear rather than lethargy has created such life-lessness, the writer needs to pay more attention to his own thinking processes than to the instructor's possible criticism. Of course, he needs to know his audience—in this case, the instructor—but here the balance has been tipped too far toward the reader.

Another area of concern for writers is the ethical implications of pandering to an audience at the expense of expressing the truth. Frequently, professionals find themselves in the awkward position of disagreeing with company policy or of helping to market a doubtful product. For instance, a technical writer realizes that the software she is documenting is not completely debugged and therefore will not perform the functions it claims to perform. The company says that the problem will be fixed before the product is shipped, but the writer has serious doubts that this is true. Does she write the manual with or without a cautionary note explaining the problem?

Ethical problems frequently arise in marketing situations. To what extent should the writers "sell" with their prose, and to what extent should they focus less on persuasion and more on the un-adorned facts? The legal ramifications of paying undue attention to the audience at the expense of the truth can be staggering. Writers who make false claims in an attempt to win the audience's favor may find themselves involved in law suits. In spite of this, the temptation remains, luring more and more writers into dishonesty.

Nonetheless, if you understand the importance of discovering your own ideas and expressing them honestly, then an understanding of the audience becomes essential to the writing process. It is ex-tremely difficult to communicate any message without knowing who the receiver is, and writing with that receiver in mind does not neces-sarily mean you are "selling out." It is a matter of degree. If you have taken the necessary time to turn your attention inward to your own thoughts, the next logical step is to look outward to the reader. How can you best communicate your ideas to that other person or group of people? There are certain things to look for as you prepare to transmit your thoughts to a particular audience. The more systematic you are about analyzing your audience, the better you will communi-cate. You already know *your* needs—you decided on these when you determined your purpose for writing. Now you need to discover the audience's needs. Many of these have been alluded to earlier, but a systematic series of questions may help you to focus better on audience analysis.

Before writing, take a few minutes to think through these questions about audience. Try not to rush the answers because it is hard to determine what the audience really needs, but it is temptingly easy to lapse into stereotypic thinking.

- Who will read what you write? More than one person? Who is the primary reader and who is secondary?

- Why are they reading what you write? To get information? For pleasure? To make a decision?

- What information do your readers need most? What do they need second? Can you prioritize according to their needs?

- Where will the audience read your prose? In a busy office? In the quiet of a study? Will your document design match the needs of their environment?

- What biases might your readers have either for or against your ideas? Can you avoid exacerbating the negative ones and emphasize the positive ones?

- What does your audience already know about your subject? Will you risk patronizing them or talking over their heads?

These questions encourage writers to see their readers from a variety of angles, making sure they have all the preliminary information necessary to make the writing task easier. Without this knowledge, most writers waste hours with drafts, hoping by serendipity to connect with the audience. If writers know what they need and know what the readers need, they should be able to match these needs by creating a voice appropriate to the situation.

PRACTICE EXERCISE 2·2

For the next writing task you are assigned, consider purpose and audience before you begin to write. It may help to use a formal structure as a catalyst for your preliminary explorations of these elements. The chart on page 31 should help you define the rhetorical situation. Fill it out completely.

	Purpose	Expectations	Needs
Writer's concerns:	• What are you trying to convey? • What problem(s) will this text address? • Is there a priority order for the arrangement?	• What do you want readers to think as a result of reading the text? • What do you want readers to do as a result of reading the text?	• What information or material do you need to write the text?
Readers' concerns:	• Why are they reading the text? • What problem(s) do they want it to address? • Is there a priority order for what they need to know?	• What do they want to get from reading the text? • What amount of detail do they expect it to have?	• What is their level of expertise in the subject? • What prior knowledge do they need to understand the text?
Effect on the text: [What will your text include to satisfy the above requirements?]			

Figure 2.1 Rhetorical Situation Chart

Voice

Think back to the actor at the beginning of this chapter and again note the parallel between his preparation for a role and a writer's preparation for writing. He knows what his goals are, and he knows who will likely be in the audience the night of the performance. Now he concentrates on expressing his part as effectively as possible to that audience.

So, too, writers consciously adopt a "voice" or writing persona that will best express their ideas to the intended audience. Because writers obviously cannot use gestures or audible inflections to communicate, they must rely solely on a written voice created with diction (word choice), syntax, punctuation, and page design. Using these tools skillfully to create the right voice is prerequisite for good communication. As noted earlier, the attorney's flippant tone was inappropriate for her rhetorical situation, and similar lack of attention to written persona is a problem for many writers. It is easy to ignore the fact that the writer's voice can make the same subject appeal to widely different audiences. For example, notice how the following two passages differ as they communicate the same information to different readers:

1. Floppy disks get their name from the fact that the disks themselves are flexible. They are made of Mylar plastic coated with a thin layer of magnetic material. They are sandwiched inside a square, thin, cardboard like protective cover that remains permanently on the disk, even when in use. The disk spins inside the cover and a slot in the cover allows the read/write head to come in contact with the magnetically coated disk. . . .

   Floppies come in two sizes, a standard size which has 8-inch square jacketed disks, and the mini-floppies which have 5¼-inch square jacketed disks. The standard size can store between 220,000 and 350,000 bytes of usable data. By "usable data" is meant space for data that is available to you, the user. The total storage capacity of a standard floppy is about 400,000 bytes. But a large number of these bytes must be used for formatting and control, so that the controller in the disk unit will know where to store and find data.
   —A Practical Guide to Small Computers

2. Here are some basic things to know about disks:
   Disks, or diskettes, are about eight inches square and they look somewhat like the old 45 rpm phonograph records. They are commonly called "floppy disks" because they are not as stiff as phonograph records. But they aren't *really* floppy—

like, say, jello. They are encased in a plastic jacket that should
never be removed. The jacket has several small openings
where the magnetic surface of the disk is exposed, and it is
through these openings, presumably, that information is put
onto the disk or taken off. Exactly how this happens I am not
now nor will I ever be in a position to say. It is enough that
the machine knows how to do it.
    —Writing with a Word Processor, *William Zinsser*

The first example sounds more businesslike than the second one
does. The first writer assumes the reader is not afraid of computers
and probably knows a lot about them already—for example, the
meaning of the terms *byte, read/write head,* and so forth are not defined. This passage is a straightforward transfer of information to a
technically inclined audience who wants to know about disks. On
the other hand, the second example targets people who are nervous
about using computers and are perhaps resistant to the idea of using
the machines. The author has to capture the audience's trust in his
role as a nontechnical person who can also effectively use a word processor. By creating a voice that seems to say, "Gee whiz, if I can do it
anyone can," the writer successfully connects with his audience. For
the writer and the reader in the second example, "It is enough that
the machine knows how to do it."
    The techniques used to create an appropriate voice are discussed
throughout this book and in detail in Chapter 7. For now, the important thing is to realize that all prose has a definite persona, even
when writers are not aware of its presence, and it is better to control
it than to offend your reader unwittingly.
    You can do several things to gain control. First, choose a voice
only after determining the purpose and the audience's needs. Otherwise you may let your choice of persona lead your writing, instead of
vice versa, and such a mistake can be costly. For example, if you are
angry when you write, you may create a hostile voice that unnecessarily offends the audience and does more damage than good. Or, in
another instance, you may attempt a humorous voice when the rhetorical situation calls for more serious writing. Second, try to create a
tone simlar to that used in a normal intelligent conversation with another person. Avoid using slang and other unprofessional language,
but also avoid using a stiffly formal manner that unnecessarily dis-
tances the writer from the reader. Such formality borders on pom-
posity in most writing situations, and it does more damage than
good in reader/writer relations. For example, in this policy statement

written to define a company's views on professionalism, the tone is much too stiff for the situation:

> The practice of a profession is an activity requiring the judicious application of knowledge and judgment that can only be acquired through specific education and experience. This fact has been recognized by the public through the enactment of statutes in most states, requiring the testing and registration of persons offering or actually practicing several of the professional services provided by RTE Company, and regulating the commercial practice of those professions.

Although this paragraph is correct in its grammar and syntax, the voice you hear as you read is that of a prim and proper official reading the rules. Why be so stilted? The point of the statement can be effectively phrased in less stiff prose without losing its sense of decorum:

> Professional practice requires specific knowledge and judgment only acquired through appropriate education and experience. Therefore, professionals must first pass examinations and then officially register with the state before beginning commercial practice. RTE professionals fall in this category.

The difference in voice between the two versions makes a subtle change in impact the prose has on readers. Most readers will pay much more attention to the second version because it is more direct and definite in its message, whereas the first version seems weighted down with formality and is difficult to understand. To achieve an appropriate persona, writers should get into the habit of reading aloud. If the author of the previous example had read his prose out loud, he might have recognized the overly formal voice. Always read prose aloud before you're satisfied with it, whether it's a technical report or just a letter home. You can't *hear* your voice unless you actually *say* the words. Find a private spot away from other listeners, and tune your ear to the prose. Does it sound natural? Could another intelligent person follow the voice patterns without getting lost in windy sentences and stiff expressions? Really listen to what you've written.

PRACTICE EXERCISE 2·3

Here is an example of prose that the author did not read out loud before it left his hands. As a result, the voice is inconsistent, creating an unintentional effect. The writer, an environmental engineer, composed this paragraph as part of a report on a coal-tar clean-up operation. His audience is made up of technical people who need to know the precise site data in order to continue the project. Read the passage and determine where the voice inconsistencies occur.

> The dense, tarlike fluid will tend to creep downward under the influence of gravity and slowly sink like slime through the saturated zone until it encounters an undeniable barrier to its downward migration. Relatively impermeable fine sand, silty or clayey soil strata that is laterally extensive will provide such an undeniable barrier and will severely impede the downwardly oozing coal tars due to their high viscosity and surface tension effects.

This sounds like Vincent Price reporting on contaminated waste. Such inconsistencies in tone can create embarrassing moments when writers are unaware of their prose voice. Revise the passage to make the voice appropriate for the intended audience.

Awareness of the rhetorical situation as inherently dramatic allows writers to better understand the artistic relationship of purpose and audience to the text. When writers take this relationship seriously and explore these elements in detail, the writing task itself is no longer an abstract concept, and they can begin to plan a strategy for communicating real information to real people.

FOCUS ON:

Your Writing Project

Choose a topic that allows you to ask for something from a specific group of people. You may ask for money, for sympathy, for consideration, for approval, for action, or whatever. It may be a letter, an editorial, a proposal, or any other type of writing that exaggerates the rhetorical situation enough to give you good practice in defining the rhetorical elements. Write down your preliminary analysis of purpose, audience, and voice.

The Writing Group

In a group of writers who are all writing about the same topic:
- Divide the group into two parts.
  1. Two or more writers focus on evaluating the purpose and presenting their results to the whole group. Research outside of the classroom may be necessary to define the problem clearly.

2. Two or more writers focus on evaluating the audience and presenting their results to the group. This, too, will probably require some outside research.

- After getting full-group input on both audience and purpose, all of the writers should discuss the ramifications of these results on voice. What voice is most appropriate, given what you now know of the rhetorical situation? List the specific characteristics you believe your writing should have to succeed in this situation. Be as detailed and as focused as possible.

In a group of writers who are all writing about different topics:

- Follow the steps listed in the first part above, but have each writer complete both the purpose and the audience evaluations for his or her own project.

- Each writer should present the results to the group and ask for help in determining what voice to use.

- The group should prepare lists of specific characteristics each writer's prose should have to succeed in the various situations. Be as detailed and as focused as possible.

Chapter 3

Invention Strategies

Classical rhetoricians believed that discourse had five parts: *inventio, dispositio, elocutio, memoria,* and *pronuntiatio,* or, in modern terms, *invention, arrangement, style, memorization,* and *delivery.* Memorization and delivery pertain to oral speeches, helping to create the speech's dramatic effect on the listeners. Writers, on the other hand, depend on written words alone to deliver the dramatic eloquence of their message. For both writers and speakers, the initial three parts of classical rhetoric are the timeless components of all discourse. These three components form the foundation of this book.

Invention comes first. Although we usually think of *invention* in its scientific or engineering sense—meaning to create something new—the concept transcends specific disciplines, applying equally to Thomas Edison and James Joyce. From the Latin *inventio* and paralleling the Greek term *heuresis, invention* means the discovery of ideas. This term describes what writers do in the initial stage of composing. Before writing, no matter what kind of writing you do, you need to discover your ideas about the subject at hand.

Consider the person who thinks she has no problem with invention because her subject has been given to her as a class assignment: for example, "The Function of Madness in *Hamlet.*" She already knows the material and has the appropriate data, yet when she begins to write, she cannot think of anything to say. The sense of security she has gained by collecting information has suddenly fallen away as she realizes that the information itself does not *say* anything; it does not have a point until she shapes it into one.

Similarly, writers in business and industry usually do not have to struggle to determine the subject matter of an assigned writing project. If the subject is "An Assessment of Hazardous Waste Levels in Flint Pond," the engineer knows that she must communicate her assessment of the hazardous waste levels in Flint Pond, but she still does not know how to present the evaluation in a form that will clarify her findings for the reader. As she does preliminary thinking about the writing task, she probably will clarify in her own mind the data's meaning so that she can communicate it better to the reader. This discovery of ideas process is often overlooked, as too many people believe that invention occurs only in academic writing. All good writers depend on invention as the first stage of the writing process, no matter what kind of writing they do.

To write well, you need to think well. This chapter focuses on ways to think critically about a subject, strategies for discovering ideas about it, and methods for analyzing the value of various approaches to it. This is the invention process. Keep in mind that these strategies are suggestions, not maxims. You may use some of these techniques or develop strategies of your own to help spark creative ideas. As you think about your writing task, remember that the invention process is recursive: you can expect to repeat parts of the process before you know with certainty what you want to write about.

Thinking Critically

Critical thinking often means creative thinking. It is hard to be creative in a world that often encourages and even rewards unimaginative thought. Paradoxically, this has been caused in part by our entry into the Information Age, an era glutted by so much new information that we spend most of our time memorizing it rather than discovering new ways to think about it. In almost every discipline, the past twenty years have brought so many changes that students of various subjects find themselves trying to learn and remember as much as possible, while the body of knowledge is quickly expanding.

In response to this problem, a group of engineering faculty members from several universities in New England recently met to discuss ways to encourage their students to be more inventive. One of the featured speakers was Paul MacCready, the contemporary inventor who designed the Gossamer Condor, the first human-powered airplane, now hanging beside the Wright Brothers' plane and the Spirit of St. Louis in the Smithsonian, and who also designed the SunRaycer, the world's fastest solar-powered car. According to MacCready, his creativity stems from his refusal to depend on the expected solutions; he is not afraid to take risks. "The plane worked," he said, "because I knew aerodynamics but not structural engineering. Every part of that plane was on the verge of breaking apart." If he had stayed within the safe limits of what was already known, stayed within the tried and true methods of structural engineering, neither the Gossamer Condor nor the SunRaycer would exist. Similarly, if writers do not exercise creativity but instead depend on the safety of prefabricated ideas, writing is no more than a copying exercise.

With knowledge expanding so fast, many people become so caught up in memorizing facts that the creative spirit is stifled. Only when people step back and gain perspective on what they know does the invention process begin. Thus, writers should examine all sides of a subject rather than trusting preconceived notions.

Finding a fresh approach to a writing assignment means that you must see the subject without the blinders of preconception. When people expect to see a thing a certain way, it usually appears that way, whether or not that is its true image. Similarly, thinking based on prefabricated ideas produces writing that says nothing new, that offers nothing important to the reader. As a writer, you have a responsibility to go beyond the expected views and present your subject so that the reader sees it with fresh eyes. Developing such a critical eye for any subject is not a mysterious process that depends on a kind of mystical second sight. Instead, critical thinking is a fairly systematic method of defining a problem and synthesizing knowledge about it, thereby creating the perspective you need to develop new ideas.

At this point, you need to determine how other people view the topic and how that topic relates to a larger context. It is a good idea to do some general reading or research first to give you enough familiarity with the subject that you can formulate your thesis. During these preliminary phases—before you have clearly defined the problem—most of your efforts will go toward understanding the situation in which the problem occurs (understanding the context for the characters' behavior in *Hamlet,* for example, or determining the extent of the hazardous waste in Flint Pond). When that is done, you will be able to ask intelligent questions about the subject matter and gradually narrow your focus to a clear thesis.

In an attempt to define their subjects and plan this initial research, many writers begin by listing possible thesis statements or by writing a series of assertions about the topics. Unfortunately, this method works against the writers by stifling the creative discovery of ideas. It is a method based on what is already known. The best way to discover a new focus on your subject is to ask questions rather than to pose answers. By asking the right questions, you broaden your vision of the subject so that the solutions you eventually find are creative and informed, not pat answers based on stale information.

Classical rhetoricians used a series of three questions to help focus an argument. Today these questions can still help writers understand the topic about which they are writing. *An sit?* (Is the problem a fact?); *Quid sit?* (What is the definition of the problem?); and *Quale sit?* (What kind of problem is it?). By asking these questions, writers see their subject from many new angles before they begin to narrow the focus to one particular aspect. For example, the writer faced with writing about "The Function of Madness in *Hamlet*" might use the questions this way:

> Does madness have a function in Shakespeare's *Hamlet*? (*An sit?*)
> If madness does have a function, what exactly is it? (*Quid sit?*)
> What kinds of madness are represented in the play? (*Quale sit?*)

The engineer writing about Flint Pond could also use these questions to help focus the report:

> Is there a problem with hazardous waste in Flint Pond? (*An sit?*)
> If there is a problem, what is its scope? (*Quid sit?*)
> What dangers does this present to the public? (*Quale sit?*)

Good questions provoke good answers. If you use these preliminary questions well, you should discover some important ideas about your subject and want to explore these thoughts even more. The answers can give you a framework for your initial research.

PRACTICE EXERCISE 3.1

Try the classical rhetoricians' questions on your own work. As you prepare for your next writing task, write the topic at the top of the page and the three discovery questions below. Use these questions as guides for collecting information about the subject. Then, based on your research and your own intuition, answer the questions as thoroughly as possible.

At this stage, writers of documents such as the Flint Pond report have all the information they need to begin writing because their task is clearcut and does not involve any further analytical thinking. They can compose a report that communicates specific information to the audience. But other, more open-ended, writing situations require further invention to help writers narrow the focus. Academic writing, for example, usually requires much more analysis than do reports or business memos.

If you are confident that you understand the nature of the specific subject, and your topic requires further analysis, you are now ready for the second half of the critical-thinking process—stepping back and seeing the problem in the light of other ideas. As critical thinkers, writers need to be sensitive to how things connect. Instead of seeing their specific subject in a vacuum, they should try to see how it fits in a larger scheme. By transcending the narrowness of a single discipline, writers can view the subject from a broader perspective and see how it relates to other things. "Have I read anything that relates to this problem?" "Does an idea from another discipline have any bearing here?" "If I were a scientist instead of a humanist, how would I view this issue?" These questions—and many others like them—generate the perspective necessary to give writers the critical vision they need.

Again, Paul MacCready serves as a good example, even though his craft is not writing. Like most inventors, MacCready has a knack for seeing connections between things. When he was in Australia doing time trials for the SunRaycer, he noticed a solitary hawk flying high above the trials. When a feather dropped to the earth, MacCready picked it up and spent hours just looking at it, noticing its natural contours and its construction, noting how nature had developed the perfect flying design. From looking at that feather, he learned more about aerodynamics than he could read in many treatises on the subject. According to MacCready, his winning aerodynamic designs today owe a lot to that feather. (Incidentally, he carries the feather with him as a reminder of what people can discover when they open their eyes to the natural relationships around them.)

Up to this point in the invention process, you have focused on a preliminary understanding of the subject you are writing about. You have systematically narrowed your critical lens to define the problem in isolation, and then have broadened the view to see the problem in its larger context. Now you are ready to generate critical ideas about it.

Developing Ideas

Your preliminary work is done, and now your task is to decide what to do with the information you have collected. How does all of this material add up to meaningful ideas? For nearly every writer asking that question, heuristics play a major role.

"Heuristics" are systematic techniques that spark new ideas or retrieve ideas buried in the subconscious mind. In other words, a heuristic is the technique writers use to jog their minds so that ideas begin to flow. Much like athletes who have set routines to "psych up" for a sport—to get the energy levels high and the blood pumping—writers have strategies to get the creative juices flowing. These techniques range from the mundane "comfort factor" of always writing in a favorite spot—the desk by the window or the kitchen table—to sophisticated methods for unlocking the subconscious mind.

One such technique most writers are probably familiar with is the set of questions journalists use when they report a story: Who? What? Why? When? Where? How? Often, just asking these questions about a topic sparks ideas and generates new approaches to the subject. Writers who use this method may use other heuristic techniques as well.

Another heuristic, one popular in today's corporate world, is the technique of "mind-mapping." Sometimes known as "branching," "ballooning," or "clustering," mind-mapping is a visually presented brainstorm that allows writers to see what they are thinking and make appropriate connections between thoughts (see Figure 3.1). This technique moves the writer closer to a precise focus on the topic, but it also assumes a thorough understanding of the problem at the outset. Although there are many variations in technique, the basic process is as follows:

Step 1: Find a large sheet of paper or other writing surface (a white board or a flip chart). Make sure that the paper is large enough to allow for extensive branches of thought.

Step 2: Write the main subject in the middle of the page, and draw a circle around it.

Step 3: Think of subtopics and write these around the main subject, but box these subissues to differentiate them from the circled main idea. Make an effort to express each idea in one or two key words that call to mind the same image each time they are used (for example, *apathy, anger, con-*

fusion, rather than *employees who may not be motivated, emotion, unclear circumstances*").

Step 4: Connect the boxes to the main topic with solid lines.

Step 5: Repeat steps 3 and 4, generating supporting points for each subtopic. (You may want to use colored pencils to differentiate the levels of ideas.) By doing this, you highlight the relationship between ideas and create a visual stimulus.

By using this heuristic technique, you not only generate new ideas but also see the relationships among them. Your task now is to sort out and arrange the ideas you have generated. These processes are easier because the ideas are already grouped in visible clusters and levels.

One of the most powerful—and most advanced—heuristic techniques is the tagmemic grid (see Figure 3.2). In simplified form, a tagmemic grid is a series of boxes containing questions that ask writers to visualize their subject within a physical system much like the particle, wave, and field system in physics. First, the subject is viewed as an isolated particle, then as part of an active process moving through time (wave), and finally as part of a broader space, a field of processes. Writers move their subject through the grid, answering questions and constructing a systematic view of the subject as they go along. By looking at the subject from these various perspectives, writers transcend one-dimensional thinking and have a much broader understanding of how their subject relates to and is affected by other parts of an interconnected system.

Using the grid or other heuristics to generate questions, you can continue adding more questions, gradually allowing you to see all the facets of the problem. The following example of this progressive questioning technique applied to the *Hamlet* problem illustrates how it works to spark creative ideas:

1. *What are all the aspects of the problem?*
   Hamlet is feigning madness, Ophelia is truly mad, Claudius is criminally mad, Laertes is maddened by anger, Hamlet is similarly angry with his mother, Yorick used madness to make people laugh.

2. *Are all these aspects important?*
   Yes, but Yorick is least important.

Mind-Map of the *Hamlet* Problem

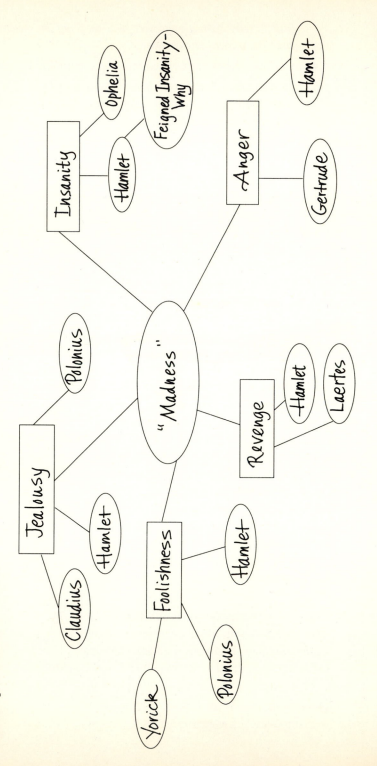

Mind-Map of a Corporate Problem*

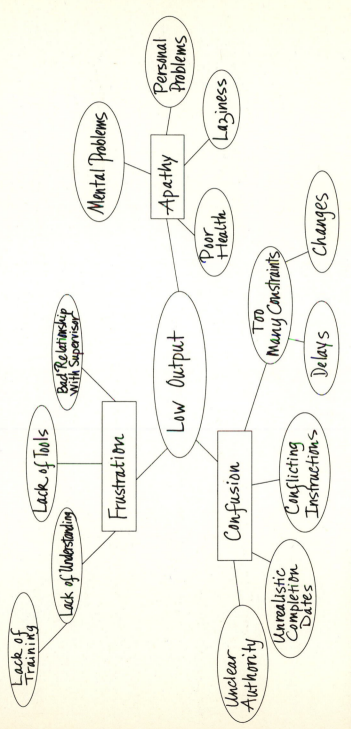

Figure 3.1 Mind-Map Examples
*Adapted from Management Skills Associates, Inc., Solvang, CA 93464. Used with permission.

	CONTRAST	VARIATION	DISTRIBUTION
PARTICLE	1. View the unit as an isolated, static entity. → *What are its contrastive features?*	4. View the unit as one among a group of instances that illustrate the concept. → *What is the range of variation? How much can the unit vary without becoming something that does not illustrate the concept?*	7. View the unit as part of a larger context. → *How is it typically classified? How is it positioned in relation to the whole?*
WAVE	2. View the unit as a dynamic object or event. → *What physical features distinguish it from similar objects or events?*	5. View the unit as a dynamic process. → *How is it changing?*	8. View the unit as a part of a larger, dynamic context. → *How does it interact with its environment?*
FIELD	3. View the unit as an abstract, multi-dimensional system. → *How are the unit's components related by class, in class systems, in temporal sequence, and in space?*	6. View the unit as a multi-dimensional physical system. → *How do particular instances of the system vary?*	9. View the unit as an abstract system within a larger system. → *What is its position in the larger system? What features make it part of the larger system?*

Figure 3.2 The Tagmemic Grid Chart from *Rhetoric: Discovery and Change* by Richard Young, Alton Becker and Kenneth Pike, copyright © 1970 by Harcourt, Brace Jovanovich, Inc., reprinted by permission of the publisher.

3. *Are any of these aspects in conflict? How?*

   Yes, they are in conflict. The many aspects of madness in the play make it difficult to pin down a true definition. Are anger and madness synonyms? Is Laertes's anger a forerunner of the kind of madness afflicting Claudius? Do the vicious types of madness inevitably create victims of insanity such as Ophelia? Does Hamlet's pretending to be mad connect him to the other kinds of madness in the play? Is he culpable for it?

4. *What related topics are not part of the problem?*

   Other characters' reactions to the various types of madness are not at issue. Only the audience's ability to see the various kinds of madness is important.

5. *Can the problem be phrased in the form of a single thesis question that does not repeat the given assignment?*

   Does Shakespeare use a continuum of madness in *Hamlet,* connecting all the characters and leaving no one guiltless?

Compare the phrasing of this final thesis question to that of the original assignment: "The Function of Madness in Shakespeare's *Hamlet.*" It is clear that the writer has focused her thoughts throughout the questioning process, beginning with a list of the problem's aspects and moving gradually to a clear definition of the issue she wants to address. At this stage, the writer does not have all the ideas in place, nor has she determined an answer for the thesis question, but she does know exactly what she is looking for, and she won't write an essay that gives a pat answer.

PRACTICE EXERCISE 3.2

Apply one or more of the heuristic procedures discussed in this section to the same subject you used in the previous Practice Exercise. Your goal should be to define clearly a thesis question that specifically focuses on what your writing will address. Keep all the scratch paper and notes you use so that you can trace your own invention process once you have reached that goal.

Once the writer knows what she is looking for, the rest of the research will be purposeful and not aimless sifting through mounds of information. Too often, writers think they are productively working by immediately gathering as much information as possible about the general topic. However, such a formidable collection of unfocused notes creates an enormous writer's block. Worse, it also adds unnecessary time to the writing process because the writer now has to sort through the material, deciding what applies and what does not. It would have been much simpler to wait until the problem definition was clear before amassing so many research notes.

This is not to say that you should look only for opinions that corroborate your own. Maintaining such a bias during research works against honest inquiry. Instead, you should continue to keep the thesis question clearly in mind and research all the material directly related to that topic. This process narrows the field to the essential research, eliminating unnecessary and unproductive work.

Some heuristic procedures will work better for you than will others. But any one of them will work best if used in a systematic way. In fact, the key to the entire invention process is systematic inquiry where you carefully put the subject through set paces to discover *all* the possibilities, not just a few. It is tempting to rush the process or to be satisfied too easily by the first spark of an idea. You may miss important issues by settling on one idea too soon. Although it is not necessary to use several heuristics, or even to use more than one, it is essential to complete at least one carefully organized inquiry into the subject. This method assures a logical rather than an emotional base for the prose, and it also encourages writers to see the whole picture rather than a distorted corner of it. In writing, as in most things, patience is a virtue.

Analyzing Approaches

Once you have in mind a definite solution to the thesis question, you face yet another question: What is the best way to approach the subject so that the readers will see the wisdom of the proposed solution? In other words, you have to analyze the many possible methods for presenting your final idea to determine which one shows it in the best light.

There are many possible approaches from which to choose. Listed below are five of the most common ones, including a brief discussion of each:

Definition —   Is your major purpose to clarify the point at issue? If your subject is ambiguous in any aspect, you may want simply to define it so that it fits a classification scheme with which the reader is familiar.

Comparison— Perhaps the best approach is to show how the subject is similar and/or different from others. A sharp contrast or easy comparison may express your subject better than other methods.

Relationship— How does your subject affect other things? If the way your subject relates to a certain system is most important, you may want to choose the approach that allows you to illustrate cause and effect, contradictions, consequences, and so forth.

Circumstance— This approach often is used in persuasive argument to suggest that something is possible or impossible based on the situation. Another technique under this heading is to argue probabilities based on previous experience: it happened this way in similar circumstances before, so it will happen this way again.

Testimony— This approach depends on external authority for proof. For example, you may support your subject with eyewitness accounts, statistics, recognized experts in the field, and so on.

As you think about these possible approaches, you may discover aspects of the subject you had not seen before. In this way, analyzing the approaches helps you to reanalyze your ideas at the same time. For example, if the writer of the *Hamlet* assignment originally had decided to present madness in the play by comparing the characters' versions of insanity, she may have sharpened her idea when she considered the "relationship" approach. Through this angle on the subject, she not only contrasts Hamlet's and Ophelia's state but also emphasizes the effect madness has on everyone in the play, including the audience. The broader approach better serves her thesis question, "Does Shakespeare use a continuum of madness in *Hamlet?*"

The ability to analyze is a product of critical thinking. In many ways, all the parts of the invention process are products of critical thinking, and all depend on systematic logic. Thomas Edison was a visionary who could see possibilities the rest of the world had not yet dreamed of. But his vision was a product of seeing things from all sides, not just from the expected point of view. Similarly, Picasso's subjects transcend the normal perspective, suggesting all sorts of possibilities and relationships not visible when the forms are in their

Figure 3.3   Pablo Picasso. *Guernica*. 1937. 11′6″ × 25′8″.
Copyright 1990 ARS N.Y./Spadem. Used with permission.

expected postures. But Picasso's figures are in perfect geometric balance, their positions carefully chosen to express the significance of the moment caught on canvas. In nearly every instance of creative genius, patience and logic lie behind the inspiration.

Like Picasso, who wanted to present the horror of the Guernica massacre (see Figure 3.3) and tried a variety of approaches before he found the perfect version, writers need to experiment with different angles and perspectives on their ideas. After all, the perspective that writers finally choose will define their ideas for their readers. When we look at Picasso's *Guernica* today, the initial impact of the figures' suffering is intensified because of their violent, fragmented poses. The artist did not permit us the comfort of a traditional view. Instead, he insisted on approaching his idea abstractly, making us see the violent suffering first and the individual people second. Writers can have just as dramatic an effect on readers if they choose their approach well. Analyzing approaches allows writers to determine which method works best to produce the desired results.

PRACTICE EXERCISE 3.3

Using the same topic you have used for the other exercises in this chapter, analyze how the five most common approaches would work for your topic. Which one would allow you to best express your answer to the thesis question?

Narrowing to the Final Choice

How do writers know when they have the best solution and the best approach? This question haunts many perfectionists who believe that an even better thought lies just over the horizon. In fact, the answer is not a difficult one. If you have followed a logical method to reach this final stage, the best choice should be obvious. When it is not, perhaps there are two equally good alternatives, or perhaps you have not been as careful with the process as you should have been. Looking again at the notes you have collected and quickly reviewing the discovery steps should solve the dilemma.

Some writers, however, get bogged down at this last stage because they hate to commit to one solution. Committing to that solution means taking a stand—a stand that might not be the best one. These writers avoid risk by delaying the final choice, by always postponing the writing to do more research, and by spending more time discussing the topic with others than developing a thesis. If you tend to procrastinate, it might help to remember that once the actual writing begins you will still have opportunities for more discovery and chances to change direction if that seems appropriate. But the best advice is to trust yourself. If you have put a topic through these logical paces, the result should be at the very least a viable solution.

The original writing assignment has evolved gradually through the invention process from a vague subject to a definite thesis. The remaining task is to state the solution in proposition form, a form that makes a point and suggests the approach the writer plans to use in the subsequent discussion. For example, the Shakespeare topic has gone through several versions as the writer has refined it to the final stage:

Subject: The Function of Madness in Shakespeare's *Hamlet*.

Question: Does Shakespeare use a continuum of madness in *Hamlet,* connecting all the characters and leaving no one guiltless?

Thesis: The many faces of madness in Shakespeare's *Hamlet* implicate all of the major characters as contributors in varying degrees to the downfall of Denmark. By extension, Shakespeare comments on the complicity we all share in the world's destructive madness.

The last version is a single-sentence proposition that is arguable and leads directly into the "relationship" approach the writer has chosen. Through the invention process, the writer has defined the specific problem, examined it critically, generated ideas, analyzed approaches, and narrowed to the final proposition. Now she is ready to write the essay.

FOCUS ON:

Your Writing Project

The goal of this project is to give you the experience of looking critically at an abstract subject and narrowing the focus to produce a clearly defined view. Perhaps the best kind of writing for this assignment is academic writing. Turn to an academic discipline that especially interests you—history, chemistry, literature, political science, and so forth—and write a critical analysis that presents your perspective on a specific problem from that discipline.

Keep in mind that a critical analysis goes beyond simple description and definition and emphasizes the "why" questions instead of who, what, when, where, or how. Make sure you allow enough time for the invention task so that your thesis question is finely tuned prior to writing. The practice exercises and the group exercise in this chapter may help you to do this.

The Writing Group

This group exercise works best with writers in pairs rather than in groups of three or more. It is an exercise based on Plato's dialectic method, which suggests that two people of like minds engaged in inductive dialogue can come to understand something better than either one could separately. The process goes like this:

1. The group divides into pairs.

2. One writer begins by asking a question pertaining to his or her paper topic. It could be one of the three discovery questions discussed at the beginning of this chapter, or it could be a general question of the writer's own invention.

3. The partner in the group offers an answer to the question and asks a narrower one about the same topic.

4. The original writer responds and then asks another question—perhaps one even more specific or another general one sparked by the previous exchange.

5. The partners continue this dialogue, noting down all the questions and answers, until they agree that they have exhausted the relevant questions and have a greater understanding of the topic.
6. The partners write the thesis question together.
7. The partners repeat the process for the other writer's topic.

Chapter 4

Writing from Sources

Most kinds of writing require at least some research, and many kinds depend on thorough documentation to maintain credibility. Although writers may be eager to rush through their research, they need to realize that researching is part of the writing process, not separate from it. Writers research topics to answer questions they have about the subject, questions generated while they decide what is important to say.

Writing from sources means more than just going to the library and flipping through the card catalogue to find enough reference books to fatten the bibliography. If you focus only on collecting as much information as you can, you will likely find yourself bogged down later as you try to incorporate the material into your text. Before beginning productive research, you must have a clear question you want to answer, and you should understand that research involves at least three tasks: gathering information, evaluating sources, and integrating the resulting information into the text. All three of these steps are essential if you want to present well-documented, thoroughly supported prose.

Gathering Information

Although the library is a good place to start research, even traditional academic research papers may require more than that, and professional projects may send the writer far afield for solid information. It is important to know how to use the library's extensive resources, but it is equally important to explore other valuable sources of information. When searching for answers to research questions, you should investigate all possible leads and not dismiss any out of hand. In many instances, although a source may not be the best one, it may lead to another that is an important resource.

The library is in the research business and therefore can provide the easiest way to begin the process. But it is important to have a research plan so that collecting information proceeds logically and thoroughly, not haphazardly. The following tips for library research might help make the process more efficient.

1. Begin with the most general sources—bibliographical source-books (for example, the *Oxford Companion to English Literature, Encyclopedia of Business Information Sources, ERIC Resources in Education, Encyclopedia of Psychology,* and so forth).

2. Check the books published on the subject, then check the articles in periodicals. The books usually contain substantial background information, and articles present the newest ideas.

3. Do a computer search for more material if the library has computer facilities. Most large libraries can tap into central data banks and provide printouts of pertinent articles (for a small fee, of course).

4. Read newspapers. This valuable source is often overlooked, although it often provides the most timely comment on the subject.

5. Use only material that relates directly to the research question. It is tempting to copy everything remotely pertinent just in case it becomes important later. Instead, concentrate on keeping the question clearly in mind and gathering information that will contribute to answering it.

6. Organize the research notes under headings so that each entry fits logically with the others and with the larger topic. If you can easily divide the overall research question into subcategories, try to define those categories before tracking down infor-

mation. That way, the process is more organized and the notes will be more usable later.

7. Document the sources directly on the notes. Including all pertinent information on the note cards saves a great deal of time and effort later in the bibliography process, and it also makes another trip to the library to check page numbers, publication dates, or other details unnecessary.

PRACTICE EXERCISE 4.1

After the invention process has helped you develop focused research questions, try your hand at some equally focused library research. The following technique is one way to do research effectively:

Write your research questions on separate note cards, and take them with you to the library. Mark each card with a different number.

① "Is Long- or Short-Term Economics the Better Approach to U. S. Economy?"

Also take a stack of additional cards with you to the library so that you can take notes directly on the cards.

Check all of the sources your library has available, including microfilm, microfiche, and computer database searches.

When you find relevant material, write the source on the note card that has the appropriate research question at the top of it. Make sure to list the source in proper bibliographic form. Give each source a letter that will identify it.

① "Is Long- or Short-Term Economics the Better Approach to U. S. Economy?"
A. KEYNES, J.M. (1930). *A TREATISE ON MONEY* NEW YORK: AMS PRESS, INC.

Place the research question card number and the source's letter in the upper right hand corner of your note-taking card.

```
                                        1A


∿∿∿∿∿∿∿∿∿∿∿∿∿∿∿∿∿∿∿∿∿∿∿∿∿∿∿∿∿
```

Take your notes, making sure to copy direct quotations exactly as they are written in the original; include the page numbers.

```
P.53- "A simple economic fact is           1A
       that as the production of an economy
     goes down, the total income of
     said economy goes down."
P.84- "The government should offset
      changes in public expenditure".
∿∿∿∿∿∿∿∿∿∿∿∿∿∿∿∿∿∿∿∿∿∿∿∿∿∿∿∿∿
```

When you are finished with this phase of research, you should have a substantial list of sources on each research question card and a stack of well-organized note cards you can work from when you begin to write your paper.

As mentioned previously, many projects require more than library research. One invaluable source of information is the personal interview. Setting up an interview may mean making several telephone calls and perhaps writing letters, as well as devising a list of good interview questions so that the interviewee does not get off track or sidestep important issues. In some cases, the interviewee may give only one-word answers instead of explaining the interesting details you want to hear about the topic. You need to have a plan for dealing with any of these possibilities. Interviewing is not as easy as it looks, and it requires more than getting two people together in the same room with a tape recorder. Here are a few things to keep in mind when planning an interview.

- *Focus on the research question.*
  As you prepare for the interview, ask yourself what specific information you need from the interviewee. It may help to write

down the primary idea you want to explore with this person as a reminder of the interview's purpose. That way, if the talk turns in other directions, you can gently bring the speaker back to the point.

- *Send the interviewee a list of questions ahead of time.*
  If you have taken the time to provide the interviewee with questions prior to the interview, he or she will have thought about them and will be able to answer more fully and carefully. An added benefit of sending questions ahead is that it gives the person time to collect pertinent material and have it available at the interview rather than having to search for such data at a moment's notice.

  Be careful not to limit yourself to the questions you have prepared for the interviewee. These should serve as a basis for discussion, not as the total package. Otherwise, the interviewee could mail his or her answers, and you would miss the opportunity for the fascinating and often valuable information that occurs in face-to-face circumstances.

- *Roughly outline the progression of questions you would like to ask.*
  Interviewers who are prepared and who get the best information from an interview go into the situation with a set of questions to serve as guidelines for the discussion. These are not an absolute structure for the interview, but they allow you to think ahead about how your questions lead into each other and elicit more detailed answers, and they also make you look more prepared and professional. Interviewers who arrive for the interview with no questions and no real sense of direction frustrate the interviewee and usually take away little but disorganized chatter.

  These questions should not be the ones you send ahead to the interviewee. This private list is much longer and more detailed than the list of major points you have put in the mail, and it serves as an organizer for the sequence of questions you will ask.

- *Phrase the questions narrowly enough to keep to the point but open enough to allow the interviewee freedom to expand on the points.*
  Comments such as "Tell me about Boston Harbor pollution" open the gates for a flood of disorganized information. On the other hand, questions like "Don't you agree that Boston Harbor is the most polluted harbor in the nation?" elicit either

"Yes" or "No" answers—hardly enough for an effective interview. Instead of these extremes, try to ask questions that are
specific enough to capture the speaker's attention but open-
ended enough to encourage the speaker's opinions rather than
your own. For example, "According to a recent study, fish
caught in Boston Harbor are safe to eat, although show more
evidence of carcinogens than fish caught anywhere else. What
does your knowledge of the harbor waters tell you about this
situation? Would you eat the fish?"

- *When the interview is over, suggest that you may need to call for
  follow-up information*.

  It is not likely that you will have anticipated all the information
  gathered in the interview. If it is a good interview, you will
  have learned quite a bit of new material that takes time to digest. As a result, expect that you will need to get back to the
  interviewee to ask for clarification on certain issues or to request additional information. It is polite to ask if the interviewee would mind a follow-up call to make sure all the facts
  are straight. Most people appreciate your care in asking and
  your concern that the information is clear.

PRACTICE EXERCISE 4.2

Conduct at least one interview with someone who is an expert on
a topic you are writing about. Before you actually meet with the
person, follow the preliminary procedures discussed above. Take
notes during the interview itself, and, when the interview is over,
write them up into a coherent record of what took place. After
you have finished the process, write a brief evaluation of your experience. What techniques worked for you? What might you have
done better?

These are just two of the many sources of information for writers.
Professional societies, special interest group meetings, private collec-
tions, controlled circulation periodicals, and many other places or
people can serve as resources for writers tracking down information
about a specific subject. Nonetheless, the good researcher not only
can find the sources but can use them effectively, knowing which
ones are trustworthy and which are suspect.

Evaluating Sources

After many years of studying or working in a specialized field, most writers develop a good eye for what is trustworthy in that field and what is not. For those writers without such experience, a few general guidelines can help in evaluating sources.

Timeliness

First, check the publication date of any written material you use. In most instances, books or articles published earlier have been superseded by new ideas or by updates on older concepts. In medicine, technology, or other similar disciplines, the early publications give a historical perspective on new developments, but they are no longer authoritative sources. In the computer industry, for example, which changes almost monthly with the new products rapidly appearing on the market, information printed in book form is often outdated before it hits the shelves. Researchers interested in this field must look to articles in trade journals, conference proceedings, and personal interviews for up-to-date material.

Publications in the humanities and social sciences also must be timely. This is especially true of literary criticism. Any research done on Shakespeare, for example, must take into account the latest opinions and trends in Shakespearean criticism, but it is also important to be familiar with the essays of L. C. Knights, A. C. Bradley, G. Wilson Knight, and other giants in the field. The subject matter they deal with has not changed, so their views retain more value than do dated opinions on fiber optics or laser technology. Nonetheless, because approaches to literary criticism evolve over time, the newer critics will probably use the most modern methods of inquiry, and you should check both current and traditional sources.

Legal research, on the other hand, relies on precedent for its value. Attorneys spend most of their time researching case law to determine where certain trends in court opinions began, and tracing the evolution of these opinions so that they can argue legal precedents for the cases at hand. If a 1949 case is seminal, but the holding has been superseded by a later case, the attorney can either depend on the later case or argue that the case at hand is not similar to the 1949 example and is therefore not governed by either opinion. Attention to publication dates is essential here, as in all other disciplines.

Familiarity with Previous Research

A second test for the authority of written material is its reliance on previous sources. An article or a book usually combines the author's experience with his or her own research in the field. If the article offers no grounding in previous research and lists insufficient references to outside sources, the author may not be familiar enough with the work already done on the subject. Perhaps, then, the article is "reinventing the wheel" so to speak, or is not valid in its assertions because they are based on nothing but experience. Books and articles that are only experiential are often not trustworthy sources. The other extreme is also true. If written material is choked with outside references, the author may have nothing original to say and may be rehashing what others have already said. Look for a balance of external references and personal experience. Both are valuable if used together.

Bias

Third, check the breadth of the argument. In weak articles, the authors offer biased opinions with no discussion of the opposing views. By doing so, they cheat the readers of making their own decisions about the material because they may fear the validity of their stance. A hallmark of poor arguments is their one-sided nature and their omission of alternative views. Good arguments, on the other hand, usually include all possibilities and suggest why the author's view is the best alternative. Be wary of articles that express narrow opinions or use emotion rather than logic to make their points. If an article depends on emotion as the primary persuasive element, it probably is not characterized by logic.

Reliability of the Source

Finally, note the credentials of the author or the interviewee. Researchers should look for people who are leading experts in the field—people who have published widely on the subject or who have extensive experience working with the material. If possible, gather information from the top experts and then move on to those newer to the field but who bring hard work and new ideas to the discipline. For example, when looking for information about the pollution in Boston Harbor, contact the engineering supervisor of the harbor clean-up project and one of the project engineers. Do not rely solely on the brochures put out by the Department of Environmental Quality Engineering or the word of a local politician up for reelection.

One of the best methods for evaluating sources is to collect as much pertinent information as possible and compare notes. Most researchers find certain authorities quoted more often than others or discover trends of thought and the important opposing opinions on the issues. The most effective way for writers to evaluate sources is to read enough to become experts on the subject themselves. From an informed perspective, they can judge more easily the validity of others' opinions.

PRACTICE EXERCISE 4.3

1. Check the list of sources you have already compiled. Is each an appropriate authority? Explain why.
2. If you have found some sources that are not trustworthy, list them too. Explain why these sources are not helpful.

Integrating Sources into the Text

When the research is done, you should have enough information to feel confident in giving an answer to the original research question, and the material you have gathered should support your assertions when you begin to write. You may have an impressive stack of notes, photocopies, tapes, and other source material spread out on the desk, or spilling off the table, onto the floor, onto the bed, onto the floor.

This is a critical stage for writers because at this point the research either pays off in well-documented text or overwhelms both the writer and the text, evidenced by prose laden with other people's ideas pasted loosely together. Looking at the stack of information, you may feel as if there is nothing original left to say, and your job is simply to organize previously stated ideas. At this stage, it helps to remember the thesis question and the ideas generated around it. If you have done the research well, you should be able to divide the stack into categories, move the categorized material into a logical order, and begin work on one category at a time. As you sift through the information in each category, you probably will find it easier to remember your original ideas and how the material you have gathered supports them. For each category, keep the primary idea in the forefront while sorting through the information to decide what specific quotations to use, what material is especially supportive, and what material is not as relevant as it seemed earlier. Organize the piles accordingly. (For more information on organizing, see Chapter 5.)

After you have organized the material and are actually in the process of incorporating these sources in the written text, you should follow some general guidelines. Begin with a strong statement of your own ideas. If you start with other people's thoughts, you lose the opportunity to engage the reader directly; instead, you back into the discussion, often giving the impression that you lack confidence in your own work. This advice may seem heretical, and it directly contradicts the popular practice of beginning with quotations. Some writers argue that the initial quotation lends more authority to their own words, catches the reader's interest, and sets the tone for the text. Effective writers ought to be able to use their own words to accomplish these same purposes, and the quotation probably would be more effective within the text itself where it could either support or refute an argument. In most situations, writers who begin with their own ideas are more forceful, more organized, and less likely to depend on quotations as crutches.

Once your own idea is expressed, then quotations and other external references work effectively to support these assertions. The function of the research material is to support the author's assertions, not to replace them. For example, the following excerpt from an article by George Gopen in the *Michigan Law Review* makes a point and then supports it with an external reference:

> There are no greater powers than those of creation and dissolution. Lawyers have both, on a daily basis, because of the nature of their relationship to language. They create binding relationships between people where none existed before—a God-like task, making something out of nothing. They create whole entities (corporations) by the Adam-like power of naming. Those powers remain with the lawyers as long as non-lawyers cannot pierce the veil of legal language.
>
> > Many people today, and presumably in the past, have seen through this mystical veil and perceived the secular nature of the law. . . . What we have to consider is that, in essence, law is little different from political policy, administrative decision and military strategy. In itself therefore it would be seen for what it is, a form of political control, without much difficulty. Now clearly such transparency is contrary to the interests of ruling

classes who always want to give their directions some universal legitimacy. It is also contrary to the interests of lawyers who need special status and esoteric services in order to continue—who would pay so much for mere political administrators?
—*C. Sumner,* Reading Ideologies, *as quoted in "The State of Legal Writing," George Gopen* Michigan Law Review 6:333, 344

If the Sumner quotation had appeared first in this example, the author would have lost the opportunity to set the powerful tone of his discussion and also would have lost the chance to focus the reader's attention on his own idea: the God-like nature of attorneys. Instead, the reader would have been confronted with a quotation about legal language and political control—in no meaningful context—followed by a much-weakened assertion that lawyers use language to maintain power. Clearly the strength of the passage would be lost.

Another effective method for integrating source material into the discussion appears in the next example. Here the author weaves the supportive quotations and references into the fabric of his own thoughts, creating a smoothly integrated unit:

The relationship between rhetoric and knowledge has always been problematic, no less so today than in the classical period. Systematic thinking about rhetoric emerged in the fifth century B.C. out of the paradoxes discovered by sophist philosophers in their contemplation of the relationship between language and belief. Their discoveries often took extreme forms of relativism, as in Gorgias' famous first principles: "Nothing is; even if it is, it cannot be known; even if it can be known, it cannot be made meaningful to another person." While such princples seem contradictory, they at least had the salient effect of making subsequent rhetoricians aware, in the words of G. B. Kerferd, that

the relationship between speech and what is the case is far from simple. While it is likely that fifth-century thinkers all were prepared to accept that there is and must always be a relation between the two, there was a growing understanding that what is very often involved is not simply a presentation in words of what is the case, but rather a representation, involving a considerable degree of reorganization in the process.
—*G. B. Kerferd,* The Sophistic Movement, *as quoted by John T. Gage, "An Adequate Epistemology for Composition: Classical and Modern Perspectives"* Essays on Classical Rhetoric and Modern Discourse, *ed. Connors, et al., Southern Illinois University Press, 1984, pp. 152–153*

Here author John Gage introduces the problem of rhetoric and knowledge, then uses the words of Gorgias and Kerferd to corroborate and extend the idea: words are reflections of reality, not reality itself. In so doing, the author remains the authority in the passage, skillfully using the quotations to reinforce his own control over the material.

Note, too, the techniques Gage uses to weave the quotations into the text. He introduces each quotation so that the reader has a clear idea of the quoted material's function in the discussion. For example, he introduces Gorgias's principles as an example of "extreme forms of relativism," in fifth-century B.C. When he uses Kerferd's words, he begins the sentence himself, introducing the idea and letting Kerferd finish the point. In the first example above, George Gopen does not use an elaborate introduction. Instead, he uses the phrase "pierce the veil of legal language" in the sentence directly before the quotation's first line, "Many people today, and presumably in the past, have seen through this mystical veil. . . ." The connection is implicit. Such techniques for integrating quotations into the discussion are essential for producing seamless prose that uses external material effectively. They allow the reader to read the quote as an integral part of the text, not as an intrusion.

Some writers assume that the quotation itself will do the job without any help. Too often, readers are jolted by quotations that appear in the text without introduction or any apparent connection to the discussion. This usually happens when writers are so close to the material that they drop in a quote, assuming that the necessary bridges are obvious. They rarely are. Keep in mind that all quotations need to be carefully yet deliberately woven into the discussion so that the reader clearly understands how they support the author's assertions.

Using Original Thought

The importance of the writer's own ideas is paramount. If you have no ideas when you begin research, you will have no original ideas when you finish the process. As a result, the document you produce will be little more than a pastiche of other people's thoughts. The primary rule in writing from sources is that you must have a clear sense of the thesis question so that the research you do is focused on solving that problem, and the resulting prose is highly focused as well. If you directly address a problem and use your external sources to support your solution, the prose will have a clear direction and purpose.

As a further precaution against depending on other people's ideas, you should get in the habit of using at least three sources for every major point. That is a fairly standard rule of thumb when researchers are looking for a real answer to a research question and are in danger of producing biased results. Three sources give you a broader view of the possible approaches to the point and make it easier to develop a unique informed approach. As mentioned previously, if you organize your discussion around major points you have developed through the invention process, and if you keep those ideas in the forefront as a framework for answering the thesis question, the resource material naturally takes on a supportive role rather than a dominant one.

Finally, when you finish a draft of an essay, you should ask yourself the following question: "If I were to present this to the experts I'm using as sources, would they say I have used their ideas fairly and have said more than each of them has said singly? Would they see that I have augmented their views with my own ideas?" These are tough questions to ask but important ones if you want to have confidence in your prose.

Documenting Sources

Writers document their sources so that readers know where the information came from and how to find it if they want to do more research on the topic or check the original source for themselves. The various documentation forms are precise because the form ensures that all the information will be there for the reader who depends on that citation to find the source. The purpose is to let readers know where to look to find the page number, the volume, the year, and whatever else they need to know. Such precision also makes the final text look professional and gives it a sense of authority.

Nearly every field has its own precise documentation guidelines, so it would not be especially helpful to present one here as the appropriate style. The Modern Language Association, the American Psychology Association, the Associated Press, the United Press International, the legal profession, and various corporations all have preferred documentation forms. The best advice is to find the documentation form appropriate to the type of writing and follow it exactly.

The following examples show three of the most common documentation forms. Each example gives both the possible references used in the body of the paper and the complete citation used at the end.

Modern Language Association (MLA)
  Reference in Text:
    Widgets have innumerable uses (Holmes 211).
    or
    According to Holmes (211), widgets have innumerable uses.
  End Reference ("Works Cited"):
    Holmes, John A. *The Uses of Widgets*. New York: Technology Books, 1989.

American Psychological Association (APA)
  Reference in Text:
    Holmes (1989, p. 211) notes that widgets have innumerable uses.
    or
    As many experts agree, widgets have innumerable uses (Holmes, 1989, p. 211).
  End Reference ("References"):
    Holmes, J. (1989). *The Uses of Widgets*. New York: Technology Books.

Endnotes
  Reference in Text:
    As many experts agree, widgets have innumerable uses.[1]
    or
    "Widgets have innumerable uses."[1]
  End Reference ("Endnotes"):
    [1] John A. Holmes, *The Uses of Widgets*. New York: Technology Books, 1989) 211.

An issue more important than documentation form is knowing what to document. In brief, anything that is copied needs to be documented. As a general rule, there are three instances where citing a source is essential, although some of the guides mentioned above suggest more than three. All agree that it is necessary to cite sources in the following instances:

- *Direct quotations:*
  Any words or visual material (maps, charts, and so on) taken directly and intact from another source should be documented.

- *Paraphrases:*
  An original idea stated in different words, though the idea remains intact, should be documented. If the information is factual rather than an original opinion and can be easily found in other sources, documentation is not necessary.

- *Specific organization:*
  When writers copy the organization of ideas in the original source, they should document that source.

Perhaps the best tip for knowing when to document is to use common sense. If writers are careful to give credit where it is due and to provide the reader with easy access to all the source material, the text is probably documented appropriately. More detailed information is available in the reference and citation guides used in the various fields.

Careful research makes you an authority on your topic and allows you to write with credibility. When you have explored the available resources and have included documented support as the foundation for your discussion, your writing task becomes much easier in two ways. First, your research gives you enough expertise to evaluate the quality of your own ideas on the topic; second, you can more readily convince readers that you know what you are talking about. Uninformed opinions cannot be disguised by clever writing.

FOCUS ON

Your Writing Project

1. Write a resource paper that summarizes the most important trends and current ideas about a topic of your choice. For example, you might explore contemporary banking methods, trends in literary criticism, computer networking, effective product marketing, and so on. Include references to the best sources on the topic, and compile a focused bibliography at the end of the paper.

2. Write an analysis of a profession that is attractive to you. Include at least one interview and as much information as you can about salaries, job security, professional growth expectations, available training, and the most important developments in that field over the last five years.

The Writing Group

As practice, use your writing group to test your interviewing techniques. A rehearsal of the interview process can ease your apprehensions about it as well as point out possible weaknesses in your method that need to be fixed before the real interview.

Have each member of the group submit a list of topics about which he or she is knowledgeable. Divide the topics among the group members, asking each person to interview someone else on his or her special topic. The interviewer should complete all the preliminary and follow-up steps discussed in this chapter and, using the information from the interview, write a short paper about the topic. After the exercise is finished, distribute copies of these papers to the whole group for comment.

Chapter 5

Arrangement

Imagine walking into your house and finding everything rearranged. What used to be the dining room is now the den; the living room has become the master bedroom; and the study now serves as the laundry. Even the furniture has been moved to new locations, so you cannot depend on old patterns to orient yourself. You know the house is the same place as before, but its new order has given it a whole new character. It no longer fits your tastes or your purposes. In fact, it does not seem like yours anymore, although you recognize all your belongings in it.

Arrangement in writing has the same dramatic effect. Two writers can take the same subject matter and arrange it differently, changing the meaning with a shift in order, so that the same material sends two different messages to the reader. That does not mean that the material changes or that either writer is presenting false information; it simply means that the way writers organize their ideas has a profound effect on how readers perceive the text's meaning. Therefore, before writers begin arranging prose, they need to understand the delicate connection between arrangement and meaning.

Understanding the Symbiosis of Order and Meaning

Part of the reason organization plays such a vital role in creating meaning is explained by reader response theory. As readers, we have developed approaches to reading that are influenced by our cultural expectations and reading environment. For example, when a text begins "Once upon a time . . . ," readers expect a story to entertain them. But when a text begins "Dateline TOKYO—Japanese auto makers announced today . . . ," readers expect a news bulletin. Similarly, prose intended for special environments has specialized organization. The business memorandum is a good example of ordering information to increase efficiency in reader response. In the business environment the memo's standard organization pattern allows readers to find the main point quickly and file the memo for easy retrieval. Deviation from the normal pattern, however, creates confusion and wastes time as readers try to find information in unfamiliar locations. The following is an example of proper memorandum format:

January 22, 1991

TO: James P. Wallace, Purchasing Dept., Dane Plastics
FROM: Cynthia Lee, Purchasing Agent, RoyCo Engineering
SUBJECT: RoyCo Hotcell Installation Billing
                Purchase Order #73200

Now that RoyCo is in the final phase of the Hotcell installation, we can itemize our specific costs for the project. Attached is a breakdown of the cost additions and deductions from the original purchase price of our P.O. #73200. Please use these figures for the final billing.
    Thank you.

Attachment
cc: J. P. Brady
      D. Rosen

Notice in this example that the four heading lines at the top clearly define all the pertinent information: date, sender, receiver, and subject. Especially important is the subject line that concisely identifies the specific purpose of the memo, thus giving the reader an immediate context for the information that follows. Such precision also is helpful later when the reader needs to retrieve the memo from a file. A weak subject line such as "RoyCo Hotcell Installation" would not set this memo apart from the hundreds of others written during the course of the project, and the writer would fail to use organization to its fullest potential.

The other standard parts of this memo allow the reader to know at a glance that additional information is attached and that copies of this memo went to two other people. If any of these essential parts were left out, arranged in a different order, or placed in a different spot on the page, confusion would result. By adhering to standard memo form, business writers use organization to meet reader expectations and increase corporate efficiency.

Because readers expect certain patterns to emerge in a discourse, shifts in those patterns create dramatic effects—whether or not that is the writer's intent. You need to be aware of reader expectations and organize your prose to meet those expectations or to thwart them if there is a good reason for doing so.

The following examples illustrate how different organization affects meaning. Both of these newspaper articles deal with the same basic information, but the organization is entirely different. Although the reporters went to the same news conference and started with the same facts, the arrangement of information in the stories creates widely different impressions on the reader. Notice how each reporter features some facts more prominently than others and includes additional information to color reader response.

Article 1: Police Net "Closing in" on Girl's Killers

An army of police working around-the-clock is "closing in quickly" on the killers of an 11-year-old girl who was hit by a stray bullet in a drug-related fight Friday night, officials said yesterday.

Boston Police Deputy Superintendent William Celester, who is heading the investigation, said "30 to 40" extra officers and 14 detectives are combing Roxbury in the wake of Darlene Tiffany Moore's death.

"We are making progress. We are questioning a lot of people," Celester said at a press conference yesterday. "We may have something [today]."

The intense sweep of Roxbury for the girl's killers yesterday netted a murder suspect wanted in connection with another drug-related killing.

Paul Larry "The Lizard" Guild, also known as Eric Arthur, 21, was arrested at 12:45 P.M. for the murder of a suspected drug dealer, Anthony Johnson of Dorchester, on June 17.

The arrest was not directly connected to Moore's death, Celester said.

Moore was killed by two stray bullets, when one group of young drug dealers ambushed another near her home.

Ironically, Moore had been sent to live with her relatives in Greenville, S.C., because her mother considered the streets around their home in Roxbury unsafe. She was back in Boston for a visit when she was shot twice, once in the head and once in the back, while sitting on a mailbox talking with friends.

Celester said 12 members of the Power Patrol and Anti-Crime units—which are assigned to especially high-crime areas—have also been added to the search for the three youths who gunned down Moore.

The bulk of the Anti-Crime unit has been assigned to Roxbury for the past three months where drug-related violence has been the worst in 20 years, Celester said.

Celester said police called yesterday's press conference "to assure the community that we are doing everything possible" to combat recent drug-related violence in Roxbury.

Concerned about the bloody surge of drug-related crime in the area and outraged at Moore's death, a group of neighborhood residents met with Celester Saturday to demand more police protection.

Celester called the meeting "very productive" and said he would present one suggestion—releasing the names of all arrested drug dealers to the press—to Mayor Ray Flynn and Police Commissioner Francis "Mickey" Roache.

City Councilor Bruce C. Bolling, a member of the group, said Flynn and Roache should hire 300 additional permanent police officers, including 30 to 40 for the Roxbury and Mattapan area. Those additions would bring Boston's total police force to about 2,300 and the Roxbury-Mattapan allocation to about 310, he said.

Celester said there had already been one by-product of stepped-up patrols and community vigilance: the arrest of Guild. He was nabbed in front of 65 Camden St. in the Lenox Street housing projects after a vicious struggle with police.

One officer suffered a sprained thumb wrestling with Guild who was attempting to get a .357 magnum revolver loaded with hollow-point Teflon-coated slugs in his waist-band, police said.

Police sources said Guild was a major drug dealer in the area and police found eight bags of what they believed to be heroin in his possession, Celester said.

He is being charged with murder, illegal possession of a firearm and ammunition, and possession of heroin with intent to sell.

His "slippery" ability to avoid the law earned him the street nickname "Lizard," said arresting officer Drew Smith, who had been investigating Guild for six months.

In addition to the murder warrant for allegedly [shooting] Johnson in the face, Guild was also wanted by police for armed robbery, assault and battery, larceny, burglary and previous illegal weapons charges, police sources said.

Guild was spotted by off-duty Area E (Jamaica Plain) detective Nick Clinton. Smith and Patrolman Edward Hairston of the Area B "Power Patrol" and Patrolman Robert Merner of the City-Wide Anti-Crime Unit made the arrest, Celester said.

—The Boston Herald, *Monday, August 22, 1988. Reprinted by permission.*

Article 2: In Roxbury, Demands to Help Curb Violence

Roxbury residents enraged by the murder of an 11-year-old girl yesterday called on authorities to take drastic steps, including the use of the National Guard, to reclaim their neighborhoods from warring gangs of drug dealers.

Some residents of the Grove Hall neighborhood said a no-exceptions curfew might curb violence by clearing the streets and sidewalks where drug deals occur. Others said a new police station should be built in the middle of the Homestead Street area, which is notorious for drug dealing.

Ben Haith, a longtime community activist, called on the state judiciary to establish night sessions of criminal courts so working people from the neighborhood can attend trials of drug dealers and urge longer sentences.

Barbara Williams, a resident of Homestead Street for 33 years, said she favors deployment of National Guard soldiers to patrol the neighborhood. "It's never been worse," she said. "With the shooting of the little girl, I've lost hope."

Haith, Williams and others planned to meet with Mayor Flynn in City Hall this morning to demand action. The meeting was arranged by a Roxbury neighborhood group after Darlene Tiffany Moore, 11, became an innocent victim Friday in an escalating war between rival drug gangs.

"I am holding city officials responsible for the killing of that child," said Amanda C. Houston, 62, Homestead Street activist. "We've been warning that this kind of thing would happen for months—years, really. The neighborhood has been vocal and organized and persistent, but nothing happened. Now this."

The victim, who was known as Tiffany, was to have returned yesterday to South Carolina, where she had lived with an aunt the past two years and attended school. Instead, she died Friday night after being hit by two stray bullets fired from a passing automobile. Police Deputy Superintendent William R. Celester, commander of Area B (Roxbury, Mattapan, parts of Dorchester), said Tiffany was the unintended victim in a ride-by attack by the Castlegate Road gang on the Humboldt Avenue gang.

Tiffany, described by family members as a "friendly, loving little girl," was sitting on a large mailbox at the corner of Humboldt and Homestead with two friends when the attack occurred at about 9:30 P.M.

Asked about suspects, Celester yesterday said detectives have "some people in mind," but declined to comment further on the investigation. "We're questioning people," Celester said in a brief news conference at the Area B station.

Another Roxbury shooting last weekend, meanwhile, is believed to be drug-related. Celester said Michael Searcy, 18, of Lamartine Street, Jamaica Plain, was shot three times in the chest Saturday at about 9 P.M. on Parker Street, which Celester called "a drug area."

Searcy was reported to be in critical condition yesterday at Brigham and Women's Hospital in Boston. Celester said police are seeking two men identified by Searcy as his assailants.

Celester, a 20-year police veteran, said the streets of Roxbury have never been more violent. He blamed the easy availability of drugs and guns to young people.

The shootings prompted police officials to assign about 40 additional police officers to patrol Roxbury, an 8-square-mile section in the very center of Boston. Foot patrols were instituted on Homestead Street on Saturday.

Houston was quoted in Boston Globe stories in March and June as saying drug dealing was out of control in her neighborhood of big, old homes on the northeast side of Franklin Park.

The corner of Homestead Street and Humboldt Avenue, where Tiffany was shot, is considered a major crossroads for young dealers. "It's seen as someplace important for anyone who's trying to muscle in on drug dealing turf," said Houston. "They were trying to get someone and this girl unfortunately was there."

The corner of Elm Hill Avenue and Homestead Street is another strategic location, she said. "Homestead Street itself is known all over New England as the place to go for all of your drug needs," she said.

Houston said, "two dear friends," Richard and Marilyn Wood, recently moved from Homestead Street to the town of Easton. "We don't let the children play in the neighborhood," Marilyn Wood told the Globe in June. "It's too dangerous. We're under constant pressure from the criminal element here. We're prisoners in our own community."

Haith, director of the anti-crime program at the Roxbury Multi Service Center, said petitions are circulating for additional police patrols, night court, and the National Guard. He said police should "get back into the community and stay there, instead of running at each crisis."

Haith said police should establish a storefront "operations room" where police and community members can easily swap information on drug dealers and use maps and charts to combat the enemy. He said the names of known drug dealers should be widely circulated.

Haith also suggested a citywide march, organized by clergy, against drugs and violence. "This thing is a cancer and it's spreading to other parts of the city," he said.

Flynn was unavailable for comment yesterday. On Saturday he visited Tiffany's mother and pledged "around the clock" efforts to arrest her murderers.
—*Courtesy of* The Boston Globe, *Monday, August 22, 1988*. *Reprinted by permission*.

A quick reading of Article 1 makes it clear that the story is about police efforts to stop the crime wave in Roxbury. By focusing first on the Deputy Police Superintendent and following up with the story of Guild's capture, the *Herald* reporter gives the impression that the police are swarming over Area B in an all-out war on youth drug gangs. Deputy Superintendent Celester would approve of this arrangement more than he would of the *Globe's* version.

The *Globe* takes the neighborhood's viewpoint. After reading Article 2, most readers would think that the police have been slow to respond to an obvious problem. By sandwiching the Tiffany Moore story between angry responses from the neighborhood activists, the reporter has created a story that demands more police action. The *Globe* ran the story of Guild's arrest in a separate box on the same page as the longer article reproduced here. That placement effectively cuts the direct connection between the two stories, while the *Herald* suggests that Guild's arrest is evidence of police response.

In both articles, arrangement plays a major part in the meaning readers take away with them. The *Herald* story begins with "An army of police working around-the-clock. . . ." On the other hand, the *Globe* begins with "Roxbury residents enraged by the murder of an 11-year-old girl . . ." and ends with mention of "around-the-clock" police efforts. Readers are getting two very different meanings from the articles—meanings created by the way the reporters organized their stories.

As this example shows, meaning and organization are inextricably linked. These two newspaper stories have been deliberately selected to make a point, but it is nevertheless fair to say that organization contributes extensively to meaning in any type of writing. Writers who believe that order does not matter as long as all the pertinent information appears in the story are deluding themselves. When you are aware of the symbiosis between order and meaning, you can achieve different effects by carefully organizing your prose to suit various purposes.

PRACTICE EXERCISE 5.1

The following two sports articles cover the same story in different ways. Read them carefully and write a short analysis of how the stories' arrangement of material creates different effects on the readers.

"It's Toronto in the American League East"

by Joe Sexton
Special to the New York Times

TORONTO, Sept. 30—The afternoon began with the SkyDome roof half-open. By 5:37 P.M., one had every expectation that it would be completely off at any second.

The Toronto Blue Jays, a team burdened by past failures to perform courageously and competently in the clutch, today won the American League East title by defeating the Baltimore Orioles, 4–3.

The victory, the Jays' second comeback triumph in 24 hours against the only team with a chance to catch them, sent the 49,553 fans into a frenzy and several dozen relieved and rejoicing Blue Jays streaming from the field.

The Blue Jays, who had trailed from the third inning on, struck for three runs in the bottom of the eighth against three Baltimore pitchers to wipe out a 3–1 deficit.

The decisive inning captured the Blue Jays in their entirety, with hits produced by stars old and traded for within the last two months. Lloyd Moseby laid down a crucial sacrifice, Mookie Wilson kept the threat alive with a chopped single, Fred McGriff laced a vital run-scoring single and George Bell, the probable most valuable player, aptly brought home the final run with a sacrifice fly.

The loss ripped up for the Orioles what appeared to be yet another remarkable chapter in their magical and completely unexpected quest for a division crown just a year after they were unqualifiedly the worst team in the major leagues.

Dave Johnson, a 29-year-old career minor leaguer had started the game after the scheduled pitcher, Pete Harnisch, was scratched after stepping on a nail en route to the hotel Friday night. He allowed just two hits through seven innings before walking Nelson Liriano to start the eighth.

Johnson was quickly gone and a dozen electric minutes later, the Blue Jays were all but champions.

The crown was inestimably sweet for the Blue Jays, who have been dogged for weeks about whether they were going to cough up yet another shot at the glory of a World Series championship. In '85, they had wasted a 3–1 lead in games against the Royals in the A. L. championship series. In '87, they lost the last seven games of the regular season to forfeit the title to the Tigers.

The Orioles, after a strange argument concerning the stadium lights before the start of the third inning, got them turned back on, and then turned up the heat on the Blue Jays a bit with a couple of runs to take a 2−1 edge.

With one out, Phil Bradley was safe on an infield single, and after another brief argument concerning Cal Ripken's ground-rule double, was permitted to score and even the game at 2−2. The umpires at first ordered Bradley back to third after a fan reached out and caught Ripken's bounding ball down the left-field line.

Moseby Friday's Hero

The momentary ruling, though, brought the Oriole manager, Frank Robinson, bounding out of the dugout. After an exchange with John Shulock, the home-plate umpire, Shulock determined that there would not have been a play at home on Bradley and allowed the run. Of course, there ensued a rather less productive exchange between Cito Gaston, the manager of the Blue Jays, and the umpires.

Gaston, however, had to relent eventually, and no sooner had he sat down in the dugout than another Baltimore run was brought home by Randy Milligan's single to left.

Bradley's speed made possible Baltimore's third run an inning later when Bradley followed Mike Devereaux's single and Bob Melvin's double off the wall in right with an infield single back of second base. Tony Fernandez made every effort to field the ball, but once he had there was no chance of nailing Bradley.

Lloyd Moseby, Friday night's hero, was the afternoon's first principle focus of interest when he walked to start the bottom of the first. He moved to second on Mookie Wilson's ground out and advanced to third when Fred McGriff pounded the ball to second. He crossed the plate when George Bell's soft single trickled into right field for a 1−0 lead.

Copyright © 1989 by The New York Times Company.
Reprinted by permission.

"Blue Jays capture AL East crown"

by Steve Fainaru
The Boston Globe *Staff*

TORONTO—The sometimes dreary march to the AL East title ended in victory yesterday for the Toronto Blue Jays, who fought off their own dubious history and the phenomenon of the Baltimore Orioles in consecutive games that raised both teams above the mediocrity the division came to represent this summer.

In the end, the Jays won it in a deafening roar, scoring three eighth-inning runs in a 4–3 victory at the SkyDome, the $600 million playpen that opened one day after Toronto came back from a 10–0 deficit to defeat the Red Sox in early June.

Thousands of fans lingered long afterwards just to gaze at the magnificent stadium. In the basement, Toronto's ornate clubhouse had become a symbol for the team's stiffness down the stretch. After the Jays clinched, however, they simply trashed the place, spilling Labatt's and champagne over the marble tables and littering the newly-carpeted floors.

"We believed in ourselves the whole year," said veteran Lloyd Moseby. "Unfortunately, people wrote bad things about us. They said we would choke again. But we believe in ourselves, and now we're where we belong, sipping champagne."

Toronto opens the American League playoffs Tuesday night in Oakland, Calif. With one more victory today, the Blue Jays would finish one game better than the Red Sox did winning the East last year. Like the Sox, who took off after firing manager John McNamara, Toronto was sparked by the firing of Jimy Williams when the team was 12–24. Since then, Toronto is 29 games over .500 under Cito Gaston, the first black manager to lead his team to a division title.

It was Gaston's soft-spoken, almost nonchalant approach that helped get Toronto through the final week, when memories of previous collapses in the 1985 playoffs and the final week of the '87 season were brought up daily. Beyond Gaston, the Jays were indebted to their bullpen, which allowed four hits over 11 scoreless innings in the two victories over Baltimore, and to first baseman Fred McGriff, who overcame an appalling September slump to drive in the tying run with a single.

For the Orioles, their unbelievable season seemed to be summed up by reliever Kevin Hickey, who after playing a crucial role in the Baltimore loss, shrugged and said, "What the heck. Columbus took a chance. He discovered America a year later. Maybe next year we'll discover the American League crown."

Yesterday was wildly typical for the Orioles (86–75), losers of 107 games last season. The regularly scheduled starter, Pete Harnisch, was scratched after he stepped on a nail while making the one-mile walk back to the team hotel Friday night with his sister and brother-in-law.

He was replaced by rookie righthander Dave Johnson, the 29-year-old Baltimore native who had descended recently from a heady flight that included his first major league victory, a huge win over the Sox in Baltimore and even a Player of the Week award in early August.

Johnson had lost his previous five decisions, but "to be honest, I think he pitched about as well as he can pitch," Toronto third baseman Kelly Gruber said. He gave up two hits in the first six innings and carried a 3–1 lead into the eighth. He walked the first batter of the eighth, Nelson Liriano, however, and the young Orioles suddenly found the SkyDome collapsing on top of them, full force.

Orioles manager Frank Robinson brought Hickey, another career minor-leaguer whose career was revived this season. Hickey walked pinch hitter Manny Lee, then went to a 2–1 count on Moseby, who was attempting to sacrifice. Before he could throw another pitch, Robinson went to righthander Mark Williamson.

Moseby, who already had failed once to get down the bunt, laid one down that looked almost as if it hit the third-base line and bounced back into fair territory. "It was unbelievable," he said. "It hit the chalk and just spun. I've never seen anything like it. You know when something happens like that, it's destiny."

With runners on second and third, Mookie Wilson drove in a run with a single through the short-third hole. That left the inning to McGriff, the league's home run leader, whose only homer of the month came Sept. 4 in Chicago. He tied the game with a sharp single to right. George Bell drove in the winning run with a sacrifice fly.

"This makes up for the whole month," McGriff said.

The Orioles came within four outs of first place Friday night. Yesterday it was five. Still loose, an attitude that extended from Robinson, who walked through the race with a knowing smile that seemed to infuse his young team with confidence, they ravaged lefthander Jimmy Key for eight hits in four innings and had five doubles in the first seven innings by five players.

Cal Ripken, who came out of his own September slump in the series, tied the game with a double in a two-run third, and Phil Bradley drove in a run with a single in the fourth, Key's last inning.

Baltimore had one hit the remainder of the game, Tim Hulett's leadoff double in the seventh off righthander Frank Wills, who pitched four scoreless innings. The end came when Tom Henke (20th save), struck out pinch hitter Larry Sheets. Henke's ERA is 0.92 since Williams, who among other things was accused of mishandling his bullpen, was fired.

In the Baltimore clubhouse, Johnson's eyes were framed in red, but the mood was decidedly upbeat. In a far corner, first baseman Jim Traber gave catcher Jamie Quirk a high five. There were a few hugs. Outside the door, above the field, the roof closed silently, cutting off the sky.

Courtesy of The Boston Globe.
Reprinted by permission.

Organizing for Emphasis

The reporters in the previous examples used organization to empha-size material they thought was important. By controlling the se-quence of information, they placed their emphatic points in the strong lead-off position, relegating other material to weaker positions relative to the overall organization. In the *Herald* story, for example, Deputy Police Superintendent Celester is in an emphatic, strong position, whereas the Roxbury citizens' group is deemphasized. The opposite is true in the *Globe* story. The initial focus in each article "sets up" the readers to view either Celester's police or Roxbury's citizens as the prime movers in the action. In any discourse, the be-ginning sets reader expectations, and the first few paragraphs are the key to creating emphasis in the whole text.

A short digression into cognitive psychology might help here. Many recent studies have shown that readers process text hierarchi-cally, giving more importance to information high in the hierarchy than to information low in the hierarchy. To put it simply, readers pay more attention to ideas or facts at the beginnings of texts. That is why Celester's position is so important in the newspaper stories. By establishing a hierarchy, writers can emphasize certain points easily because the hierarchies affect the readers' perception of the material.

When you organize, you walk a tightrope between your own ex-pectations and those of the readers. The task here is to learn to read from the readers' point of view. This means you must take responsi-bility for remembering that the readers know only what you tell them. Unfortunately, in the heat of composing it is easy to for-get that the readers have not yet thought through the ideas and do not share your sense of how all the pieces relate. It is important to remember that the beginning of the text is the place to establish the reader-writer relationship and the hierarchy of the ideas you are going to present. As you organize your prose, keep in mind that effective organization should appear seamless, not patchworked to-gether. That means you should know ahead of time what informa-tion is most important, and you should prepare the reader from the beginning to see its importance.

There are more sophisticated techniques for emphasizing infor-mation than the simple "what comes first is most important" rule, particularly when the writer cannot depend on chronological order as an organizing principle. Generally, writers use one of two basic strategies to organize their material: deductive or nondeductive (*inductive* is not the right word to use here) organization. Each influences reader response differently, creating totally different effects.

Deductive Organization

Read the following passage about a famous New York Apellate Court case and think about why it is hard to follow:

> **Palsgraf v. Long Island R.R. Co.**
> **Court of Appeals of New York, 1928**
> **248 N.Y. 339, 162 N.E. 99**
>
> *Cardozo, C. J.* Plaintiff was standing on a platform of the defendant's railroad after buying a ticket to go to Rockaway Beach. A train stopped at the station, bound for another place. Two men ran forward to catch it. One of the men reached the platform of the car without mishap, though the train was already moving. The other man, carrying a package, jumped aboard the car but seemed unsteady as if about to fall. A guard on the car, who had held the door open, reached forward to help him in, and another guard on the platform pushed him from behind. In this act, the package was dislodged and fell on the rails. It was a package of small size, about 15 inches long, and was covered by a newspaper. In fact it contained fireworks, but there was nothing in its appearance to give notice of its contents. The fireworks when they fell exploded. The shock of the explosion threw down some scales at the other end of the platform many feet away. The scales struck the plaintiff, causing injuries for which she sues.

This passage is hard to follow because it is not organized deductively. Because the major point appears in the last sentence, readers have no context in which to understand the previous information. As they read the passage, they probably have questions such as, "Why is the fact that there were two men pivotal?" "Is Rockaway Beach important?" "What do the guards have to do with the story?" Actually, the passage is more of a mystery story than a legal fact pattern, because it keeps the reader in suspense until the final sentence. But it is not even a good mystery, because readers have no context set for caring about or identifying with the characters.

If the information in the last sentence was moved to the beginning of the passage—"The plaintiff is suing the railroad for injuries she received when a dislodged package at the railway station caused scales to strike her"—the reader could follow the rest of the text easily, understanding the importance of each fact. Presenting the main point first is the hallmark of deductive order.

Most writers of informative or critical prose use this organizational strategy to increase reader understanding of their ideas. Deductive organization initially sets the context for subsequent text so that the reader understands how the pieces fit together. To set the stage effectively, you should make sure the introductory paragraphs state the text's main purpose and, depending on the situation, the text's conclusions as well. By beginning with a clearly stated goal and/or conclusion, you put everything in a frame of reference for the readers, allowing them to read with a purpose in mind instead of wandering aimlessly through the prose. For example, the following introductory paragraph deftly and directly expresses the author's main purpose and the conclusions he holds:

> Despite the horrors, futilities and destructiveness of war, there are nevertheless certain virtues and truths associated with it which humanity cannot afford to lose. In any discussion of new ways of settling conflicts, these military virtues cannot safely be disregarded.
> —*Richard B. Gregg, "An Effective Substitute for War"*

After reading this paragraph, you know the author's view and understand the emphatic point the rest of the text will make. This framework allows you to better judge the relative importance of each point that follows. On the other hand, if the author had begun with the sentence "Combat soldiers know how to face death," you would have been at a loss about how to interpret it.

Nondeductive Organization

Read this introduction and determine how it serves to set the scene and establish the author's emphasis:

> On a very hot evening at the beginning of July a young man left his little room at the top of a house in Carpenter Lane, went out into the street, and, as though unable to make up his mind, walked slowly in the direction of Kokushkin Bridge.
> He was lucky to avoid meeting with his landlady on the stairs. His little room under the very roof of a tall five-story building was more like a cupboard than a living-room. His landlady, who also provided him with meals and looked after him, lived in a flat on the floor below. Every time he went out, he had to walk past

her kitchen, the door of which was practically always open; and every time he walked past that door, the young man experienced a sickening sensation of terror which made him feel ashamed and pull a wry face. He was up to the neck in debt to his landlady and was afraid of meeting her.

It was not as though he were a coward by nature or easily intimidated. Quite the contrary. But for some time past he had been in an irritable and overstrung state which was like hypochondria. He had been so absorbed in himself and had led so cloistered a life that he was afraid of meeting anybody, let alone his landlady. He was crushed by poverty, but even his straitened circumstances had ceased to worry him lately. He had lost all interest in matters that required his most immediate attention and he did not want to bother about them. As a matter of fact, he was not in the least afraid of his landlady, whatever plots she might be hatching against him. But rather than be forced to stop on the stairs and listen to all the dreary nonsense which did not concern him at all, to all those insistent demands for payment, to all those threats and complaints, and to have to think up some plausible excuse and tell lies—no! A thousand times better to slip downstairs as quietly as a mouse and escape without being seen by anybody.

—*Fyodor Dostoevsky,* Crime and Punishment

Clearly, Dostoevsky has set the scene dramatically so that you have a definite sense of the young man's mental state, but you don't have a clue about the main point or the conclusions. In creative writing and other kinds of prose that depend on touching the readers' emotions, deductive organization often does not work. Instead, writers may draw the reader into the scene by painting a picture to capture the imagination, relying on drama to achieve emphasis. This nondeductive strategy assumes that readers will make discoveries during the course of reading and come to conclusions on their own rather than knowing the conclusion first and then looking only to understand *why* it is true. In this organizational pattern, the journey is more important than the destination.

Both strategies work well in different circumstances. When you want to organize your prose so that your points are emphasized in a transactional or persuasive situation, deductive organization is appropriate. On the other hand, if you want to lead your readers gradually to a discovery of the main point, as in creative and some expository essay writing, nondeductive order is the best plan. Your purpose, in both cases, will determine your choice of strategy.

PRACTICE EXERCISE 5.2

Find a short piece of writing (one or two pages) that you think is especially well organized. What makes it work so well? Is the order deductive? Does it present the context of information first and then proceed to the details? Or, if it is organized nondeductively, why is that strategy appropriate? Write a brief analysis of its organizational strengths.

Outlining Effectively

An outline is essential to the art of organizing. Although even the mention of the word may cause groans from many who think of outlining in its most rigid sense, learning more useful outlining techniques can save you a lot of time and energy in the writing process. You do not have to write a rigidly formal outline, but it genuinely helps to create a planning structure that allows you to test ideas and organizations until you find the right one.

Writing a good outline gives you the opportunity to think through your ideas before you commit them to the page in paragraph form. The skeletal outline makes it easier for you to see how the parts of your document fit together and allows you to critique it more effectively. If you see something in the outline that you do not like, you can rearrange it immediately instead of having to revise long passages of prose. It is not only less work to revise your thoughts in outline form than when they are in full-fledged composition form, it is also less damaging to the ego. Once prose appears in paragraphs, writers often think of it as an inviolate finished product at that stage, even though it could benefit from reworking. That does not happen with outlines, perhaps because there is less of the writer invested in the prose at that point.

All of these advantages depend on writing a useful outline. Keep in mind that the key to effective outlining is to develop a skeleton of the document that allows you to work out your thoughts as thoroughly as possible before creating a lengthy prose passage. That means that instead of jotting down short descriptive words or phrases in your outline, you should develop an outline containing complete thoughts. For example, look at the outline below and ask yourself whether it is useful to the writer.

ENVIRONMENTAL RESTORATION PROGRAM
INTEGRATED ALTERNATIVES DOCUMENT

I. INTRODUCTION
   A. References
   B. Review of Process Pathway
   C. Public Participation Summary

II. SITE DESCRIPTION
   A. Location
   B. History
   C. Characteristics

III. RISK ASSESSMENT
   A. Public Health
   B. Environmental

IV. ALTERNATIVES
   A. No Action
   B. Alternatives Considered
   C. Selected Alternative Rationale
   D. Environmental Impact of Selected Alternative

V. CONCLUSION

VI. REFERENCES

A writer could not gain much direction from this outline. Phrases like "Public Health" or "Environmental Impact" do not tell you what you want to say about these ideas; at best, this outline serves only to divide the document into manageable parts. It does not help the writer with developing ideas.

A more useful outlining technique involves taking the process a step beyond dividing the discussion into parts. A good outline provides a clear picture of your document, allowing you to think through your ideas and check for possible trouble spots before you are overwhelmed by hefty prose passages.

To write an effective outline:

1. State the issue you are writing about in question form. (This is the place to use the thesis question you have developed.)

2. Divide the discussion into manageable subsections.

3. Write the subheadings for each section in complete sentences that lead to definite conclusions.

4. List supportive evidence or material under each subheading. These can be listed in short phrases or jotted notes.

5. Write a short conclusion that directly answers the question you asked at the beginning.

To check the outline's effectiveness, ask yourself the following questions:

- Does each subheading contribute to answering the question stated at the top of the page?
- Do the subheadings follow one another logically? Are they in the best sequence?
- Do the subsections seem balanced? Is there enough supportive material under each subheading, or are some lightweight whereas others seem overburdened with evidence?
- Do the subheadings lead directly and inevitably to the conclusion?
- Does the conclusion answer the question given at the beginning?

Here is a short "before and after" sample that shows how the above suggestions can turn outlining into a genuinely helpful writing tool.

Version 1

MISLEADING MYTHS ABOUT COMPUTERS

I. INTRODUCTION

II. THE MYTHS
    A. The Arithmetic Myth
    B. The Obedient Slave Myth

III. CONCLUSION

Version 2

DEBUNKING THE MISLEADING MYTHS ABOUT COMPUTERS

ISSUE: Is the widely held belief that computers are inherently stupid true?

    A. Misconceptions about a computer's limitations seem to be based on two widely accepted but basically untrue premises: the Arithmetic Myth and the Obedient Slave Myth.

    B. Although many people believe that computers are nothing but arithmetic calculating machines, they can do more than solve mathematical problems.
      1. Most computer operations are nonarithmetic (store, load, test, shift, read, write, skip, move, match, transfer, and so on).

2. Computers spend most of their time positioning, comparing, choosing, and copying—not things a calculator does. (Example: using a computer to prepare paychecks.)
3. It is more accurate to say that a computer is a general-purpose symbol-manipulating machine.

C. Even more widespread is the belief that computers are obedient slaves that do only what they are told to do and do not have the capacity to "think," even though we can program computers to originate ideas.
   1. The paradox: In a literal sense a computer must be given its program of instructions, yet this is not a real restriction on the intelligence of computers.
   2. A. L. Samuels of IBM programmed a computer to play checkers so well that it consistently beat its creator.
   3. The Stanford Research Institute's robot "Shakey" was programmed to solve for itself a wide class of problems.

CONCLUSION: Contrary to popular belief, computers are more than large, obedient calculators. They are smart machines that depend on us to help make them even smarter. Doing so will allow them to increase our knowledge as well.

[The complete version of this paper appears in the first chapter of Bertram Raphael's book, *The Thinking Computer*.]

Note how thoroughly this second version indicates the writer's plan for the prose and how much easier it is to work from than the first version. The writer has already thought through his ideas and has definite points to make about them. With this outline, he can use the rest of his writing time to concentrate on refining the prose rather than on formulating and arranging the basic ideas behind it.

Investing time in an outline at the beginning of the writing process ultimately saves writers hours of composing time and prevents the headaches that can occur when writers realize too late that they have taken their discussion in the wrong direction. It is much easier to rearrange a few lines of outline than it is to move massive chunks of prose—or worse, to have to scrap a whole day's work.

Organizing Text by Levels

Once you have decided on the major arrangement for your ideas, you should then turn your attention to the many organizational levels inherent in every discourse and try to get all of them working in concert to make your point effectively. All discourse is organized at four levels: large-scale, small-scale, paragraph, and sentence levels. To organize a text effectively, you need to be aware of each level as well as the interplay among them. For instance, a document that is well organized overall but has weak paragraph organization does not work as it should, nor does a text that has carefully crafted paragraphs but weak individual sentence structure.

Although the rest of this book deals with these levels in greater detail, the following section briefly defines each of them to give a sense of how each contributes to the arrangement of the whole text.

Large-Scale Organization

This organizational level pertains to the overall discourse and focuses on the arrangement of the text's major parts. Classical rhetoricians, with their penchant for systematizing the universe, believed discourse should have five distinct parts organized in the following sequence:

1. Introduction
2. Statement of facts to set the context
3. Proof or support of the case
4. Refutation of opposing views
5. Conclusion

This arrangement worked well for ancient rhetoricians who used rhetoric primarily in legal argument, and it underlies much of the discourse written today. In fact, these five parts are standard organization for nearly all informative and persuasive discourse, from business memoranda to critical essays, because they assure that the writer will proceed deductively, and they guide the reader logically through the text. Greek and Roman orators believed that this type of deductive organization—in which the main point is clear from the beginning—was essential for logical discourse.

Some types of writing do not lend themselves to deductive organization. Creative writing may be organized differently, as may some essay forms and prose designed for purposes other than to inform or persuade. In these cases, writers may take great liberties with organization to create special effects. They may want to begin with a series of examples, keep the reader in the dark about the point until it becomes self-evident, or use chaotic prose to create a sense of chaos within the reader. There are also other possible arrangements or organization patterns.

Whatever your choice about large-scale organization, it is important that the arrangement is appropriate for your purpose and the reader's needs. It is also essential that you have thought through the organizational decisions and have made an informed choice.

Small-Scale Organization

Once you know how to arrange the major parts, you are faced with decisions about how to organize the material within each part. Keep in mind that readers can digest a limited amount of material at one time. They respond best to discussions that are divided into self-contained segments they can read and understand completely before moving on to the next point. Before you begin thinking about arranging on this smaller scale, you should again examine the main ideas of your text and make sure they are really the most important points you want to express. Ask yourself whether each of these ideas is important enough to warrant a section all to itself and whether you have enough information to write a complete discussion about each point. When you are comfortable with these ideas, you are ready to organize them so that they become logical building blocks to support your overall thesis.

Techniques for small-scale organization can apply to a section or a subsection or even a long paragraph, depending on the depth, completeness, and complexity of the discussion. The arrangement ordinarily should parallel the five parts of the large-scale organization, thereby reinforcing the overall logic of the discussion and ensuring that you have treated each point completely. For every main idea you wish to express, apply in miniature the pattern of introduction, statement of context, support, refutation (if appropriate), and conclusion. Such an arrangement will make the whole process of small-scale organization much easier and will balance the text.

The following tips may help you to organize more effectively on the small scale:

1. Make sure that each subsection has a clear reason for standing as a unit.
2. Make sure that each subsection is of equal importance. Although the lengths of the sections may vary, each should be important enough to warrant a separate emphasis.

3. Organize each segment using techniques parallel to large-scale organization: introduction, statement of context, support, refutation, and conclusion. (Note that the refutation may not be appropriate in every subsection.)

4. Complete an entire point within the section before moving on to another section.

5. Make sure that you have written a clear conclusion for each section to signal the readers that this is the end of one main point and to allow them to digest the information presented.

To make these techniques clearer, here is an example of a subsection excerpted from *Mother Earth News*. Note how the author presents his point in a complete package that allows the readers to understand and respond to this idea before moving on to the next one:

INTRODUCTION & STATEMENT OF CONTEXT

It's not simply the environmental movement that has failed in the 20 years since the first Earth Day. The government programs have also failed. The approach strategy taken by the EPA and all of the state environmental regulatory groups has been wrong. It hasn't worked. As a result, there's been very little improvement in the environment, and certain things have gotten worse.

SUPPORT

This isn't just a hand-waving conclusion on my part. It's based on actual numbers. Look at the changes in emissions and pollutants. In 1970, the Clean Air Act Amendments called for a 90 percent reduction in urban levels of carbon monoxide, hydrocarbon, and ozone, setting a 1977 deadline for achieving this goal. In 1977, with compliance not even in sight, the deadline was moved to 1982. When that was missed, the deadline was delayed once more to December 31, 1987. Now, with nearly 100 million people breathing substandard air in urban areas that are still in noncompliance, the deadline may be extended up to 25 years *more!*

REFUTATION

In a very few instances, we have succeeded. These allow us to examine the specific reasons for environmental success or failure. The answer is simple: If you don't put something into the environment, it's not there. Air emissions of lead have declined by 86 percent because much less lead is now added to gasoline and therefore that much less lead is contaminating the environment. The environmental levels of DDT and PCB have dropped sharply because their production and use have been banned. Mercury is much less prevalent in the environment because it is no longer used in manufacturing chlorine. Strontium 90 has decayed to low levels because the United States and the Soviet Union have had the simple wisdom to stop the atmospheric bomb tests that produce it.

CLUSION { The moral is, controls don't work. When a pollutant is attacked at its point of origin, it can be eliminated. Once produced, it's too late. . . .
—*Barry Commoner,* Mother Earth News *(March/April 1990)*

As this passage illustrates, effective organization of a discussion's components creates a logic and clarity that might be missing if the writer organized only on the large-scale level. Likewise, if you organize the smaller sections of your prose well, the clarity of your ideas will be immediately apparent, although readers may not be aware of how carefully you have crafted this inner structure.

Paragraph-Level Organization

Chapter 6 discusses writing paragraphs in detail. At this point it is sufficient to note the relationship of paragraphs to the other levels of textual arrangement.

Although they must have effective transitions between them and they must work together to build toward a major point, paragraphs are units unto themselves. In the larger context of the discourse, paragraphs function as the logically constructed building blocks that make up the small-scale chunks. If writers ignore this function and, instead, use paragraphs as a dumping ground for loosely connected ideas, the whole discourse caves in because the basic support units cannot hold up the structure.

Sentence-Level Organization

Chapter 8 presents a detailed discussion of sentences. For now, note only that sentence design is as much a form of arrangement as is large-scale organization and the other organizational levels. Even though the other levels of organization work well, if the sentences are all the same length, or overuse a particular structure, or are otherwise poorly designed, they can destroy the entire text because the readers have to struggle too hard to grasp the writer's meaning.

When you become aware of the four levels of organization, you also realize the extent to which arrangement affects discourse, and you become more aware of the power to control meaning by using effective organizing principles. As anyone walking into the rearranged house mentioned at the beginning of this chapter would know, organization is a prime factor in the creation of meaning and in the impact of that meaning on the reader.

Guiding the Reader

Communicating well in any kind of writing means you must lead the readers through the text. A technical writer, for instance, guides users through the steps of a process; an academic writer guides readers through a complex argument; a business writer guides department managers or consumers; a legal writer guides attorneys, judges, and clients; and so on. To do that, they have three basic tools:

- Statement of organization
- Signposts
- Format

Statement of Organization

Usually placed in the first or second paragraph, the statement of organization is a direct admission of the writer's organizational plan. It states the purpose of the document and indicates the arrangement of the discussion to follow. In so doing, it becomes part of the context statement suggested by classical rhetoricians (Part 2 of the five parts of discourse) as the writer uses it to create a framework for the rest of the text. This direct approach sets reader expectations and creates a preliminary road map through the prose. In other words, the statement of organization tells the reader where you are going and how you plan to get there.

The following lead paragraphs show how the statement of organization makes even a complex text seem more manageable for the reader.

> We can distinguish various kinds of theories in physics. Most of them are constructive. They attempt to build up a picture of a more complex phenomenon out of the materials of a relatively simple formal scheme from which they start out. Thus the kinetic theory of gases seeks to reduce mechanical, thermal, and diffusional processes to movements of molecules—i.e., to build them up out of the hypothesis of molecular motion. When we say that we have succeeded in understanding a group of natural processes, we invariably mean that a constructive theory has been found which covers the processes in question.
>
> Along with this most important class of theories there exists a second, which I will call "principle-theories." These employ the analytic, not the synthetic, method. The elements which form their basis and starting-point are not hypothetically constructed but

empirically discovered ones, general characteristics of natural processes, principles that give rise to mathematically formulated criteria which the separate processes or the theoretical representations of them have to satisfy. This the science of thermodynamics seeks by its analytical means to deduce necessary conditions, which separate events have to satisfy, from the universally experienced fact that perpetual motion is possible.

The advantages of the constructive theory are completeness, adaptability, and clearness; those of the principle theory are logical perfection and security of the foundations.

The theory of relativity belongs to the latter class. In order to grasp its nature, one needs first of all to become acquainted with the principles on which it is based.

—*Albert Einstein, "What is the Theory of Relativity?"*

It may seem curious that a person whose whole professional effort is devoted to psychotherapy should be interested in problems of communication. What relationship is there between providing therapeutic help to individuals with emotional maladjustments and the concern of this conference with obstacles to communication? Actually the relationship is very close indeed. The whole task of psychotherapy is the task of dealing with a failure in communication. The emotionally maladjusted person, the "neurotic," is in difficulty first because communication within himself has broken down, and second because as a result of this his communication with others has been damaged. If this sounds somewhat strange, then let me put it in other terms. In the "neurotic" individual, parts of himself which have been termed unconscious, or repressed, or denied to awareness, become blocked off so that they no longer communicate themselves to the conscious or managing part of himself. As long as this is true, there are distortions in the way he communicates himself to others, and so he suffers both within himself, and in his interpersonal relations. The task of psychotherapy is to help the person achieve, through a special relationship with a therapist, good communication within himself. Once this is achieved he can communicate more freely and effectively with others. We may say then that psychotherapy is good communication, within and between men. We may also turn that statement around and it will still be true. Good communication, free communication, within or between men, is always therapeutic.

It is, then, from a background of experience with communication in counseling and psychotherapy that I want to present here two ideas. I wish to state what I believe is one of the major factors in blocking or impeding communication, and then I wish to present what in our experience has proven to be a very important way of improving or facilitating communication.

—*Carl R. Rogers, "Communication: Its Blocking and Its Facilitation"*

As both of these examples illustrate, the writers have introduced their purposes for writing, have set those purposes in specific contexts, and have directly stated their organizational plans. By using these techniques, they have given the reader directions about what to expect. In addition, in the process of crafting such careful statements of organization, the writers are forced to create a logical arrangement to their texts.

When the statement of organization is clear, the rest of the document is easy to organize because it follows the map set out at the beginning. By referring back to that statement as they proceed through the text, writers reinforce the appearance of order and keep the readers "located" in the prose. In the first example above, Albert Einstein gives the background for his theory of relativity and then states directly how he plans to proceed: "In order to grasp its nature, one needs first of all to become acquainted with the principles on which it is based." Similarly, Carl Rogers establishes a context for his discussion and then announces that he will present two ideas: "I wish to state what I believe is one of the major factors in blocking or impeding communication, and then I wish to present what in our experience has proven to be a very important way of improving or facilitating communication." In both texts, the writers have used the statement of organization effectively, and the rest of their texts fulfill the organizational promises made at the beginning.

As is clear from these examples, writers who make a good first impression are going to have an easier time convincing the readers of the discussion's validity. It is important to make it easy for the readers to know what is expected of them. No matter how accurate the logic is, if readers have to work too hard to understand it, they will resist.

Signposts

Like the statements of organization, signposts are prose indicators that orient the reader in the discourse. These "reader cues" periodically recap where the discussion has been and where it is going, constantly reminding the reader of the larger picture. Because readers can be expected to keep only a limited amount of information in mind at once, it is a good idea to provide these continuing reminders of how the pieces of the discourse relate to each other. Signposts direct attention back to the larger pattern, placing all the pieces in logical context. They also provide reflective pauses in the discussion, allowing the reader to digest small units of information instead of being overwhelmed by the whole document at once.

Poorly written signposts sound forced and lack grace. Novice writers who have just discovered this technique sometimes use it much too blatantly. For example:

> Having demonstrated the broad applications of the exclusivity rule to all injuries caused by work-related events, this memorandum will now address the plaintiff's individual claims in the light of the court's application of the Michigan Workers' Compensation Act in similar cases.

Compare that paragraph to one on the same subject that uses signposts effectively. It more subtly indicates where the argument has been and where it will go.

> Unlike the language defining disabling injury, the Michigan Workers' Compensation Act provides no guidance on nondisabling injuries. Similarly, there is no explicit indication of whether contract damages are compensable under the Act. In the following cases, the Michigan Court of Appeals probes these two categories and provides the basis for analyzing the plaintiff's contract damages and nondisabling injuries.

The key to effective signposts is to include them without making them obtrusive. Remember, writers need to guide their readers logically through the discussion, but a clumsy attempt at this can sound patronizing. Signposts such as "The previous section discussed X, and the next section discusses Y" seem so mechanical that they insult both the writer's and the reader's intelligence. Although readers do not like to feel as if they are being mechanically led, they are appreciative when writers gently point the way.

To further illustrate this point, here are a few more examples of good signposts found in various kinds of writing. As you read them, think about how each allows the reader a breathing space to reflect on the previous material before moving forward on a clearly marked path. Note, too, that each one is forceful as an orienter but is not overly mechanical.

> To implement this professional practice policy, company employees shall adhere to the following procedures for identifying, signing, and sealing our work products.
> —*from an internal memo in an engineering firm*

So far I have described research into various theoretical concepts and textual features that relate to readability as if the results of that research applied in about the same way to all readers in all reading situations. However, there are also some very important differences among readers that affect the way they would interpret a communication and, consequently, affect the readability of that communication for them. Two of these reader variables are the reader's familiarity with the communication's subject matter, and the reading style adopted by the reader.

—*Thomas N. Huckin "A Cognitive Approach to Readability"*

If then this way of approach is an effective avenue to good communication and good relationships, as I am quite sure you will agree if you try the experiment I have mentioned, why is it not more widely tried and used? I will try to list the difficulties which keep it from being utilized.

—*Carl R. Rogers "Communication: Its Blocking and Its Facilitation"*

Discipline, a willingness to take risk, and commitment both to a vision and to the people you've selected to help you get there—without those traits in abundance, it usually doesn't work. Consider the head of another mid size company, a participant in a nationwide service industry, though not one of the companies we studied for this book. We'll call him Tom Walters and the company XYZ, Inc.

—*Donald K. Clifford, Jr. and Richard E. Cavanaugh* The Winning Performance

Format

The third tool writers have for guiding the reader is the design—the format—of the text. The way prose appears on the page directs the readers' eyes to the important points and leads readers to see the organization even before they begin to read. When they look at the arrangement of the text on the page, readers should be able to see what is most important, what is subordinate, and what is the best reading pathway through the information. This is especially true in functional documents where the writer is trying to communicate essential information and the reader is a busy person who has no time to waste. For example, the following passage makes its point quickly because of its clear design:

Among the options open to the Document Review Committee, these three were the most practical:

- Maintain the present document as it stands.

- Revise and clarify the present document.
- Construct a new, replacement document.

By indenting the three options and highlighting them with bullets, the writer has guided the readers' eyes to the important points and has made the prose much easier to read.

Writers of primarily functional texts can test the effectiveness of their document design by trying the following experiment. First, find one page of prose—a memo, a report section, a business letter, a set of instructions—and pin it to a bulletin board. Next, ask a colleague who is not familiar with the text to stand just far enough away from the page so that she cannot read the words. Then ask if the organization of the text is clear from that distance. Can the reader see the relationship of the parts? Which section is most important? Least important? Are there clear steps through the document, indicating a good reading path? Or does the whole page look dense and forbidding to read?

Most writers learn a lot from that experiment, especially about reader attitudes. Readers who are confronted with a dense block of single-spaced text dread the prospect of having to wade through such thick prose. Without realizing it, the writer has put the reader off before any words are read or any information is passed. Furthermore, some page design gives false signals, suggesting to readers that certain material is top priority because of its position on the page, when it really is undeserving of such attention.

To avoid this blocking of communication, writers should pay particular attention to these simple formatting rules for good document design:

1. Use headings liberally.
2. When possible, use specific, informative headings, not one- or two-word descriptive blurbs.
3. Make sure that each level of heading has a distinct placement and format so that the major headings differ from the subheadings, and the minor subheadings differ from those of greater importance.
4. Make sure that headings and subheadings exactly match the Table of Contents.
5. Do not use "bald heads"—a heading immediately followed by a subheading. Always place at least one sentence after each heading.

6. Center only information that is important enough to warrant such attention. The reader's eye will be drawn to that material.

7. Do not use bullets for long lists. Pages of bulleted items create a false impression that the information has no depth or substance.

8. Use bullets when the order of information is not important. Use numbers when the sequence is important.

9. Make sure that paragraphs vary in length and are not all dense "blocks" of information, nor strings of short "blurbs."

10. Use enough white space between information to allow the reader to see where each idea begins and ends.

A thorough discussion of document design requires much more space than is available here. Nonetheless, because it is so important for at least 75 percent of the writing done today (and that is probably an extremely low estimate), effective formatting techniques should be in every writer's repertoire. Otherwise, simple writing tasks such as the following memorandum create undue difficulty in communication. Take a minute to put yourself in the shoes of the company employees who received this message; read it as they would:

December 9, 1991

TO: All Employees
FROM: J. M. Knight
SUBJECT: Meeting on "Management by Objective,"
December 10–12

On December 10–12 the corporation will host a conference of Management by Objective, which will be held in the Building Six Auditorium. Approximately 500 conference participants are expected, which will cause crowding at some of the Corporation's facilities. The Building Six Parking Lot will be reserved for conference attendees. Employees who normally park there should make an effort to use other lots. Also, between 11:30 A.M. and 12:00 P.M., the Administrative Building Cafeteria No. 3 will be occupied by conference attendees. Corporation employees should plan accordingly.

    As always, your cooperation in these matters is greatly appreciated.

Because of this memo's poor organization and format, most employees initially had the impression that they were being invited to the conference. The subject line announces the *conference,* not the true topic of the memo. The body of the text further reinforces that mistaken impression by beginning with information on the conference. Buried in the lower half of the main paragraph is the memo's real point, that employees not only were not included in the conference but they also had to park and eat in remote locations. It is no wonder that the company morale was low. A better version, using format to greater benefit, is shown below:

December 9, 1991

TO: All Employees
FROM: J. M. Knight
SUBJECT: Alternate Parking and Cafeteria Arrangements
for Employees not Attending the Conference
on December 10–12

Because of the 500 guests expected for the "Management by Objective" conference to be held at the company on December 10–12, those employees not attending should note the following special arrangements:

1. *Building Six Parking Lot will be closed.* Please park in the adjacent lots during those three days.

2. *Administrative Building Cafeteria 3 will be closed between 11:30 and 12:00.* Please plan to use Cafeteria 2, or schedule your lunch after noon on those days.

Thank you for your help in easing the crowded conditions during the conference. If you have any questions, please call me at X2512.

Note that the reformatting clearly signals the true subject of the memo and makes it easier to find what the company is requesting. By indenting and numbering the two "action items," the writer focuses the reader's eye on those important points and lets the reader know immediately that there are two items to consider. This version also does not create false expectations. In this revision, the writer has used the effective format to emphasize the memo's organization visually, even though the text is so short. In longer documents, such page design techniques become increasingly important guides for leading the reader through complex material.

PRACTICE EXERCISE 5.3

ABC Company, a multinational engineering firm, has been plagued by cost overruns and shoddy workmanship from their subcontractors on a major project. After much debate at the administrative level, the company has decided to take legal action to solve the problem. The following draft is a summary of events that was written by an ABC engineer to send to an attorney who is preparing litigation procedures. Using all of the techniques in this chapter, rearrange and revise this draft report so that it is clear, deductive, and readable.

ABC Company Report

The overhead door installation has caused delays and cost overruns to ABC Company. The door motor terminal strip was not labeled, and the terminals were not consistent as to N.O., N.C., and so on. This required significant time for the electrical contractor to troubleshoot and complete accurate terminations. The O.H. door installer was not able to provide assistance, since he had no way of knowing how they were factory wired. In addition, at least one motor was factory wired incorrectly, which was corrected by the electrical contractor. The door limit switch and safety edges have had to be periodically reset on frequent failures of operation.

The door seals have also been a problem. During the Hotcell installation period, the Hotcell installation contractor (Robertson Airtech) encountered a problem with fit up of the Hotcell final face panel. The dimensional tolerances were not as described in the "Owners Manual"; that is, "'Cam-Action' latches are precisely located and foamed into place for perfect alignment of panels when connected together." This discrepancy was called to the attention of the Chemrox field installation representative while he was at Bethune providing installation assistance. The directive given by Chemrox was to pull the face panel in to meet the edge of the ceiling panel and latch it together as a best effort. This was done by the contractor. Because this caused a slight bowing of the face panel, the question was asked about consequent possible effect on the door installation. Chemrox's reply was that it should not cause a problem. Subsequently, we contacted the panel manufacturer to question why the panel dimensional tolerance was so large. We were told that this is normal and that had we been advised of this normal occurrence it could have been handled by positioning the front top panel flush with the face panel, leaving the tolerance gap spread out between the ceiling panels. Because the cells had already been assembled, there was no practical way to accomplish this other than disassembly of the cells.

During installation of the O.H. doors, it was observed that the door seals would not take up the tolerance gap caused by the bowed face panels and therefore would not provide a suitable seal. In addition, the seal was constructed of an extruded plastic base retainer with a "stick-on" surface that would not suitably adhere to the face panel. The 3/8-inch diameter bulb seal and seal retainer appeared to be of a low-quality design and was unlikely to hold up under the imposed operating conditions even with "perfect" fit up. ABC had repeatedly asked for the best quality seal for reliably limiting air infiltration into the cell. Chemrox assured us they would provide a suitable seal for this application, however, this seal was not the best quality.

The best fix for the overall seal problem was to find and test a seal of suitable design and quality that would allow for tolerance imperfections on the door and door opening and provide reliable and suitable sealing. The first new seal tried was not suitable because of the design type, although it was of good quality. The second new seal provided excellent sealing with the tolerance gap and was of high quality, consisting of an extruded rigid aluminum base screwed to the face panel. The seal was a long rubber flapper type that was pulled in tight under cell negative pressure to provide positive sealing.

In ABC's view, this is the type and quality seal that should have been provided by Chemrox aside from the panel tolerance problem.

During the testing and evaluation of a suitable seal, Chemrox was kept informed but never offered assistance and never indicated an alternative solution until a fix was found and the cost burden became a question. At this time, Chemrox decided that the panel tolerance problem was due to the installation contractor not following instruction for assembly. This is under dispute at present.

The door installation began June 18, 1990 and has not been completed as of October 4, 1990. The installer has worked on and off during this period but has failed to show up during critical periods despite frequent telephone reminders. This has caused overruns during the start-up period because the start-up crew could not accomplish tasks that were scheduled based on door completion time commitments, which were not honored by the door installer. This includes the real problem delays that were caused by a slow response by Chemrox in authorizing the order for the new seals despite ABC's repeated requests for urgent completion.

Organizing is not easy. But writing well is not easy either. Just remember that the care writers give to each part of the writing process is directly proportionate to the quality of the finished prose, and, with practice, the task gets easier.

FOCUS ON

Your Writing Project

1. For this project, write a paper that explains "Why _____ is true." (Choose your own title; this one is just a suggestion.) Be sure to carefully guide readers through your thoughts and explanations to a well-supported conclusion by organizing the discussion into digestible chunks and using subheadings if you think they would be helpful. As a first step, write an outline for this project and submit it to the instructor or to the writing group for comments.

2. Change the audience for your project. Assume your new readers are hostile to your ideas and are daring you to convince them that your position is correct. Reorganize the discussion to make it work well for this group. List the changes you have made and why.

The Writing Group

Professional writers who work in groups in business and industry have developed a technique that works well for writing groups in other situations, too. "Storyboarding" is a technique that allows an entire group to help organize a document and to brainstorm. To adapt storyboarding for your writing purposes, follow these simple steps:

1. Begin with a structured outline as discussed in this chapter. You may want two people to develop this preliminary outline, or you may decide to have each person develop one. You can use only one outline at a time for the storyboarding process.

2. Write each subheading for the document in a complete sentence at the top of a large sheet of paper or a posterboard. Use one subheading for each board.

3. Begin with the first subheading. As a group, discuss the wording for the subheading and then contribute ideas for the supportive evidence that should appear under that heading. If any drawings or other artwork (tables, figures, charts) would help, include samples here.

4. Continue the same process for each subheading on subsequent posterboards.

5. Arrange the boards visibly around the room so that the group can see the entire document.

6. As a group, rearrange the document by physically moving the boards from place to place and by adding and subtracting information from each board.

7. When the group has agreed on the organization of the whole piece, the process is complete. (Often in industry, each member of the group is given one of the boards and is asked to write that section of the project. Storyboarding promotes group consensus on a document ultimately written by many individual writers.)

Chapter 6

Beginnings, Middles, Endings

Well-written prose appears almost seamless in its careful integration of the necessary components. Readers move naturally through the text, progressing from the introduction through the subtopics to the conclusion without being unduly aware of the divisions. Although good writing requires clear organization—organization often signaled by headings and other formatting techniques—readers should view this order as inherent to the subject, not as an imposed pattern straining to contain the diverse components.

Good prose makes reading easy, and it makes writing *look* easy. Such apparently seamless prose, however, takes a great deal of effort to compose, and writers must understand the nature of the individual parts coming together to form the whole. Ironically, writing that appears labored probably took less time to compose than text that seems to read naturally. In order to write well, you need to spend some time considering the parts you have to work with and thinking about how to integrate them naturally into the prose.

Beginning Well

The first few paragraphs of the text create the critical first impression on the reader. As most people would agree, first impressions of anything are hard to overcome. When people meet someone for the first time, they immediately form opinions based on initial impressions: A new person's handshake, voice, and style either make a positive impact or create a negative impression that is difficult to counteract. The same thing is true in writing: the beginning makes either a positive or a negative impact on readers, and this initial response colors their view of the rest of the text.

Consider these powerful beginnings:

The problem lay buried, unspoken, for many years in the minds of American women. It was a strange stirring, a sense of dissatisfaction, a yearning that women suffer in the middle of the twentieth century in the United States. Each suburban housewife struggled with it alone. As she made the beds, shopped for groceries, matched slip cover material, ate peanut butter sandwiches with her children, chauffeured Cub Scouts and Brownies, lay beside her husband at night—she was afraid to ask even of herself the silent question—"Is this all?"
  —*Betty Friedan* The Feminine Mystique

In our house on North Congress Street in Jackson, Mississippi, where I was born, the oldest of three children, in 1909, we grew up to the striking of clocks. There was a mission-style oak grandfather clock standing in the hall, which sent its gong-like strokes through the living room, dining room, kitchen, and pantry, and up the sounding board of the stairwell. Through the night, it could find its way into our ears; sometimes, even on the sleeping porch, midnight could wake us up. My parents' bedroom had a smaller striking clock that answered it. Though the kitchen clock did nothing but show the time, the dining room clock was a cuckoo clock with weights on long chains, on one of which my baby brother, after climbing on a chair to the top of the china closet, once succeeded in suspending the cat for a moment. I don't know whether or not my father's Ohio family, in having been Swiss back in the 1700s before the first three Welty brothers came to America, had anything to do with this; but we all of us have been time-minded all our lives. This was good at least for a future fiction writer, being able to learn so penetratingly, and almost first of all, about chronology. It was one of a good many things I learned almost without knowing it; it would be there when I needed it.
  —*Eudora Welty* One Writer's Beginnings

Home medicine is a big industry these days. A recent network survey by one of the major evangelical organizations indicates that one out of every three Americans will experiment this year with a variety of do-it-yourself home cures and quack remedies ranging from self-induced vomiting kits to alpha/beta brain wave scans and multihead, blood-magneto suction drums to measure percentage of true body fat.

Others will test themselves daily, in towns and ghettos all over the republic, for potentially fatal levels of blood glucose, or use strange and expensive litmus tests to screen each other for leg cancer in the femurs and the ankles and the knees.

We are all slaves to this syndrome, but in some ways it is a far, far better thing. . . . Last Saturday night I went out to the snack bar at the Geneva Drive-In near the Cow Palace and performed tests on a random selection of customers during the intermission period between "Rocky IV" and "Pale Rider."

The results were startling. . . .

Huge brains, small necks, weak muscles and fat wallets— these are the dominant physical characteristics of the 80's . . . The Generation of Swine.

—*Hunter S. Thompson* Generation of Swine

Each of these beginnings makes a definite impact on readers: whether the response is positive or negative, the prose gets a reaction. To achieve these effects, the authors have gambled that their words will capture the reader's attention by establishing a connection between the writer and the reader. Friedan begins with the mystery of the "unspoken problem" and hopes to draw in many who will recognize themselves or people they know. Welty depends more on creating a world so real and so filled with reminiscences that readers put themselves in the prose, hearing the clocks and remembering similar vivid images from their own childhoods. Thompson, on the other hand, uses biting sarcasm to catch audience attention. His no-nonsense approach to the world appeals to the readers' rebellious side—the side that would like to break the bonds of politeness and "tell it like it is" just once.

In addition to connecting with their readers, all three of these beginnings clearly signal the main purpose and the "voice" of the prose to follow. The authors simultaneously capture readers' attention and give them a sense of what to expect. With the words "It was one of a good many things I learned without knowing it; it would be there when I needed it," Welty lets the reader know that her stories of childhood are the key to understanding her writing. Friedan's prose brings into the open the unspoken question "Is this all?" and clearly indicates that the rest of the book will attempt to answer it. Thompson's prose indicates not only his strong "voice" but also the unflattering view of America that becomes the theme of his book.

Everyday writing operates in much the same way. Although only a few writers publish novels or essays for the public, most people are called on regularly to prepare memos, analyses, reports, and so forth. For example, an engineer who wants her prose to begin well must do the same things the writers of the earlier examples did: connect with the reader, establish the purpose, create an appropriate voice, and set reader expectations. The first lines of her report's introduction might look like this:

> This report presents the methods and results of a Preliminary Assessment and Phase 1 Site Investigation of the TCA Tank Site. The main objectives of the report are (1) to define the lateral and vertical extent of soil and ground water contamination caused by a leaking trichlorethane storage tank and (2) to classify the site according to the Massachusetts Contingency Plan's regulations.

Although the voice in this report is not meant to entertain, as are the voices in the earlier examples, the author has developed a no-nonsense tone appropriate for the situation, and she has set her audience's expectations of what is to come. They can immediately understand the report's purpose and can read on without wasting time wading through unnecessary words. Because she has written these first lines so succinctly, the rest of the report is much more likely to succeed.

As this example suggests, nonfiction writing—whether it is an essay, a report, or a critical analysis—begins well when it gives the reader a sense of confidence in both what you have to say and how you say it. Readers respect clarity of purpose and tone, and they are much more willing to trust writers whose prose exhibits these qualities.

The following critical analysis illustrates this point. Although the subject matter—Irish migration patterns—may not strike you as a riveting topic, you should be able to follow the author's ideas without difficulty. Unfortunately, this opening paragraph proves more frustrating than helpful:

Version 1

> Migration optimally is a mechanism of adjustment that functions to reduce the inequalities between two areas. The subject of this study is the extent to which this may have been so for Irish persons who were migrating between Ireland and England during the first half of the nineteenth century. This study proceeds from the assumption that by following a regular pattern of temporary migration between the two communities, the mostly agricultural people of Ireland were, at least temporarily, able to preserve valued aspects of their existing social system. The monetary returns from migration enabled them to maximize desired benefits and minimize losses of valued social institutions that would have been necessary if they had broken the links with Ireland permanently.

Does this introduction give readers a clear sense of what the rest of the text will cover? Does it inspire confidence in the writer's ability to handle the subject? The answer to both of those questions is no. In fact, this passage's convoluted sentences and lack of direction give the impression that the writer is as confused as the prose.

Now look at the revised version of the same text, and notice the difference a few simple changes make:

Version 2

Migration at best is a mechanism of adjustment that reduces inequalities between two areas. This discussion studies the extent to which this mechanism functioned for Irish people who were migrating between Ireland and England during the first half of the nineteenth century. By following a regular pattern of temporary migration to England, the agricultural people of Ireland were, at least temporarily, able to preserve valuable aspects of their existing social system. The cyclical migration enabled them to earn money while maintaining ties to their valued social institutions, ties that would have been lost if they had broken the links with Ireland permanently. For the Irish, this early migration was a positive adjustment rather than a forced choice.

In this revision, the writer has cut out unnecessary words and has trimmed the number of complex phrases, thereby creating a more direct and conversational voice. Phrases such as "proceeds from the assumption" and "maximize desired benefits" are omitted or changed to simpler forms so that the reader does not have to expend so much energy on translation. Changes such as these immediately establish a better rapport with the reader of any text, no matter what the subject matter. But the most important change the writer of this paragraph has made is to add the last sentence. That sentence serves to focus the whole paragraph by emphasizing the idea presented in the first sentence and giving the reader a concise statement of the main point: early Irish migration was a positive adjustment. By changing the voice and adding that one sentence, the writer has given the introductory paragraph a sense of direction and has created a complete unit of thought that the reader can use as a focus for the rest of the discussion. The passage now exudes a sense of confident authority, earning the reader's respect instead of causing unnecessary frustration.

To make sure your prose begins well, remember that readers appreciate such directness and confidence. They also respond best to paragraphs that invite reading, not those that bury their points in densely worded phrases. Beginnings work best when they:

- Catch the reader's attention
- Create an appropriate "voice"
- Set readers' expectations for what follows
- State the main purpose

PRACTICE EXERCISE 6.1

Keeping in mind the preceding checklist, read the following openers and analyze their effectiveness. Make sure you discuss how each of the four points in the checklist applies.

> Moments after they had begun handing out the stack of opinions to the unruly reporters in the Supreme Court press room, hours before the lawyers had finished dissecting 85 pages of opinion and dissent, the phones began to ring at pro-choice offices across the country. They carried one anxious question: How bad is it?
> —*Ellen Goodman, "Privacy, Reproduction Now Political Questions"* The Boston Globe, *July 4, 1989*

> I freely admit that the spotted, or laughing, hyena is not the loveliest animal to behold. Still, it scarcely deserved the poor reputation imposed upon it by our illustrious forbears. Three myths about hyenas helped to inspire the loathing commentary of ancient texts.
> —*Stephen Jay Gould, "Hyena Myths and Realities"* Hen's Teeth and Horse's Toes

> In many important ways, what we think of as business strategy finds its roots in military strategy. One tenet of military strategy, of course, is that the successful warrior finds his adversary's weak spot and takes him off guard—guerrilla warfare. Midsize growth companies, lacking the advantages of scale and resources, have become masters of guerrilla warfare. Like the American revolutionaries two centuries ago, they base their strategies on selection of the battlefield, speed and surprise, fanatical spirit, concentration of effort, and the triumph of ingenuity and common sense over heavy odds.
> —*Donald K. Clifford and Richard E. Cavanagh,* The Winning Performance

Good openers set the stage for what is to come. If the beginning is weak, nobody will want to read on. On the other hand, if the beginning is strong but makes promises the rest of the text does not keep, the reader will feel justifiably betrayed. Your best strategy is to write an opener that is like a firm handshake. It signals confidence, friendliness, and an honesty that attracts readers' trust. Your job as a writer is to make sure the rest of the prose warrants that trust.

Writing Middles

For many writers, the middle of the text—that is, the part immediately after the introductory section—is where they dump everything haphazardly after they have spent hours crafting an introduction. On the other hand, more advanced writers realize that the middle of any document requires special skill because it is the longest part of the prose, and it should indicate a progression of ideas. This means the readers need guidance. They need to see a clear path ahead.

When you reach the middle of your text your major task is to guide readers through your thought processes so that they understand your point of view and why you think that way. The beginning introduces the main idea, and the ending wraps up the argument, but the middle makes your point comprehensible and gives it logical support. You must concentrate on keeping the reader with you as you move from thought to thought. To do that well, you should remember the suggestions about arrangement given in Chapter 5. Craft the paragraphs so that their logic is undeniable and the links between them are solid.

Most important, readers should always have a clear sense that your prose is going somewhere. Weak prose has a middle section that does not seem to lead to anything. Often the paragraphs are disconnected and could be rearranged without changing the meaning of the text, leaving the readers to determine how the material fits together to support the writer's thesis.

Think of the middle of your text as a path to your major point. When you began to research your idea, you had no clearly marked way to reach your goal—you had to explore several paths and make side trips before you finally reached your conclusion. As the writer, it is your job to see that readers do not have to repeat your meanderings to come to the same point. Instead, you should clearly state the destination at the outset and mark the path throughout the text with indicators that tell where the readers are in the journey. If readers are well oriented, they can follow the path effortlessly and reach your position quickly. If they are not well oriented, they will probably end up in a different location from the one you had in mind.

Knowing how to write paragraphs well and how to connect your paragraphs with effective transitions are essential skills for writing good middles.

Paragraph Anatomy

Understanding paragraph anatomy makes writing middles much easier. Because paragraphs are the basic units of thought, the middle of any document is nothing more than a logical arrangement of these paragraphs. The key word here is *logical*. Paragraphs, after all, are the units that express the logic of any prose. Good paragraphs are an essential prerequisite for effective writing. Nonetheless, paragraphs are the most abused component of the writer's craft. Even seasoned writers admit that they neglect these building blocks because they are more concerned with the overall organization of the prose or the precise wording of individual sentences. They simply indent wherever it "feels right." However, by paying more attention to the structure of successful paragraphs, writers can become more conscious of the great power residing in these blocks of prose.

Each paragraph should have *unity* and *coherence*. Simply put, this means that every paragraph should focus on one main idea—usually a subtopic of the larger discussion—and the sentences should link together logically. Although that sounds easy, it is often hard to recognize the boundaries of your main idea and know how to present it as a unified block. In the following example, the writer has ignored cohesive unity and has composed an "unglued" paragraph:

> Ron Harre (1984) states that primates are extremely limited in the types of information that they can communicate. Compared to humans, primates' communication systems are inferior since they cannot refer to the environment or a sense of time. However, Seyfarth (1984) warns that we must not be too hasty to form these conclusions. He points out the problems in studying animal communication. Researchers begin with the belief that primates' sounds mean nothing and these sounds must prove functional before they are granted meaning. Another problem is the difficulty of measuring the effectiveness of primate sounds. Seyfarth states the only way to measure effectiveness is to measure the physical reaction to a given sound. If the same approach was applied to human speech, its effectiveness would be greatly underestimated. Hence, Seyfarth theorizes that we may also underestimate the effectiveness of primates' communication by focusing only on their physical reactions.

It is hard to determine this paragraph's main topic. Although the general subject is primate communication, this paragraph has no clear focus. Is it that primates' communication skills are inferior to those of humans? Is it that researchers cannot measure the sounds appropriately? Is it that the research methods are ineffective? Or do all of these scattered ideas cohere under one main point not directly stated in the paragraph? Even though the writer has apparently linked his ideas with transitional words (such as *however* and *hence*), this paragraph lacks the glue to keep its ideas together. To communicate effectively, the writer needs to focus these thoughts for the reader so that the priority of ideas are clear. Without sharp focus, too many thoughts compete for the reader's attention, creating a three-ring circus effect.

Here is how the above paragraph might look if the proper glue helped to keep the cohesive unity intact:

> Although Ron Harre (1984) states that primates' communication systems are extremely limited and inferior to those of humans, Seyfarth (1984) argues that this conclusion may be too hasty. Perhaps it is the research methods used to study animal communication that are limited, rather than the primates' ability to communicate. Seyfarth theorizes that we underestimated the effectiveness of primates' communication because researchers believe that primates' sounds mean nothing until they are proven functional, yet the only way to measure a sound's functionality is to measure the physical reaction to it. As Seyfarth points out, if this same approach were applied to humans, we might underestimate the effectiveness of human speech as well.

Writers often have to fight the urge to keep at least three rings in action all the time, making it hard for the reader to focus on one. From your experience, you probably know that when you write you are often juggling so many ideas that it seems impossible to deal with only one at a time. Everything seems to overlap. But to write powerful prose, you must view every paragraph as a unified expression of a definite idea. You need to determine your point and focus the reader's attention on it.

Each paragraph must be inherently logical. If you establish a cohesive pattern for development in each paragraph, the whole text becomes easier to read because it moves in a series of logical steps. Your reader can concentrate on every major idea without too many ancillary thoughts vying for attention. To organize your paragraphs into cohesive units, consider these suggestions:

- Organize your material deductively so that your main idea is at the beginning.

- Write one sentence that powerfully expresses your point.
- Use the rest of the paragraph to support and explain the point.
- Begin and end with transitional material that indicates where you have been and where you are going.

Now look at how these four suggestions work together in the following passage about the treatment of female slaves in pre–Civil War America:

> Women slaves were not immune to the lash, nor were they spared the horrors of more brutal tortures. Even those who were pregnant had to work in the fields, and little was done to ease the burden. Dr. E. C. Hyde, a white physician who practiced in the Carolinas for thirty years, reported that "The slave women were forced to labor from pregnancy to maternity. I have known births between the cotton rows; they were compelled to hoe out their row, and then given an hour to recover" (McKaye, 5). While this may be extreme, it was generally unusual for a new mother to receive more than one month of recuperation time before returning to the field. The harshness of the life was so much to endure that one slave mother may have spoken for many when she wished her newborn baby girl had died at birth (Feldstein, 128). For the truth was that the female slave received special and additional tortures peculiar to her sex.
>
> At puberty, the female slave became more than a potential field worker. She became a breeder, similar to the cattle the Master owned. She was also subject to the sexual advances of the Master, the overseer, and any other white male who had access to the plantation. Though records do not exist as to how often forced interracial sex took place, statistics estimate that there were three hundred thousand mulattos in the South (Feldstein, 130), ample testimony to the fact that the female could do little to protect herself from the sexual advances of white men. Rejection of such advances often led to whippings and, in cases of repeated refusal, sale. And because they so feared being sold to a Mississippi plantation, many women gave in rather than risk this potential punishment.

Applying the specific suggestions to this example gives you a better idea of how they work in practice:

1. *Organize your material deductively so that your main idea is at the beginning.*

   The first paragraph of the example begins with the main idea, thereby giving the reader a context for the rest of the discussion: "Women slaves were not immune to the lash, nor were they spared the horrors of more brutal tortures." From that sentence, the reader knows the paragraph topic and expects a discussion of how women slaves were treated so brutally. The purpose of the paragraph is apparent, creating a framework for the point the writer wants to make.

The second paragraph uses two sentences to introduce its main point: "At puberty, the female slave became more than a potential field worker. She became a breeder, similar to the cattle the Master owned."

2. *Write one sentence that powerfully expresses your point.*
This powerful statement goes beyond the introductory "context setter" of the previous suggestion. Instead of establishing a framework for the paragraph topic, it specifically expresses the crucial point. Here, the writer expresses her point in the paragraph about female slaves' treatment: "The harshness of the life was so much to endure that one slave mother may have spoken for many when she wished her newborn baby girl had died at birth." Notice how this statement connects logically to the context-setting first sentence, but it is much more direct in its meaning. Every paragraph should have at least one direct sentence, and it may occur anywhere in the paragraph.

In the second paragraph, the statement of the key idea occurs close to the middle of the paragraph: "Though records do not exist as to how often forced interracial sex took place, statistics estimate that there were three hundred thousand mulattos in the South (Feldstein, 130), ample testimony to the fact that the female could do little to protect herself from the sexual advances of white men."

3. *Use the rest of the paragraph to support and explain the point.*
Make sure that you support your assertions with sufficient explanatory material and check to make sure every sentence serves as support for the main idea. Do not include any sentences that do not directly and logically relate to the point. In the paragraphs above, note how the sentences in each focus directly on the main point. Not one is out of place or irrelevant.

4. *Begin and end with transitional material that indicates where you have been and where you are going.*
The last sentence of the first paragraph—"For the truth was that the female slave received special and additional tortures peculiar to her sex"—makes a neat transition to the first sen-

tences of the next paragraph—"At puberty, the female slave became more than a potential field worker. She was now a breeder, similar to the cattle owned by the Master." A more thorough discussion of transitions appears later in this chapter, but the idea of guiding the reader carefully over the paragraph breaks is essential to consider at this juncture as well.

PRACTICE EXERCISE 6.2

Apply the four steps for writing a sound paragraph to these sample passages from a variety of published and unpublished sources. Analyze why they are or are not focused. Be as specific and as detailed as you can.

There are three methods you can use to detect if a chemical is being released from its container when it should not be. The first is visual. If you see a leak occurring, take the proper steps to stop the leak and then to clean it up. The steps differ for each chemical, so you must know the specific steps for the chemical that is leaking. Sometimes you cannot see a leak, but can smell it. If you smell an unusual odor, figure out what the odor is and then take the proper actions to stop the leak and then to clean it up. There may be a monitoring system installed in your workplace that warns you if the chemical leak occurs. If there is, learn where the monitor is and how to use it.
—*a chemical company's Safety Manual*

"I don't get ulcers; I give them!" says the obnoxious boss in the cartoon. Any psychologist will tell you that lack of control—real or imagined—is a prime source of stress. It seems to me that lack of control—perceived or real—is behind much of the negative reaction experienced by the so-called "rest of us" to computers. Hackers know how the machines work; they can manipulate them, use them to do things; they know about the ones and zeros behind the magical graphical user interface. But the typical user does not. He may know that there's only a dumb machine in there, but he's afraid of breaking it. He's scared of making a mistake. He's afraid of doing something stupid that the computers won't understand. He blames his problems on himself, not on computer errors or poor design. He forgets that there's a magician—a person—behind the magic in the computer. For moral, aesthetic, and practical reasons, we should not forget the people behind it all. They make the rules; they control things. Computers only carry out orders. People, not computers have responsibility. (People may make mistakes and may not always have the intention of achieving a particular result, but that's another matter.)
—*an unpublished draft of a newspaper column*

It may also have been during this period that changes in the cultivation of the potato aided new aspects of Irish social development when the interval between planting and harvest was lengthened, thus facilitating the peasants' freedom to leave earlier and return later in the agricultural season in order to take advantage of opportunities for work elsewhere, either in Ireland or in England. A writer in 1794 observed that cottiers were planting their potatoes earlier in the season because of their obligations to their landlords (MacAodha, 1956). Planting potatoes in the technique known as "lazy bed" was considered elsewhere in Europe to be characteristically Irish. The ridges in which potatoes are grown in their Andean homeland appear to be similar to Irish lazy beds and tuber crops throughout the tropics are planted in ridges or mound, but the ridge technique in Ireland is certainly older than the cultivation of the potato there because it was used for growing cereal crops from early times (Evans, 1957). Although some consider the term the scornful epithet of the English, Bourke says it is far more likely that it was derived from the French "laisser" meaning to do least violence to the soil. In this form of cultivation, the earth was piled in ridges with trenches between. Although requiring more intensive cultivation in the initial stages, it required almost no maintenance until the potatoes were harvested in October or November. Evans suggests that the name may derive from the fact that the sod under the ridge is not dug: the bed is built up on top of the grass with sod and soil dug from the trenches between the ridges. Not only does this method make full use of the humus and decaying grasses but it prevents the potato sets from becoming waterlogged and rotting, for the whole bed is raised above the water table. In addition, the unbroken sod checks the downwash of valuable plant nutrients. Trenches or furrows between the ridges provide open drains and the lazy beds are always carefully aligned with the slope of the land, thus providing for minimal soil erosion.
—*a critical study of Irish history*

Envirotech will provide a construction observer for the duration of capping and closure activities, who is trained for procedures in field observation and documentation of capping activities. The observer would be able to make on-the-spot judgment as to the adequacy of the component installation. Daily construction activities and samplings would be logged with details of construction noted for conformance to the plans and specifications, and also nonconformance. On completion of the construction, data would be compiled into a certification report, which, if passing, would be signed and sealed by a licensed Rhode Island professional engineer. If an area is ruled as insufficient quality for passing, the corporation would have the option to have that nonpassing feature reconstructed. The certificate would apply only to original construction and not be extended to include maintenance. Certification would not be interpreted as a warranty to use the installation of the landfill cap, final cover, or any other construction item, but would serve to verify that within the constraints of the CQA program, the construction was performed as specified.

—an engineering proposal

The boxing ring is the ultimate focus of masculinity in America, the two-fisted testing ground of manhood, and the heavyweight champion, as a symbol, is a real Mr. America. In a culture that secretly subscribes to the piratical ethic of "every man for himself"—the social Darwinism of "survival of the fittest" being far from dead, manifesting itself in our ratrace political system of competing parties, in our dog-eat-dog economic system of profit and loss, and in our adversary system of justice wherein truth is secondary to the skill and connections of the advocate—the logical culmination of this ethic, on a person-to-person level, is that the weak are seen as the natural and just prey of the strong. But since this dark principle violates our democratic ideals and professions, we force it underground, out of a perverse national modesty that reveals us as a nation of peep freaks who prefer the bikini to the naked body, the white lie to the black truth, Hollywood smiles and canned laughter to soulful Bronx cheer. The heretical mailed fist of American reality rises to the surface in the velvet glove of our every institutionalized endeavor, so that each year we, as a nation, grind through various cycles of attrition, symbolically quenching the insatiable appetite of the *de facto* jungle law underlying our culture, loudly and unabashedly proclaiming to the world that "competition" is the law of life, getting confused, embarrassed, and angry if someone retorts: "Competition is the Law of the Jungle and Cooperation is the Law of Civilization."

—Eldridge Cleaver, "Lazarus, Come Forth"

Transitions Between Paragraphs

Every paragraph has two opportunities for transitional sentences: the lead sentence and the last sentence. These two serve as both the boundaries for the paragraph and its links to the rest of the text. Yet each functions in a slightly different way.

The First Sentence as Bridge   Your first sentence is probably the most important one in the paragraph because it must bridge the gap between the last paragraph and the new one. To do so, it should either explicitly or implicitly refer to the preceding material. The lead sentence from the second paragraph of the example on page 116 illustrates this technique: "At puberty, *the female slave became* more than the potential field worker." The italicized phrase refers directly to the last thought in the previous paragraph, but it also pulls the reader into the new topic to be discussed. The reader naturally questions what the female slave became and wants to read on to discover the answer.

This "bridge sentence" pulls the reader into the paragraph by subtly asking a question that the rest of the paragraph answers. This sentence does not have to be in actual question form, but it should create a question in the reader's mind. Usually, these unspoken questions are the common *who, what, when, where, why,* and *how.* For instance, the previous example encourages the reader to ask "*What* did she become?" and the reader wants to finish the paragraph to get the answer.

Here are a few more bridge sentences that perform double duty—they refer to the previous paragraph and pull the reader into the meat of the new unit:

Sentence	*Question*
Holmes did not rely on appearances alone.	On what did he rely?
This phenomenon cannot be explained by the inaccessibility of the village.	Why?
The styles, working habits, and quirks of winning CEOs vary across the entire human spectrum.	How?
But the media is not entirely at fault.	Who is?

Compare these effective bridge sentences with the following leads that give no indication of what has gone before and fail to draw the reader into the material:

The Waltons is a television show that started during the Nixon Administration.

Tuft (1979) tells us that divorce was high during the 1970s, the time period when the show aired, and that unemployment was on the rise.

The last television program to be discussed is the situational comedy *Kate and Allie,* which aired first in 1982.

Note that these sentences make self-contained statements that offer little or no sense of movement. They fail to create questions in the reader's mind, and, in fact, seem to discourage any reader involvement at all. Yet many writers who have been taught that every paragraph must begin with a topic sentence write such static prose routinely. In doing so, they prevent the reader from engaging meaningfully in the text, and they also encourage skimming. If the topic sentence perches as a self-contained unit at the top of every paragraph, most readers will begin to read only those sentences, skipping all the rest. It is a better idea to introduce the paragraph's context at the beginning and draw the reader into the heart of the paragraph for the direct topic statement.

The Last Sentence as Forecaster   Although the lead sentence usually serves as a transitional device, the final sentence in each paragraph can also indicate direction. The last sentence may contain the seeds of the next main idea, but it should remain firmly attached to its own unit. In other words, this sentence should not be a total change of subject—a lead sentence moved up a notch. Instead, it should naturally suggest the direction in which you are taking the reader. Again, look at the sample paragraph from page 116. The final sentence in the first part, "For the truth was that the female slave received special and additional tortures peculiar to her sex," indicates direction. It is almost inevitable that the lead sentence of the next paragraph will be about the tortures peculiar to her sex.

Readers may not immediately recognize the gracefulness of a forecaster sentence (remember, effective guidance is inobtrusive), but they will respond to a less than graceful forecasting sentence that rudely changes the topic and creates more confusion than clarity. Be careful about using your last sentence as a transition. If you can do it subtly, it is a highly effective technique; but if it fails, it can startle readers, causing them to lose their train of thought.

Novice writers sometimes have difficulty mastering the art of subtle transitions. For instance, look at these awkward sentences from writers who know they should provide directional signals but who do so with heavy hands:

As discussed in the following paragraph, the courts consider control over employment decisions key when determining legal status.

This report will now turn to the problem of toxic waste's effect on the local environment.

We have already described the skeleton of the show, but now it is time to look at what is really being presented to the audience.

Each of these is a forced transition. Sentences like the three above may serve a purpose during the composing process and may be left on the page until something more subtle can be worked out. However, transitions must be unobtrusive in the final product. Remember that mechanical techniques are most efficient when the reader is unaware of them. Once your mechanics begin to show, the reader may be distracted and lose trust in you.

Transition Words   One sure way to let your mechanics show is to use transitional words constantly. Words such as *also, however, nonetheless, therefore,* and *additionally* creep into a writer's vocabulary and quickly become omnipresent. If you are too tired to compose more subtle transitions, these "quick and dirty" explicit links seem like a good alternative. But such transitions often look forced. If you habitually use transition words in place of implicit connections, remove them totally for a while until you break the habit and can use them again sparingly.

If you think your connectors are overly obvious, if you are not sure whether you qualify as an amateur in this category, check your prose. Do you begin a majority of sentences with one word followed by a comma? Do you have a favorite transition word (such as *however*)? Do you create multiple opportunities to use the "first . . . second . . . third" pattern in your discussions? If you answer "yes" to any of these questions your mechanics are showing.

Implicit Transitions   Using implicit transitions instead of explicit ones creates more professional and polished prose than prose welded together with transitional words. *Implicit* as used here means that the logic is so smooth the reader understands the natural connections without *therefore* or *however*. Bridge sentences are one form of implicit transition, as are last sentences used as forecasters. There are many other forms as well, a few of which are listed below. These forms work together in many combinations to increase the implicit logic of the text.

1. *Statement of Organization:* When the writer includes a sentence in the introduction explaining how the rest of the document is organized, readers then expect the order that follows. By re-

vealing the organizational strategy at the beginning, the writer gives readers a clear view of the logic and makes their movement through the text much easier. Notice in the examples how the writers suggest the organization clearly but not clumsily. (In each example, the first sentence of the next paragraph is included to illustrate how the transitional signals work.)

Example

Electronic data processing, as corporations use it today, is so complex that controlling it is almost too difficult for words. Through our work with a number of companies, however, we have reached certain conclusions about how EDP departments grow and how they should fit into the company's organization. There are four distinct stages in the growth of all EDP facilities.
   Stage 1: Initiation. The first computer is. . . .
   —*Cyrus F. Gibson and Richard L. Nolan "Managing the Four Stages of EDP Growth,"* Harvard Business Review, *Jan.–Feb. 1974*

Example

Frank Morgan is a time machine, a cautionary presence, and a laboratory animal. He also plays an alto sax better than any man alive. But if not for the first three things, we probably wouldn't even know who he is.
   The fifty-five-year-old Morgan is a time machine because. . . .
   —*Daniel Okrent, "Thirty Years of Hard Practice,"* Esquire, *July 1989*

2. *Given/New:* Perhaps the easiest method for writing internally logical material is for the writer to follow the "given/new" sequence. If the sentences within the paragraph proceed from "given" or already explained information to "new" information, the reader can more easily follow the train of thought. This technique works especially well when the material is argumentative or inflammatory in some way. By easing readers into the new information, the writer encourages agreement.

Example

We hold these truths to be self-evident, that all men are created equal, that they are endowed by their Creator with certain unalienable Rights, that among these are Life, Liberty and the Pursuit of Happiness. That to secure these rights, Governments are instituted among Men, deriving their just powers from the consent of the governed. That whenever any Form of Government becomes destructive of these ends, it is the Right of the People to alter or abolish it, and to institute a new Government, laying its foundation on such principles and organizing its powers in such form, as to them shall seem most likely to effect their Safety and Happiness. Prudence, indeed, will dictate that Governments long established should not be changed for light and transient causes; and accordingly all experience hath shown, that mankind are more disposed to suffer, while evils are sufferable, than to right themselves by abolishing the forms to which they are accustomed. But when a long train of abuses and usurpations pursuing invariably the same Object evinces a design to reduce them under absolute Despotism, it is their right, it is their duty, to throw off such government, and to provide new Guards for their future security. Such has been the patient sufferance of these Colonies; and such is now the necessity which constrains them to alter their former Systems of Government. The history of the present King of Great Britain is a history of repeated injuries and usurpations, all having in direct object the establishment of an absolute Tyranny over these States. To prove this, let Facts be submitted to a candid world.

—*Thomas Jefferson*, The Declaration of Independence

3. *Internal Transitions*: Similar to the "given/new" sequence, this technique focuses on the sentences within the paragraph. Internal logic is just as important as the links between the paragraphs themselves, yet many writers ignore the connections between the sentences. Because writers already understand the connections, they sometimes assume that the reader can make the transition between sentences that are not linked well. Remember that the reader cannot read your mind, and you must fill in all the gaps. Every sentence ought to hinge naturally to the one before it so that the reader moves easily from one to the other without having to read between the lines. It is a good idea for writers to check each sentence to make sure the hinge is there. The example uses a variety of "hinges" to link the sentences and create successful internal transitions.

Example

A major thesis of defendant landlord's motion for summary judgment is that she lacked actual knowledge of the open foyer door and the dangerous hole in the renovation area. However, defendant Wharton knew of the extensive damage to the floor, and she knew for several weeks that the contractor planned to remove rotten floorboards in the renovation area near the foyer. A jury might reasonably infer that Wharton thereby had actual knowledge of the hole and choose to disbelieve her self-serving assertion to the contrary. Similarly, Wharton had ample opportunity to observe the open foyer door when she entered the premises. Opportunity to observe is sufficient to permit the jury to infer that Wharton had actual knowledge of the means of access to the dangerous renovation area. Once Wharton has actual knowledge of the defects, she has a clear duty to safeguard them or to issue proper warnings, both of which she failed to do.

—*excerpt from a trial brief,* Revere v. Wharton

5. *Transitional Paragraphs:* Entire paragraphs often serve as transitional devices between large sections of the document. In texts that have subsections, the final paragraph in each section should serve to conclude that part and ease the reader into the next part. In texts that are long but have no subdivisions, short paragraphs sometimes signal the end of one major thought and the shift to another. No matter what the situation, transitional paragraphs have two functions: closure and introduction. These paragraphs work best when they are short.

Check the examples below to see how they indicate where the text has been and signal the new direction it will take. In many ways, these transitional paragraphs are similar to the "signposts" discussed in Chapter 5.

Example 1

They were two strong men, these oddly different generals, and they represented the strengths of two conflicting currents that, through them, had come into final collision.
  —*Bruce Catton, "Grant and Lee: A Study in Contrasts"*

Example 2

This much we pledge—and more.
  —*John F. Kennedy, "Inaugural Address," January 20, 1961*

Example 3

The picture probably isn't quite that rosy. To keep growing in an industry that is showing the first signs of maturity, Turner faces challenges that may be his toughest ever. For years, cable system operators have been able to sign up new subscribers simply by expanding into previously unwired towns or neighborhoods. But now that cable is finally available to more than half of the country's viewers, operators must tackle a different task: They have to persuade potential subscribers—not to mention current subscribers—that cable offers them something special.

> —*Scott Ticer, "Captain Comeback: Ted Turner is Back from the Brink and Thinking Big Again,"* Business Week, *July 17, 1989*

Example 4

But what is the origin of such ethical axioms? Are they arbitrary? Are they based on mere authority? Do they stem from the experiences of men and are they conditioned indirectly by such experiences?

> —*Albert Einstein,* The Laws of Science and the Laws of Ethics

Transitions Between Sentences

Just as the transitions between paragraphs make a big difference in how smoothly your writing flows, so do the connections between sentences. Even simple techniques such as beginning sentences with *and* or *but* create a relaxed stylistic impression, just as beginning with numbers (*first, second,* . . .) or with transitional words such as *therefore,* or *however* makes a more formal statement. (As always, over-doing any of these transitional techniques makes your prose seem mechanical and repetitive.) A major key to writing effective middles is the way you establish your writing's sentence-level coherence.

For instance, if you begin every sentence with its subject, with no transitional links between it and the previous sentences, your prose may seem to hammer home your point, but it may also have a clipped, choppy effect that keeps the reader on edge because each sentence is an isolated unit. On the other hand, if you write sentences that connect in various ways, such as by implication or by introductory references to the preceding material, your prose may seem more relaxed and natural, and it also may seem more unified.

Some examples might help. The first is an example of "linear" prose where every sentence begins with its grammatical subject, making the connections between them less apparent. In the second example, the transitions are more complex, producing prose that appears more dimensional.

> Sex is central to human biology and a protean phenomenon that permeates every aspect of our existence and takes new forms

through each step in the life cycle. Its complexity and ambiguity are due to the fact that sex is not designed primarily for reproduction. Evolution has devised much more efficient ways for creatures to multiply than the complicated procedures of mating and fertilization. Bacteria simply divide in two (in many species, every twenty minutes), fungi shed immense numbers of spores, and hydras bud offspring directly from their trunks. Each fragment of a shattered sponge grows into an entire new organism.
—*Edward O. Wilson, "Sex"*

So it's natural to swing to the opposite extreme and say that literature is really a refuge or escape from life, a self-contained world like the world of a dream, a world of play or make-believe to balance the world of work. Some literature is like that, and many people tell us that they only read to get away from reality for a bit. And I've suggested myself that the sense of escape, or at least detachment, does come into everybody's literary experience. But the real point of literature can hardly be that. Think of such writers as William Faulkner or Francois Mauriac, their great moral dignity, the intensity and compassion that they've studied the life around them with. Or think of James Joyce, spending seven years on one book and seventeen on another, and having them abused or banned by the customs when they did not get published. Or of the poets Rilke and Valery, waiting patiently for years in silence until what they had to say was ready to be said. There's a deadly seriousness in all this that even the most refined theories of fantasy or make-believe won't cover.
—*Northrop Frye, "The Keys to Dreamland"*

As the preceding examples show, the character of prose depends heavily on how the writer makes connections. For straightforward scientific information or other practical material, the direct, subject-driven technique is probably the most efficient method. This linear arrangement is ideal for step-by-step material leading to a clear conclusion. But for analytical prose, or prose that makes an argument, the transitions should be more multidimensional, revealing the relationship among all of the parts, not just the ones immediately adjacent to the sentence in question, so that the reader can better understand the logic of the whole piece.

Crafting subtle transitions at all levels of your writing weaves your ideas together in a pattern that seems logical and forceful. It is difficult to argue with such interlocking prose because it gives the impression of inevitable "rightness." Smooth transitions contribute significantly to your prose's positive effect on readers.

PRACTICE EXERCISE 6.3

Read the following passage and analyze its use of transitions. Determine which transitional techniques discussed in this chapter are used here:

> Why does the American public refuse to let King Kong rest in peace? It is true, I'll admit, that *Kong* outdid every monster movie before or since in sheer carnage. Producers Cooper and Schoedsack crammed into it dinosaurs, head hunters, riots, aerial battles, bullets, bombs, bloodletting. Heroine Fay Wray, whose function is mainly to scream, shuts her mouth for hardly one uninterrupted minute from first reel to last. It is also true that *Kong* is larded with good healthy sadism, for those whose joy it is to see the frantic girl dangled from cliffs and harried by pterodactyls. But it seems to me that the abiding appeal of the giant ape resides on other foundations.
>
> Kong has, first of all, the attraction of being manlike. His simian nature gives him one huge advantage over giant ants and walking vegetables in that the audience may conceivably identify with him. Kong's appeal has the quality that established the Tarzan series as American myth—for what man doesn't secretly imagine himself a huge hairy howler against whom no other monster has a chance? If Tarzan recalls the ape in us, then Kong may well appeal to that great-grand-daddy primordial brute from whose tribe we have all deteriorated.
>
> Intentionally or not, the producers of *King Kong* encourage this identification by etching the character of Kong with keen sympathy. For the ape is a figure in a tradition familiar to moviegoers: the tradition of Quasimodo, or Karloff in the original *Frankenstein*. As we watch the Frankenstein monster's fumbling and disastrous attempts to befriend a flower-picking child, our sympathies are enlisted with the monster in his impenetrable loneliness. And so with Kong. As he roars in his chains, while barkers sell tickets to boobs who gape at him, we perhaps feel something more deep than pathos. We begin to sense something of the problem that engaged Eugene O'Neill in *The Hairy Ape:* the dilemma of a displaced animal spirit forced to live in a jungle built by machines.
>
> —*X. J. Kennedy, "Who Killed King Kong?"*

Ending Well

Scientist and writer Stephen Jay Gould sums up the importance of ending well as follows: "As a rough rule of thumb, I always look to closing paragraphs as indications of a book's essential character." For

Gould, and for most of us, the final paragraphs of any prose signal most clearly the strength or weakness of the discussion. It is the place the writer has been leading us for the duration of the document, so the ending had better be worth the trip.

The end of a written discussion gives you the opportunity to finish with flair. Strategically, the concluding paragraph is the most emphatic place in the argument because what you say here will be the chief idea the reader will carry away. Now is the time to restate your position confidently, trusting the rest of the document to support your logic. The audience likes to have the ideas put into a final perspective in a clean, crisp fashion—it is a courtesy to the reader and an opportunity for you.

This is the place where you can say to the reader, "See? This is how it all adds up." You need not go into detail because the body of your prose has done that, but you should use the last paragraph or two to summarize the main points of your discussion. After all, the reader (you hope) has been carefully thinking about your ideas and needs a quick review to pull it all together. Be brief. Do not be tempted to retell the entire story, but express the major points once again with conviction.

Strong conclusions generally have four things in common:

- They summarize the discussion.
- They are concise.
- They carry conviction.
- They are memorable.

Take a look at this concluding paragraph from Stephen Jay Gould's essay on evolution theory, and check the author's use of the four elements:

> Final cause inspired the greatest of all geological theories, but we may use it no longer for physical objects. This creative loss is part of Darwin's legacy, a welcome and fruitful retreat from the idea that some divine power made everything on earth to ease and inform our lives. The extent of this loss struck me recently when I read a passage from the work of Edward Blyth, a leading creationist of Darwin's time. He wrote of the beauty and wisdom "so well exemplified in the adaptation of the ptarmigan to the mountain top, and the mountain top to the habits of the ptarmigan." And I realized that this little line expressed the full power of what Darwin had wrought—for while we may still speak of the ptarmigan adapting to the mountain, we may no longer regard the mountain

as adapting to the ptarmigan. In this loss lies all the joy and terror of our current view of life.

—*from the essay, "Hutton's Purpose," in* Hen's Teeth and Horse's Toes

Gould summarizes the main thrust of his essay's argument in the first sentence, "Final cause inspired the greatest of all geological theories, but we may use it no longer for physical objects." Although he has not gone into detail about this idea here, his entire discussion has paved the way for him to make this statement at the end. It serves as a final focusing of the argument he has just completed, and it does not need to be more extensive. Gould has met the middle two criteria for good conclusions: he is concise, and the paragraph carries conviction. Most interesting is the final sentence's dramatic flair. That sentence echoes in the reader's mind, making the entire article more memorable by the ending's "punch." Gould's own conclusion would stand up nicely to anyone following his advice to check the final paragraph as a reflection of the book's essential character.

Final sentences do not have to be this dramatic. In fact, many writers who attempt such drama tip into melodramatic comedy, thereby undercutting their prose. Conclusions that merely sound authoritative and confident can also be effective. For example, the following paragraph contains no drama, but it does conclude the discussion extremely well:

> This is a time of vast change in the international environment and of unprecedented response to such change. But old national values, cherished and protected over long periods of time, are not to be abandoned in the wink of an eye. The challenge for U.S. business and government is to find new responses that serve both our tested values and the drastically changed international environment in which they must be put to work.
> —*Raymond Vernon, "Can the U.S. Negotiate for Trade Equity?"* Harvard Business Review, *May–June 1989*

Finally, the last example illustrates how a good writer combines a sense of drama with authority to craft a strong ending.

Kate Chopin, a wise and worldly woman, had refined the craft of fiction in the nineties to the point where it could face her strong inner theme of the female rebellion and see it through to a superb creative work. *The Awakening* was also an awakening of the deepest powers in its author, but, like Edna Pontellier, Kate Chopin learned that her society would not tolerate her questionings. Her tortured silence as the new century arrived was a loss to American letters of

the order of the untimely deaths of Crane and Norris. She was alive
when the twentieth century began, but she had been struck mute by
a society fearful in the face of an uncertain dawn.
   —*Larzer Ziff,* The American 1890s: Life and Times of
      a Lost Generation

PRACTICE EXERCISE 6.4

Although it is hard to judge endings without reading the whole
essay, read the following closing paragraphs and decide if they
work well. Do they seem to summarize the main point? Are they
concise? Do they have enough "punch" to be memorable?

> When we behold a wide tuft-covered expanse, we should
> remember that its smoothness, on which so much of its beauty
> depends, is mainly due to all the inequalities having been slowly
> leveled by worms. It is a marvelous reflection that the whole of
> the superficial mould over any such expanse has passed, and will
> again pass, every few years through the bodies of worms. The
> plough is one of the most ancient and most valuable of man's
> inventions; but long before he existed the land was in fact
> regularly ploughed, and still continues to be thus ploughed by
> earth-worms. It may be doubted whether there are many other
> animals which have played so important a part in the history of
> the world, as these lowly organized creatures.
>   —*Charles Darwin, "Worms and the Soil"*

> Hard as it is for many of us to believe, women are not really
> superior to men in intelligence or humanity—they are only
> equal.
>   —*Anne Roiphe, "Confessions of a Female Chauvinist Sow"*

> The essential condition for the existence, and for the sway of
> the bourgeois class, is the formation and augmentation of
> capital; the condition for capital is wage labor. Wage labor rests
> exclusively on competition between the laborers. The advance
> of industry, whose involuntary promoter is the bourgeoisie,
> replaces the isolation of the laborers, due to competition, by their
> involuntary combination, due to association. The development
> of Modern Industry, therefore, cuts from under its feet the very
> foundation on which the bourgeoisie produces and appropriates
> products. What the bourgeoisie therefore produces, above all, are
> its own grave diggers. Its fall and the victory of the proletariat
> are equally inevitable.
>   —*Marx and Engels, "The Communist Manifesto"*

> That doesn't mean prices aren't real—simply that they're more
> volatile, and sometimes behave in ways divorced from the

underlying economic situation. Just as exchange rates reflect a lot more than currencies' purchasing power in different countries, stock prices are reflecting a lot more than the discounted present value of future earnings. The market's scope and impact have clearly changed in recent years—making it foolish to over interpret certain events but dangerous to become too complacent. One thing, it seems, never changes, and that is the market's unpredictability.

> —*Karen Pennar, with Christopher Farrell, "Does the Market Matter?"* Business Week

Perhaps the goal of social reformers should be not love, but respect—for others and, most of all, for self.

> —*Lawrence Casler, "This Thing Called Love is Pathological"*

In June of 1876 Gray saw Bell demonstrate his telephone at the Centennial Exhibition in Philadelphia. He later told an associate: "As to Bell's talking telegraph, it only creates interest in scientific circles. [Its] commercial value will be limited." So did the professional Gray continue to misjudge the importance of the telephone even after its successful realization. In contrast, the amateur Bell wrote his father two weeks after filing his patent application (and nearly two weeks before he was first to hear human speech through his instrument): "The whole thing is mine—and I am sure of fame, fortune, and success."

> —*David Hounshell, "Two Paths to the Telephone"*

Every day in the week on a screen somewhere in the world, King Kong relives his agony. Again and again he expires on the Empire State building, as audiences of the devout assist his sacrifice. We watch him die, and by extension kill the ape within our bones, but these little deaths of ours occur in prosaic surroundings. We do not die on a tower, New York before our feet, nor do we give our lives to smash a few flying machines. It is not for us to bring to a momentary standstill the civilization in which we move. King Kong does this for us. And so we kill him again and again, in much-spliced celluloid, while the ape in us expires from day to day, obscure, in desperation.

> —*X. J. Kennedy, "Who Killed King Kong?"*

Beginnings, middles, and endings all have their own functions. Skillful writers use techniques specific to these different sections without drawing attention to them. You will not see a professional writer saying, "Look ahead now. This is a forecasting sentence." Nor will you see an expert saying, "See?" It is exactly the way I told you it was." Effective prose is so well written that readers can follow the writer's lead without being aware of the techniques behind the prose. Using the appropriate tools for the various parts allows writers to produce well-oiled prose that moves smoothly without the clang and bang of obvious machinery.

FOCUS ON

Your Writing Project

Take the middle of a paper you are working on or one you have already finished. Look at it with fresh eyes to see how well it fits together. Are your paragraphs logical units? Do you use transitions effectively? What kinds of transitions do you use? Can the reader follow your ideas? Write a brief (two to three pages) analysis assessing the strengths and weaknesses of the techniques you have used in this paper.

The Writing Group

Make copies of your paper's beginning and ending paragraphs for the whole group. Ask the group members to read and critique these paragraphs before the next group meeting. Then, use the meeting time to discuss the paragraphs' strengths and to suggest ways of making them even stronger.

Chapter 7

Issues of Voice and Style

This chapter focuses on the stylistic elements that create the ultimate impression on your reader. These elements call attention to themselves whether you realize it or not. A person dressed in an Armani jacket, Dior shirt, and checked polyester pants makes a negative stylistic impression, whereas a person dressed in jeans that fit, a matching sweater, and Reeboks makes a positive visual statement. Likewise, when you write, if your organization and logic are impeccable but your style is sloppy, the reader will carry away a negative impression, no matter how impressive your ideas are. Conversely, when you write with style, your credibility immediately increases because the reader is more willing to trust a writer whose sentences maintain an air of sophistication. The next few sections discuss how to "dress for success" in your prose.

Creating an Appropriate Voice

Voice is one of the most noticeable parts of writing. From your own experience as a reader, you probably realize that all prose has personality—some dull, some more interesting—and that you can actually "hear" the voice speaking as you read the words on the page. Just as speakers' voices create different effects on the audience, prose voices affect readers differently, too. Listen to these voices as you read, or better, listen to your own voice as you bring these written words to life:

> But even television has failed to run *King Kong* into oblivion. Coffee-in-the-lobby cinemas still show the old hunk of hokum, with the apology that in its use of composite shots and animated models the film remains technically interesting. And no other monster movie in history has won so devoted a popular audience. None of the plodding mummies, the stultified draculas, the white-coated Lugosis with their shiny pin-ball machine laboratories, none of the invisible stranglers, berserk robots, or menaces from Mars has ever enjoyed so many resurrections.
> —*X. J. Kennedy, "Who Killed King Kong?"*

> Bus No. 405 was 40 minutes into its late-morning run from Tel Aviv, laboring up the steep hills surrounding Jerusalem, when driver Moshe Elul was approached by a passenger. "For a minute, I thought he wanted to ask a question," said Elul. Suddenly, the man—later identified as a 28-year-old Palestinian from the Nuseirat refugee camp in Gaza—lunged for the wheel and jerked it hard to the right. As the bus careened through a guard rail and into a rocky ravine, he shouted "Allahu Akbar": God is great. Passengers were thrown to the ceiling as the bus tumbled down the incline and burst into flames. "Some people were limbless and with distorted faces," said one of the first medics on the scene. "There was terrible smoke. It was impossible to breathe. It was like hell."
> —*Adam Platt,* Newsweek

> One Christmas was so much like another, in those years, around the sea-town corner now and out of all sound except the distant speaking of the voices I sometimes hear a moment before sleep, that I can never remember whether it snowed for six days and six nights when I was twelve or whether it snowed for twelve days and twelve nights when I was six; or whether the ice broke and the skating grocer vanished like a snowman through a white trap-door on that same Christmas day that the mince-pies finished Uncle Arnold and we tobogganed down the seaward hill, all the afternoon, on the best tea-tray, and Mrs. Griffiths complained, and we threw a snowball at her niece and my hands burned so, with the heat and the cold, when I held them out in front of the fire, that I cried for twenty minutes and then had some jelly.
> —*Dylan Thomas, "Memories of Christmas"*

In these examples, the writers' voices dominate the prose, becoming as much a part of the telling as the information itself. Through this dominance of voice, writers reach for the readers' emotions and pull them into the prose.

Not all prose benefits from such drama, of course. Instructions or technical reports require the prose to be straightforward with little interference from the writer's personality. In these cases the voice, like the personality of a speaker charged with imparting information, becomes more businesslike and less emotional:

> Sometimes you may want to set certain lines or sections of text against the left margin, against the right margin, or centered between the left and right margins. For example, the title of a document may be centered on a line at the top of the page while the first section heading may be flush to the left margin. Certain commands make your text appear exactly where you want it. The FL (Flush Left), FR (Flush Right), and FC (Flush Center) commands are useful in formatting your text. These formatting commands are executed from the command line and are represented by command triangles in the text at the location of the cursor.
> —*a word-processing manual*

> Information collected from borings for soil samples and well placement indicate a fairly uniform sand and gravel formation to the depth of the explorations, a maximum of 148 feet. Gardiner's Clay, which is a regional aquitard for the water table aquifer, is not present in the two deep wells. In other respects, the local geology conforms to reported regional patterns.
> —*an engineering report*

At first reading, you may not think these passages have voices at all, but they do. By rereading them, you can probably "hear" the difference between the two, as the voices make themselves clear. In the first, the voice is friendly and simple, putting computer-phobic readers at ease. In the second, the voice speaks more technically, but with authority, giving the reader a sense of confidence in the engineer's professional ability. In both, the reader hears the *information* more than the writer's voice, whereas in the earlier examples the reader hears the voice at least as loudly as the information conveyed.

Most writing falls somewhere between dramatic writing and informational writing. Academic writing, for instance, has a twofold purpose: to convey information and to sound convincing. As a result, most academic writers use voice to lend authority to the text, choosing language that suggests familiarity with the scholarly field, carries conviction, and expresses opinions clearly. But some scholars become so involved with abstract concepts that they neglect voice altogether. The resulting poor prose often moves in a slow, multisyllabic fashion, plodding along with a total lack of grace. These writers have ignored voice and are mired in academic jargon. For example:

The probability of representing diverse revision processes increases with the diversity of the theoretical views brought to bear on the subject and with the conflicting or overlapping findings they generate. The multiple viewpoints of researchers from different disciplines produce a happy diversity of variables in the creative process.

When professors write like this, it is not surprising to find students trying to write like this, too. For instance:

Pursuant to the extensive research completed for this assignment, this researcher suggests that Gauss's principle is indubitably appropriate in this instance.

Now take a look at an example of effective academic prose. Notice how the writer uses the terms of her field clearly and confidently, while simultaneously creating a voice that engages the reader's intellect and interest:

When we talk about "Art" with a capital "A"—that is, about any or all of the arts: painting, sculpture, architecture, the potter's and goldsmith's and other designers' arts, music, dance, poetry, and prose fiction, drama and film—it is a constant temptation to say things about "Art" in this general sense that are true only in one special domain, or to assume that what holds for one art must hold for another. For instance, the fact that music is made for performance, for presentation to the ear, and is simply not the same thing when it is given only to the tonal imagination of a reader silently perusing a score, has made some aestheticians pass straight to the conclusion that literature, too, must be physically heard to be fully experienced, because words are originally spoken, not written; an obvious parallel, but a careless and, I think, invalid one. It is dangerous to set up principles by analogy, and generalize from a single consideration.

But it is natural, and safe enough, to ask analogous questions: What is the function of sound in music? What is the function of sound in poetry? What is the function of sound in prose composition? What is the function of sound in drama? The answers may be quite heterogeneous; and that is itself an important fact, a guide to something more than a simple and sweeping theory. Such findings guide us to exact relations and abstract, variously exemplified basic principles.
—*Susanne K. Langer, "Expressiveness"*

As is evident, written voice is an important factor in any prose. It can engage readers or put them off, just as happens with the spoken voice. When you write, it is important to recognize the personality of your work and make sure it is appropriate for the situation. A businesslike tone in a personal letter is offensive, as is an overly personal voice in business situations. Nor is it appropriate to use humor when writing a legal brief, but humor may enhance an essay for the company newsletter. The best advice is to be aware that your prose has a voice and to make sure that it works for the situation and is consistent. Prose with a personality that shifts in mid-paragraph jars the reader into focusing on the text's split personality rather than on the intended meaning.

To control voice, you need to understand the elements that create it. Unlike speakers, writers cannot depend on inflection, body language, and audience interaction to help them convey their personalities. Instead, they must rely on words and punctuation to create the voice their readers hear. The following is a list of some of the elements writers can use to develop their prose voices. It is also a good idea to check these elements at the revising stage to be sure they work well together.

Elements of Voice

Modifiers   Adjectives, adverbs, and other modifiers give color to the writing by painting pictures in the reader's mind. The more you use, the more colorful and more specific the writing becomes, but the more emotionally charged it becomes as well. Avoid overusing modifiers; it is important to strike the right balance.

Examples: I want to buy a car.
I want to buy a rag-top, fire-engine red MG.
I desperately want to buy a rag-top, souped-up, fire-engine red MG—a gorgeous hunk of car.

Charles Stone does his job.
Charles Stone does his work adequately.
That slacker Charles Stone barely manages to do even his menial job.

At dawn, the sun rose.
At dawn, the hazy sun rose silently over the horizon.
In the glistening dawn, the hazy sun rose silently, languidly over the far distant horizon.

Verbs   Prose that uses vigorous verbs has more character than prose dependent on the verb *to be*. Because verbs carry the energy of sentences, they are an essential part of the voice, and *is, are, was,* and *were* add little to the aggregate effect. On the other hand, prose that overdoes the vigorous verbs becomes too loud and boisterous for most situations. You also must make sure that the verb creates the appropriate image. Attempts to use energetic verbs sometimes result in conflicting images or inappropriate messages.

> *Examples:* The whistle was loud.
> The whistle screeched loudly.
> The whistle pierced the air with its loud screech, drowning out the morning's calm.
>
> Carrying a tray, he walked across the room.
> Balancing a tray, he teetered across the room.
> Balancing a tray, he pirouetted across the room.

Metaphor   Metaphor and simile allow writers to explain abstract ideas by comparison with other things. In so doing, they add an emotional dimension to the prose. Again, be careful not to overuse these devices, and do not mix metaphors.

> *Examples:* Tom was a tower of a man. (metaphor)
>
> He fought like a tiger. (simile)
>
> It's time to take the bull by the tail and face the situation. (mixed metaphor)

Person   Use of first, second, or third person makes a big difference in the prose voice. None of these choices is wrong; each is appropriate in different situations. Determine what is the most efficient and polite way to speak to the audience, and then remain consistent with this choice. Keep in mind that third person is the most formal, second person is usually used in direct address and in instructions, and first person is appropriate if the writer feels comfortable inserting herself in the prose. Keep in mind that overuse of the third person results in stiff, stilted prose, especially prose that uses the pronoun *one* instead of *I* or *you.*

> *Examples:* I am confident of these conclusions. (first person)
>
> You can be confident of these conclusions. (second person)
>
> A person may be confident of these conclusions. (third person)
>
> When one is caught in these situations, it is important not to panic. (third person)
>
> Do not panic in these situations. (second person)

Sophistication   As you write, speak to the audience in terms that they will understand, but be careful not to patronize them. Develop a voice appropriate for the rhetorical situation. Slang, for example, is usually inappropriate unless you are writing a personal letter or fiction. Ultraformal language is rarely useful either and often makes the writer seem like a bore rather than an interesting and intelligent person. In general, think of your readers as intelligent, friendly people, and address them accordingly.

> *Examples:*   In light of my recent promotion, I am writing to request a salary review.
>
> Since I recently got kicked upstairs, it's time you guys forked over the big bucks.
>
> In keeping with the increased responsibilities attendant to my recent promotion, I respectfully submit that a review of the company's salary obligations to me is in order.

The voice you project in your prose should always reflect your personality, but it should also change to fit the various writing situations you encounter. Like a public speaker, you must be aware of your voice's impact on the audience and be able to use it to your advantage.

PRACTICE EXERCISE 7.1

Analyze the voices in the following passages. How would you describe their effects? In what situations are these voices appropriate? Is each voice consistent within the passage, or do some of them shift?

> We have had the opportunity to study the spatially guided locomotion of one 2 1/2-year-old blind child in several experimental settings. After the child had been taken along several paths connecting four objects in a small room, she was able to move directly between the objects along paths she had never taken. Sighted adults and 3-year-old children, all blindfolded, performed with similar accuracy. These observations demonstrate that the locomotion of children, with or without visual experience, is guided by metric knowledge of space. This knowledge makes possible the derivation of further spatial information.
> —*Barbara Landau, Henry Gleitman, Elizabeth Spelke,*
> *"Spatial Knowledge and Geometric Representation in a Child*
> *Blind from Birth"*

We're shooting a scene for a corporate videotape in an idyllic setting—a park in full bloom. It'll be used for recruiting—to sell prospective employees on the joys of living on Long Island. We've captured on tape a man peacefully sleeping under a tree. The camera dwells on his face, which has a look of serene contentment. Then the producer says to the cameraman, "Wake him up, we need a release."

The preceding is pure invention. It never happened. But it should have. For any time the camera invades an individual's privacy, a release may be required.

—*Allen Cobrin, "Ethical Considerations in Corporate Video Production"*

The traffic studies reveal an urgent demand for a crossing for vehicular traffic in the vicinity of the proposed bridge to relieve the present intolerable traffic situation. The traffic volume is of more than sufficient magnitude to make it financially feasible to construct, operate and maintain, from tolls, such a crossing, not considering the broader benefits to the people of both States as well as to the local community.

—*Othmar H. Ammann, "Tentative Report on the Hudson River Bridge"*

Another novelty that I hadn't expected is that the word processor makes writing a public act. Like all writers, I'm self conscious about the words I put on paper and I don't want anybody else to see them until I think they're right. (Then, like all writers, I can't wait to see them in print and to have everybody else see them.) In this miserable state the writer has always been protected by the social codes governing behavior. It's just not polite—so we are instructed at an early age—to look over someone's shoulder when he or she is writing by hand or at a typewriter. The committing of thoughts to paper is a deed that by civilized consent we are allowed to do alone.

No such constraints apply to writing done on a terminal screen. I had no sooner started to work at my word processor, tentatively pecking out sentences and shyly experimenting with the various special keys, than I discovered that I was performing a spectator sport. People were standing behind me looking at the screen. They gave every appearance of being fascinated by what I was causing to happen.

—*William Zinsser,* Writing with a Word Processor

Stabilized line of sight gimbals used in airborne vehicles must ameliorate vibrational and maneuvering g's to reduce jitter in the sight to a level that will allow acceptable image quality. This is accomplished in the gimbal design by forcing the lowest natural frequency to as high a level as possible. Since the gimbal mass reduces the natural frequency while the gimbal rigidity increases it, it is desirable to obtain the highest possible stiffness to weight ratio. This is what makes the gimbal structure such a logical application for high modulus composite materials. A lesser known but equally important reason is damping, or diminished amplitude of the oscillations because each of the resonances within the spring mass system is perturbed by the vibrational input. Since more damping causes less response at each of the resonances, the jitter is reduced.

—*U.S. Army Technical Report*

Identifying Components of Style

Consider the following passage:

If you really want to hear about it, the first thing you'll probably want to know is where I was born, and what my lousy childhood was like, and how my parents were occupied and all before they had me, and all that David Copperfield kind of crap, but I don't feel like going into it, if you want to know the truth. In the first place, that stuff bores me, and in the second place, my parents would have about two hemorrhages apiece if I told anything pretty personal about them. They're quite touchy about anything like that, especially my father. They're *nice* and all—I'm not saying that—but they're also touchy as hell.

As you identify the elements of this voice, you are really focusing on the larger issue of style, or the form of expression that writing takes. A text's style gives it its voice and stamps it with character. From the above passage—the opening of J. D. Salinger's *Catcher in the Rye*—you know that the speaker is young, unhappy, and cocky. You know this because of the writer's choice of words: He uses slang such as *lousy* and *crap* coupled with the unsophisticated adjectives *pretty* and *touchy*. These components of voice fall under the categories mentioned previously, but other elements come into play as well. For instance, the sentence structure creates a rhythm that sounds like a spoiled child's speech pattern, and the arrangement of the words within the sentences contributes to the passage's childish character. The combination of these techniques creates the effect Salinger intended, and that combination is the piece's style.

According to classical rhetoricians, style has two major components: diction and sentence structure. The writer's choice of words and the arrangement of those words within sentences create the text's personality.

Style affects readers immediately. Writing that is ornate and filled with unnecessary flourishes and redundancies makes an enemy of the reader who must cut through the rococo sentences to find the writer's point; equally negative are stark, lifeless sentences that communicate clearly but lack any character. Between these two poles lie many stylistic possibilities.

Every sentence you write makes a statement beyond its literal meaning because the structure speaks as loudly as the ideas. Most writers have a natural style unique to their writing. Some prefer short, staccato sentences, whereas others write longer ones; some are addicted to the semicolon, whereas others are addicted to the dash; some write in polysyllabic words, whereas others use simplistic terms; and so on. The point is that writers develop stylistic habits, often without knowing it. To be a good writer, you need to recognize your stylistic habits so that you can retain the effective ones and break the others. Otherwise, your prose will create impressions beyond your control. The style should be appropriate for the specific situation, which means that you must be able to retool your prose to work in different ways. Certain trademark elements may remain, but the overall form must be flexible.

Analyzing your natural style—or that of others—requires an understanding of the following components: *diction,* including figures of speech; and *sentence structure,* including sentence lengths, sentence types, punctuation, and transitional devices. The last element on the list, transitional devices, has been discussed previously, but the others need some explanation.

Diction

Diction refers to the writer's choice of words. As you write, you are constantly making choices from a wide variety of possible words that may be used to express your meaning. Read the following sentence to get a better sense of the extent to which diction affects the reader's response to your prose. As you read, think about how the words create their effect.

> Amongst any other population, or at a later period in the history of New England, the grim rigidity that petrified the bearded physiognomies of these good people would have augured some awful business in hand.

The preceding sentence illustrates how the word choice creates a mood and even indicates a time period. If the sentence were written in contemporary style, it might read: "Among any other people, or in a later time in New England's history, the grim stiffness that petrified these people's bearded faces would have meant there was some terrible trouble at hand." But Hawthorne's original firmly sets this scene from *The Scarlet Letter* in the stark Puritan era. The words *physiognomies, amongst,* and *augured* propel the reader into the world Hawthorne describes, a world filled with rigidly proper people who harbor immense guilt for the infrequent pleasures they have experienced.

Diction can also indicate the level of sophistication and even control the reader's view of the material. For fiction writers, this is an essential technique. But the following passages suggest how word choice in nonfiction writing is as important as it is in creative writing:

> Some lands are flat and grass-covered, and smile so evenly up at the sun that they seem forever youthful, untouched by man or time. Some are torn, ravaged and convulsed like the features of profane old age. Rocks are wrenched up and exposed to view; black pits receive the sun but give back no light.
> —*Loren Eisely,* The Immense Journey

> I went to the woods because I wished to live deliberately, to front only the essential facts of life, and see if I could learn what it had to teach, and not, when I came to die, discover that I had not lived.
> —*Henry David Thoreau,* Walden

> Never in my memory has a plurality announced a judgment of this court that so foments a disregard for the law and our standing decisions.
> Nor, in my memory, has a plurality gone about its business in such a deceptive fashion. At every level of its review, from its effort to read the real meaning of the Missouri statute, to its intended evisceration of precedents and its deafening silence about the constitutional protections that it would jettison, the plurality obscures the portent of its analysis.
> —*Supreme Court Justice Blackmun's dissent,*
> Webster v. Reproductive Health Services

The authors of each of these passages use words that are exactly right for the situation. Eisely's adjectives *ravaged* and *convulsed* personify the land and its terrible victimization. Thoreau's "fronting" the essentials of life gives the impression of fearlessly meeting life head on, and Blackmun's note about the "deafening silence" creates exactly the right irony between sound and silence. These words express more than just information; they capture precise images and feelings. Consider what Blackmun's opinion would lose if he had deleted the word *deafening* or changed *evisceration* to *gutting*. How would Eisely's prose be affected if he had written "harsh old age" rather than using the adjective *profane*? As Mark Twain has suggested, "The difference between the almost right word and the right word is really a large matter—'tis the difference between the lightning-bug and the lightning."

Figures of Speech

The Roman orator Quintilian, one of the first great teachers of rhetoric, defined *figures* as "a form of speech artfully varied from common usage." For him, and for most great writers and speakers throughout history, figures of speech provide the "art" of writing—the means by which writers make their prose memorable. By making slight changes in the commonplace practices of writing, you can pleasantly surprise the reader into paying more attention to what you have to say. As novelist Ford Madox Ford noted, "Carefully examined, a good—an interesting—style will be found to consist in a constant succession of tiny, unobservable surprises."

Rhetorical scholars have listed at least thirty-six kinds of "figures"—language constructions that provide these surprises—such as metaphor, ellipsis, synechdoche, alliteration, and so on. Although the list is much too long to discuss here, it is important to note that effective writing is almost always memorable, using turns of phrase or inventive structures that the reader does not gloss over. This sentence from John F. Kennedy's first inaugural address is an example:

> Now the trumpet summons us again—not as a call to bear arms, though arms we need; not as a call to battle, though embattled we are; but a call to bear the burden of a long twilight struggle, year in and year out, "rejoicing in hope, patient in tribulation," a struggle against the common enemies of man: tyranny, poverty, disease and war itself.

In this passage, Kennedy captures the audience's attention in several ways: the use of the metaphorical trumpet summoning us to a new kind of war; the repetition of the structure "not . . . though"; the play on the words *battle* and *embattled;* the image of the "long twilight struggle"; and the final list of the common enemies of man, culminating not simply in war but in "war *itself*." Kennedy's speech would have had less effect if he had spoken in more commonplace words and structures, such as, "Now we are called again to fight against tyranny, poverty, and war."

A word of caution: Using figures of speech does not mean using flowery language or overwriting. Rather than encouraging melodramatic prose, figures of speech make writing freshly powerful. Another example—less "rhetorical" than Kennedy's momentous speech—illustrates how these techniques empower language in more everyday situations. In the introduction to a *Newsweek* "My Turn" column, journalist Dan Rather captures readers' attention by a more subtle use of figures:

> For two full months television's pictures have riveted America's attention on China. We've seen the power of television before, when a young president was gunned down, when America's sons were dying in a green-jungle hell or the barracks of Beirut. The students in Beijing were not our children. The government was not our government. The White House tried to keep a low profile and say as little as possible. This then was a truly foreign story.
>
> Television brought Beijing's battle for democracy to Main Street. It made students who live on the other side of the planet just as human, just as vulnerable as the boy on the next block. The miracle of television is that the triumph and tragedy of Tiananmen Square would not have been any more vivid had it been Times Square.

Notice the repeated words, structures, and sounds, the slow build to the climactic "This then was a truly foreign story," and the ultimate connection between Tiananmen Square and Times Square. By using a series of "constant unobservable surprises," Rather has hooked readers on the prose and caused them to want to read on.

In your own work, try to find new ways to express your meaning. Do not be content with hackneyed phrases or clichés; strive for fresh language and structures. If your phrases roll off your pen or keyboard like a car from an assembly line, the resulting prose will have a prefabricated look. Take the time to craft sentences that demand to be read, that defy precut patterns—sentences such as this one from Gail Sheehy's *Passages:* "Without warning, in the middle of my thirties, I had a breakdown of nerves."

Sentence Length

The length of your sentences can make a big difference in your writing's effect. A series of short sentences keeps the reader on edge, whereas longer sentences invite the reader to settle in and take the time to absorb large amounts of information at once. When you are writing about action, it makes sense to use shorter sentences that will increase tension. On the other hand, descriptive passages almost always contain long sentences filled with images and precise detail. Note the difference in the following two examples:

> We hunted old bottles in the dump, bottles caked with dirt and filth, half buried, full of cobwebs, and we washed them out at the horse trough by the elevator, putting in a handful of shot along with the water to knock the dirt loose; and when we had shaken them until our arms were tired, we hauled them off in somebody's coaster wagon and turned them in at Bill Anderson's pool hall, where the smell of lemon pop was so sweet on the dark pool-hall air that I am sometimes awakened by it in the night, even yet.
> —*Wallace Stegner, "The Town Dump"*

> Just yesterday a man was killed. He was assigned to Rescue Company 1, and he was working on the roof of a burning warehouse. The roof had been weakened by the fire, and it gave in. The man fell through the roof into an air shaft. He passed eight floors before he hit bottom.
> —*Dennis Smith, "Malicious False Alarms"*

Sentence lengths establish the rhythm of the prose and in doing so tap the reader's emotions. This technique is discussed in more detail later in the chapter, but it is important to note now that the various lengths create corresponding moods in the reader. In a famous passage from *A Farewell to Arms,* Hemingway mixes the sentence lengths as he takes the reader with him through a near-death experience. Read the narrative and think about how the rhythm contributes to the emotional impact:

> Through the other noise I heard a cough, then came the chuh-chuh-chuh-chuh—then there was a flash, as when a blast-furnace door is swung open, and a roar that started white and went red and on and on in a rushing wind. I tried to breathe but my breath would not come and I felt myself rush bodily out of myself and out and out and out and all the time bodily in the wind. I went out swiftly, all of myself, and I knew I was dead and that it had all been a mistake to think you just died. Then I floated, and instead of going on I felt myself slide back. I breathed and I was back. The ground was torn up and in front of my head there was a splintered beam of wood. In the jolt of my head I heard somebody crying. I thought somebody was screaming. I tried to move but I could not move.

Sentence Types

All sentences fall into one of four categories: simple, complex, compound, and compound-complex. Most writers habitually prefer one type over the others, and their prose can become dulled by repeating one pattern. If you know the basic types, you can avoid the temptation to use one type of sentence exclusively. But before learning the basic types, you may need to review the components that make up every sentence: clauses and phrases.

A *clause* is a group of words containing a subject and a verb. There are two kinds of clauses: main clause (independent clause) and subordinate clause (dependent clause).

Main clause: a group of words containing a subject and a verb and able to stand alone as a complete sentence or thought.

Example: The successful bidder will submit two reports.

Subordinate clause: a group of words containing a subject and a verb but unable to express a complete thought. Often subordinate clauses begin with subordinate conjunctions such as *after, although, before, while, since, because,* and so on.

Example: Although the successful bidder will submit two reports . . .

A *phrase* is a group of two or more words that act as a unit but have no subject or verb. There are many kinds of phrases, but the most common are prepositional phrases and participial phrases.

Example: The cat is *under the table.* (prepositional phrase)
                 Running home, he tripped and fell. (participial phrase)

The four sentence types and examples of each follow.

Simple Sentence   A simple sentence contains one main clause and may contain any number of phrases.

Example: On award of the contract, Sullivan Company will perform the work in two phases.

Complex Sentence   A complex sentence contains one main clause, one or more subordinate clauses, and any number of phrases.

Example: Because I grew up in a small town, my childhood had more of a nineteenth-century flavor.

Compound Sentence   A compound sentence contains two or more main clauses, plus any number of phrases. There are no subordinate clauses.

Example: The roof had been weakened by the fire, and it gave in.

Compound-Complex Sentence   A compound-complex sentence contains two or more main clauses, one or more subordinate clauses, and any number of phrases.

Example: The 6670 laser printer can print on both sides simultaneously, and it can print and collate multiple copies electronically, though it is prone to mechanical failure.

Pull out a recent sample of your own writing and check to see if you have a favorite sentence type. Chances are you do. Keep in mind that these types are a powerful stylistic tool and should be used with care, not haphazardly or habitually. Used well, they combine with other elements of style to produce easily readable and effective writing. Used poorly, they create dull, repetitious prose.

Punctuation

The main purpose of punctuation is to clarify meaning. For example, read this famous sentence from *The Great Gatsby,* minus the commas:

And so we beat on boats against the current borne back ceaselessly into the past.

Beat on boats? Current borne back ceaselessly into the past? Without the punctuation, Fitzgerald's marvelous words serve only to confuse. But surrounding the appositive phrase with commas clarifies the meaning and restores the effect of the images:

And so we beat on, boats against the current, borne back ceaselessly into the past.

In this sentence, the word choice and arrangement perfectly express the author's point, and the commas allow the reader to understand how the parts fit together. As a stylistic device, then, punctuation serves a subsidiary role.

Some writers rely on exclamation points, dashes, and so forth to put emphasis in their text, rather than finding the right combination of words to express meaning. In writing where punctuation becomes the primary carrier of emotion, the words seem frail beneath the heavy weight of the marks. As a result, readers may remember only the breathless effect of the exclamation points or the continuous whispers provided by so many parentheses, instead of remembering the meaning the text was supposed to convey. The writing resembles a melodrama, filled with exaggerated emotions:

> Defendant Wharton had sufficient notice of the open hole and open doorway for the court to infer her actual knowledge! (Even without actual knowledge, however, defendant landlord had ample opportunity to inspect and safeguard the dangerous renovation area during her three hours in the building.) At the very least, she could have warned the plaintiff and others about the ongoing renovations! Instead, she issued an open invitation to disaster!!

Such overdone punctuation gives a serious subject almost a comic effect and undercuts the intended argument. "Emotional" punctuation, such as exclamation points, dashes, ellipses, parentheses, and even underlining or italics, rarely has the effect you intend and should be kept to a minimum in your writing. If the words are well-chosen, punctuation as an expression of emotion is redundant.

These are the basic components that make up writing style. With these tools you can make your prose pugnacious, relaxed, congenial, businesslike, ingratiating, pompous, or just plain folksy. But no matter how you use these components, if the combination does not fit the rhetorical situation and does not have the proper effect on the reader, you have not used your tools to your best advantage.

PRACTICE EXERCISE 7.2

Find two pieces of published nonfiction aimed at different audiences and written for different purposes. One might be an article for a professional journal and the other a newspaper column, or a technical report and a chapter from a nonfiction book. Make sure that the pieces you choose are sufficiently different to warrant significant differences in style.

1. Analyze the style of each, identifying how the stylistic components work together to create the overall effect.

2. Evaluate the success of the style for each rhetorical situation.

3. Compare the two. What are the major stylistic differences?

Establishing Effective Sentence Design

What makes a good sentence? When readers think about what they appreciate in good sentences, three elements are primary: voice, focus, and rhythm. Writers whose sentences please the majority of readers have learned to handle these three elements successfully. Voice is a topic you should be familiar with by this time, but the other two may need some explanation.

Both focus and rhythm are essential for good sentence design, but writers can easily overlook them in the heat of composing. A sentence's *focus* means that the topic is clearly and efficiently defined, and the reader does not have to read the sentence twice to understand how it contributes to the discourse as a whole. *Rhythm* is a more abstract term referring to the pace of each sentence within the text. Does the pace move too quickly for the reader to follow? Is it too slow? Is one structural pattern repeated over and over, making the prose monotonous? These are questions you probably ask as a reader, and it is only fair that others ask the same of your writing.

Focus

As you are writing each sentence, ask yourself, "Whose story is it?" Readers expect sentences to be about the person (or thing) who is introduced first. As one writing professional has said in his work on sentence design:

> Readers expect a unit of discourse to be about whoever shows up first. "John loves Mary" and "Mary is loved by John" are two different sentences about the same facts. The first tells us something about John, the second about Mary. Despite the passivity of the second, both are good sentences. "John loves Mary" is actually an inferior sentence to "Mary is loved by John" if the former sentence appears in a paragraph that is telling us all about Mary. We need, therefore, to put at the beginning of each unit of discourse the people (or things) whose "story" that unit intends to recount.
> —*George D. Gopen, "Let the Buyer in the Ordinary Course of Business Beware: Suggestions for Revising the Prose of the Uniform Commercial Code,"* The University of Chicago Law Review

Extensive introductory material or other information at the beginning of a sentence misleads the reader into thinking that the sentence is about something else. Also, readers expect that the verb will contain the sentence's action and that it will appear clearly connected to the subject. "*John loves* Mary" connects the two nicely; the focus of that sentence is clear. But as you write, the rules of effective sentence design may fade into the background. The following passage is an extreme example—but not an invented one—of how prose can defy reader expectations. It is, by the way, one sentence:

> Any sanitary district formed under this chapter, for the purposes of accomplishing its objectives, or paying and refunding its indebtedness of paying unnecessary expenses and liabilities incurred under this chapter, including organizational and other necessary expenses and liabilities whether incurred by the district or any municipality therein, or any person residing in unorganized territory encompassed by said district, the district being authorized to reimburse any municipality therein or any person residing in unorganized territory encompassed by said district for any such expenses incurred or paid by it or him, and in acquiring properties, paying damages, laying sewers, drains and conduits, constructing, maintaining and operating sewage and treatment plants, or systems, and making renewals, additions, extensions and improvements to the same, and to cover interest payments during the period of construction, by resolution of its board of trustees, without district vote is authorized to borrow money and issue, from time to time, bonds, notes or other evidences of indebtedness of the district in one series, or in separate series, in such amount or amounts bearing interest at such rate or rates, and having such terms and provisions as the trustees shall determine.
> —*State of Maine, MRSA Title 38, Subchapter IV, Section 1201*

Whose story is it? It is the *sanitary district's* story. What is the action involved to create the plot for the story? You have to wade down to nearly the end of the passage to find the verb: *is authorized to borrow money and issue . . . bonds.*" All of the intervening material disguises the "plot," as it were, and confuses the poor reader who simply wants to know who or what is involved and what the action of the story is. To clarify this tangled mess, the writer could put the main actor and the action up front and provide a list for the rest of the document:

> Any sanitary district formed under this chapter may issue bonds, notes or other evidences of indebtedness, without district vote, under the following conditions: . . .
>
> These bonds or other evidences of indebtedness may be issued in one series or in separate series in the amount bearing the appropriate rate; the trustees shall determine the appropriate terms and provisions.

The revision focuses the sentence, meets readers' expectations, and renders the design effective. Although this example is extreme, the same principles apply to any writing. Just two suggestions will help with establishing voice:

- Determine whose story it is and put that person or agent first.
- Clearly connect the action to the actor.

In so doing, you will have sharply focused your prose and made the reader's job a lot easier.

Rhythm

The sentence from the preceding Maine legislature example was nearly impossible to read. The rhythm was off. Sentences, like music, have timing and phrasing that work together to produce a rhythm that helps the reader pace his reading. If the sentences are all the same length or repeat the same structural pattern, the resulting pace is monotonous and irritating because the reader reads the material in unvarying rhythmic units. The preceding example has poor rhythm for several reasons. First, it is a 191-word sentence; that alone makes the pace much too slow for reading comfort. Add to that the proliferation of short phrases inside commas, and you can see why these units—with no promise of the finishing verb—stack on top of one another. Readers confronted with that passage cannot find a comfortable rhythm to help pace them through the sentence. In the revised version, the rhythmic units allow readers to move through the sentence more naturally and easily.

Used well, sentence rhythm can reinforce the theme of a passage and help create the mood. State legislators, perhaps, cannot be expected to write peerless rhythms. For an example of well-crafted rhythms, turn to one of the masters of English prose. In Hemingway's *A Farewell to Arms,* notice how the repeated patterns and the continuous use of *and* suggest the weary troops dragging along the dusty road:

> In the late summer of that year we lived in a house in a village that looked across the river and the plain to the mountains. In the bed of the river there were pebbles and boulders, dry and white in the sun, and the water was clear and swiftly moving and blue in the channels. Troops went by the house and down the road and the dust they raised powdered the leaves of the trees. The trunks of trees too were dusty and the leaves fell early that year and we saw the troops marching along the road and the dust rising and leaves, stirred by the breeze, falling and the soldiers marching and afterward the road bare and white except for the leaves.

As this passage illustrates, the words within sentences create a music by their sounds and syllables, and the sentences themselves have rhythm because of their length, their punctuation, and their structure. In those four sentences, Hemingway's deft combination of simple words, minimal punctuation, and repetitive rhythm keeps pace with the weary soldiers, drawing the reader into a world exhausted from war.

Everyone is not going to write like Hemingway, but everyday writers need to be aware of rhythm. The Maine regulation reproduced earlier exemplifies prose that seems to trudge down the page with the readers. At the other extreme, the following paragraph's pace is much too quick, causing the readers to rush through the prose:

> Corporate winners almost universally live by a clear sense of mission. They are value driven. They have an unusually clear vision of their roles. They also have an unusually clear vision of their limitations. Similarly, they work hard to maintain a common set of company values.

This text's staccato rhythm is caused by its string of short sentences, almost all beginning with subject and verb and almost all being exactly the same length. If some of these were combined by means of subordinate clauses, the rhythm would change for the better:

> Corporate winners almost universally live by a clear sense of mission; they are value driven. While they have an unusually clear vision of their roles, they also have an equally clear sense of their limitations and work hard to maintain a common set of company values.

See the difference? With this change of pace, the prose seems more intelligent and trustworthy and less simplistic. Readers need sentence variety and clearly marked rhythmic units to pace their reading speed and comprehension. Otherwise, the sentences become a jumble of sounds and ideas that work against reader comprehension rather than enhancing it.

PRACTICE EXERCISE 7.3

To get a better sense of how writers establish different rhythms in their prose, you may want to try your hand at imitating some passages. Read the following passages carefully. Then, revise them using your own words, but make sure you use exactly the same parts of speech, approximately the same number of syllables, and the same punctuation.

> Isadora Duncan, born in San Francisco of Irish-American parents in 1878, was prepared for life by a mother who gave music lessons all day to support her family, and who played Beethoven, Mozart, and Chopin or read Shakespeare, Keats, and Burns to them in the evening. A handsome father was seldom home.
> —*Winthrop Palmer, "Isadora Duncan"*

> You ask, what is our policy? I say it is to wage war by land, sea, and air. War with all our might and with all the strength God has given us, and to wage war against a monstrous tyranny never surpassed in the dark and lamentable catalogue of human crime. That is our policy.
> You ask, what is our aim? I can answer in one word. It is victory. Victory at all costs—victory in spite of all terrors—victory however long and hard the road may be, for without victory there is no survival.
> —*Winston Churchill, "Speech to the House of Commons,"*
> *May 13, 1940*

> Through the bloody September twilight, aftermath of sixty-two rainless days, it had gone like a fire in dry grass—the rumor, the story, whatever it was. Something about Miss Minnie Cooper and a Negro. Attacked, insulted, frightened: none of them, gathered in the barber shop on that Saturday evening where the ceiling fan stirred, without freshening it, the vitiated air, sending back upon them, in recurrent surges of stale pomade and lotion, their own stale breath and odors, knew exactly what had happened.
> —*William Faulkner, "Dry September"*

> Consider the Hershey Bar—a most worthy standard bearer for the general phenomenon of phyletic size decrease in manufactured goods. It is the unadvertised symbol of American quality. It shares with Band-Aids, Kleenex, Jell-o and the Fridge that rare distinction of attaching its brand name to the generic product. It also has been shrinking fast.
> —*Stephen Jay Gould, "Phyletic Size Decrease in Hershey Bars"*

> They love it. The insolence! The insolence sets off another eruption. He peers through the scalding glare of the television lights. He keeps squinting. He's aware of a great mass of silhouettes out in front of him. The crowd swells up. The ceiling presses down. It's covered in beige tiles. The tiles have curly incisions all over them. They're crumbling around the edges. Asbestos! He knows it when he sees it! The faces—they're

> waiting for the beano, for the rock fight. Bloody noses!—that's
> the idea. The next instant means everything. He can handle it!
> He can handle the hecklers! Only five-seven, but he's even better
> at it than Koch used to be! He's mayor of the greatest city on
> earth—New York! Him!
> —*Tom Wolfe,* Bonfire of the Vanities

Maintaining Clarity

The final element of style discussed in this chapter is the problem
of clarity. Writers nearly always overwrite in their first drafts: They
use more words or more complicated words than they have to. Like
a sculptor hacking away at an unwieldy block of marble, writers
must chisel through the initial layers to reach the clear, simple lines
underneath.

This is not an argument for simplistic prose. Such language in-
sults intelligent readers. But anytime writers can express their meaning in language that is *simple* and *concise,* they do both their readers
and their own writing a great favor.

Dense, abstract prose breeds in a variety of ways, but its main
source is a failure to rely on verbs. When you speak, verbs dominate
your language: direct, active verbs that grab the listener's attention
and hold it. But when you write, these verbs often get lost in the
background as nouns and other constructions dominate, creating
language heavy with abstract concepts and light on action. It is easy
to understand why this happens. As you write, you concentrate on
the ideas you want to convey, usually ideas that you have categorized
and labeled in some fashion. In the process of defining these concepts for yourself, you have concentrated on naming them and re-
ducing them to a list of important nouns. For example, the study of
law reduces people bringing suit against each other to *litigation,* and
the study of geology reduces the earth's shifting and compressing to
stratification. After such careful study to define these concepts, you
naturally begin to write about them by using the abstract nouns:
"Litigation by the people is proliferating" instead of "More people
are suing each other"; and "The rock stratification has been caused
by millions of years of pressure and earth movement" instead of
"Millions of years of the earth's moving and pressuring the rock has
stratified it."

Readers like verbs. Verbs—especially active ones—give energy to
the sentence and make it easier for readers to understand and remem-

ber. It is always easier to read about something containing direct action than it is to read about abstractions. If you learn to use verbs as strongly in your writing as you do in your speaking, your prose will markedly improve. The following tips on controlling abstraction include ways to make your writing more verb centered.

Nominalizations

A nominalization is a noun made out of a verb or an adjective. When people write, they often turn verbs into nouns and thereby make the prose more distant from the reader. Someone may write, "We had a meeting" instead of "We met," although the latter expresses the thought more directly and concisely. To make your prose more efficient and easier to read, try to use verbs to make your point, rather than nominalizations or adjectives. Verbs are more powerful and more direct than any other part of speech. The list below shows how statements grow in strength as nouns are replaced by adjectives and adjectives by verbs.

- These facts have direct application here. (noun)
  These facts are directly applicable here. (adjective)
  These facts directly apply here. (verb)
- The crowd had a violent reaction to the speech. (noun)
  The crowd was violently reactionary to the speech. (adjective)
  The crowd reacted violently to the speech. (verb)
- What is the point of determination for shutting down the system? (noun)
  What is the determinative point for shutting down the system? (adjective)
  What determines when we shut down the system? (verb)

PRACTICE EXERCISE 7.4

Turn these nominalizations back into adjectives or verbs to make the sentences more concise.

1. Given the factual similarities between the two cases, an application of a standard similar to the *Lynch* case is appropriate.

2. Testing the contribution of methods of invention to the acquisition of complex cognitive skills is exceedingly difficult to do well.

3. All process wastes entering the in-plant sewers from floor drains,

overflows, and cleaning operations are processed through oil skimmers for oil removal, followed by neutralization with acid or caustic at the plant, before going to one of the three settling lagoons for preliminary clarification.

4. In order to ensure company-wide compliance with the following procedure, Accounts Payable will be instructed not to process invoices without an attached purchase order.

5. There can be no question of the connection between psychology and writing.

Passives

Although the passive voice is grammatically correct, writers often misuse it. Passives are appropriate when you want to downplay the agent in the sentence or when the agent is unimportant. For example, an attorney for the defendant in a vehicular homicide case would probably say: "John Smith was hit by a car on the corner of Hollywood and Vine," rather than "My client's car hit John Smith. . . ." An article on current medicine reads "AIDS research is carried on in most major universities and medical centers," because it is not important who the researchers are. But in most sentences, the active voice is the better choice. Think about this example, written first in the active voice and then in the passive voice:

> Boggs hit a low drive. Carter snagged it and fired it to first for the out.

> A low drive was hit by Boggs. The ball was snagged by Carter and fired to first for the out.

In your own writing, use the active voice. It is easier to read, and it makes your prose more powerful and more memorable.

PRACTICE EXERCISE 7.5

Rewrite the following sentences, changing passives to actives where necessary. In addition, use what you have learned about nominalizations to help you reduce these sentences to more readable size. Sometimes you will need to invent a subject.

1. Vehicle stops for traffic violations occur countless times each day, and on these occasions, licenses and registration papers are subject to inspection and drivers without them will be ascertained.

2. After much discussion, it was decided that this would be the preferred format.

3. John S., convicted of growing marijuana in his backyard, objected that his right to be free from unwarranted police searches was violated by the airplane search.

4. With two police officers trained in drug identification on board the plane, the illicit crops were observed.

5. The roaring flames could be seen for miles as the building was devoured by fire.

Noun, Adjective, and Preposition Strings

Another stylistic habit that impedes clarity is using long strings of nouns, prepositions, or adjectives. When you are aiming for precision, it is easy to use too many qualifying phrases or words in one sentence. In an attempt to include all important facets of an issue, writers often embed several qualifying constructions within the framework of a sentence. In many cases, subordinating information in prepositional phrases or condensing terms into adjectives is efficient, but writers run the risk of stringing together so many of these qualifiers that they obscure the important ideas. The following examples illustrate how these strings of modifiers gradually entangle the sentences to such an extent that they become unreadable.

- Diabetic patient blood pressure reduction may be a consequence of renal extract depressor agent application. (adjective strings)

Key to Revision: Separate the strings by adding prepositions or rearranging the words into clauses. Check, too, for any nominalizations or passives that may be adding to the wordiness.

Example: Physicians may be able to reduce blood pressure in diabetic patients by applying an agent that depresses renal extract.

- The issue of the case at bar was whether the exclusivity clause precluded Donovan from recovery through civil action when the injury was inflicted by an intentional tort of the employer and did not result in disability. (preposition string)

Key to Revision: Replace "of the" with a possessive apostrophe and turn other phrases into adjectives, thereby eliminating all seven prepositions.

Example: The issue was whether the exclusivity clause precluded
Donovan's civil recovery because the employer's intentional tort inflicted a nondisabling injury.

Writers who avoid using strings of nouns, prepositions, or adjectives create sentences that are easier to read. Again, the key to revising tangled prose of this sort is to look twice at any series of qualifiers. If it is possible to phrase your sentence another way, do so.

PRACTICE EXERCISE 7.6

Find the "strings" in the following sentences and eliminate them.
Notice that you can also use what you have learned about nominalizations and passives to help your editing, because nominalizations and passives spawn various types of strings.

1. Renewal of the contract is conditional on the continued availability of State funds for this purpose and on the approval by
   the New York State Division of Budget.

2. Ultimately, such an evaluation of the process of juvenile delin-
   quent social problems identification would raise the real possibility of special restricted forms of interests and purposes being
   the basis of social problems identification rather than some
   generalized normative system.

3. The Department shall be obligated to pay the Grantee only for
   the expenditures made and noncancelable obligations incurred
   by the Grantee until such time as notice of termination from
   the Department is received by the Grantee.

4. The temperature-dependent modified cytoplasmic microtu-
   bules of the cold-adapted antarctic fishes must assemble at tem-
   peratures well below those necessary for polymerization of the
   tubulins of homeotherms.

5. The familiar ways of conveying the impression of distance are
   by the perspective of line and of color; in line by diminution of
   size in identical objects and in color by diminution of tone or
   change of line.

6. Because of the meat wholesaler's district's workers dependence
   on this bank, the public interest requires that this branch remain open.

Although the many elements of voice and style may seem like a lot
to think about as you construct your sentences, remember that the

goal of sentence design is to create a voice that suits your purpose and your readers' needs. If you are aware of the impression you are making and of the various methods of altering it, you have more control over the writing situation.

Your readers' only impression of you is through the words you put on the page, words that collectively create an image of you in readers' minds. Your technique at the sentence level—the level where voice and style emerge—is the most noticeable aspect of your writing. Readers make judgments about your prose and the logic behind it by looking at how you craft your sentences. Well-constructed sentences give readers confidence in your ability both as a writer and as a thinker; carefully crafted sentences reflect equally well-considered thoughts. It is worth the time it takes to create such an impression.

FOCUS ON

Your Writing Project

Using the following categories of evaluation, analyze the style of a piece you have recently finished writing:

A. Diction
    1. kinds of words (formal/slang, short/long, abstract/concrete)
    2. figures of speech
B. Sentence Structure
    1. sentence beginnings
    2. sentence lengths
    3. sentence types
    4. punctuation
    5. transitional devices
C. Grammatical Patterns
    1. verb types (active/passive)
    2. repeated use of specific parts of speech (adjectives, adverbs, noun strings, prepositions)

What does this analysis tell you about your written voice? Write a short paper presenting the results of your self-study.

The Writing Group

Ask each member of the group to read aloud a passage of his or her writing—two to three pages should be enough. After each person has read, the rest of the group should tell the writer about their impressions of the voice they heard. Was it pompous? Friendly? Combative? Confident? Funny? Sly? Then try to determine what writing techniques created such impressions. Finally, decide if the voice is appropriate for the rhetorical situation. What could make it better?

Chapter 8

Revising

Revising makes writing better. Nonetheless, some writers consider revising the dregs of the writing process—an afterthought, something to do if there is enough time and energy left over. But writing is a continuing activity, and revision is an essential component of writing. In fact, many writers view revision as the most productive step in the writing process—they finally have something down on paper to work with. Some consider revision the point where their real talent comes into play as they take rough ideas and hone them to their sharpest form.

Revising *can* make writing better, and for that reason alone it is worth doing. Another reason is that learning to revise is learning to write.

Writing as a Recursive Process

Everyone revises to some degree. When you first sit down to write, you are ready to begin the revision process. As soon as you have a few words on paper—or in your head—you begin to edit so that the prose is the best it can be at that stage. This erasing and rewriting continues as you progress through the lines of your text. Even writers who claim they do not have time to revise participate in this rewriting process as they compose their prose. In a sense, then, revision is continuous as writers rewrite phrases, words, and whole paragraphs before they finish the entire text. The idea that revision is a stage that occurs only after the text is complete is a false notion, although reviewing the whole piece at the end is part of a more formal revising process.

Common sense says that all of writing is a recursive process. In other words, all the various stages of writing—invention, arrangement, revision, and so forth—occur repeatedly as writers compose. No one sits down and proceeds through the writing process in a series of isolated steps. Instead, writers move back and forth among the stages as necessary, tinkering with this phrase, rearranging that paragraph, and inventing new ideas as they go along. As a result, revision occurs throughout the process as well as at the end where it can happen in its fullest form.

Because revision happens continuously in the writing process and not just at the end, it is important to understand how to revise effectively from the very beginning of the text.

Methods of Revision

Two general principles govern the art of revising:

1. The reviser needs to keep the reader in mind.
2. Revising one part affects the whole text.

"Keep the reader is mind" is a general rule, but it is an especially important rule during the revising process. In fact, the primary goal of revising should be to make the text as clear and as crisp as possible for the reader.

Like a mother's view of her child, a writer's view of her prose is subjective. The argument makes sense to you because you created it and understand exactly what you mean to say. But before reading the text, your reader does not have the benefit of knowing what you mean. You cannot ship yourself with the prose to its final destination and look over the reader's shoulder, explaining what you really meant to say. The prose must do that for you. That is why it is so important for you to see the text from the reader's perspective before it leaves your hands and becomes the only explanation of your ideas the reader has.

With this in mind, put yourself in the reader's place and try to read the prose from that point of view. Are there gaps in the logic? Do you have to read between the lines to understand the text? Do you feel confident of the writer's authority? Does the prose progress smoothly without making you struggle to read it? These and other similar questions allow writers to see their prose through different eyes and reshape it to look its best.

As you look at the prose from a fresh stance and begin to make changes in it, remember that the text is an interconnected document, and a change to any part probably will affect the whole. This second major principle of revising pertains to many aspects of the prose, including headings, tone, ideas, format, and even numbering systems. All too often professional writers have been embarrassed when their final versions return from the typesetter with errors in numbering or in organization because they neglected to account for the impact one small change had made on the whole document. When you revise, remember to check the entire text to make sure the revision is an appropriate "fit" with the whole discourse and to see if the revision necessitates any other changes.

Because revising occurs at so many different points within the writing process, it might be helpful here to suggest methods of handling revision both during the composing stages and after the first draft is finished.

Revising During the Composing Stages

Writers naturally revise as they go along in the composing process. Whenever you communicate a message, your brain screens the words before they become public. If the message is a few spoken words, you probably revise them so quickly that you are not even conscious of having done so. And if the message is written but short, you may wait until the text is complete before turning your attention to revision. But when writers are involved in composing long texts, the screening needs to be more systematic.

Systematic revision works best when writers stop after every "chunk" of the text to revise that piece. Such a system usually requires that you incorporate the revising process into your writing schedule and determine in advance how to segment the prose for revision. That means preparing some sort of an outline—either a jotted one or a complete one—prior to beginning the writing. If you know the general shape of the document, it is easier to determine convenient stopping places for revision. For example, in a text that has multiple subheadings, the segments are built in. Your task is simply to maintain the discipline of revising after you finish each subsection. If the text does not have these obvious breaks, turn to the outline and mark some places where the prose naturally completes one idea and moves to another. These are excellent points for a revising break.

When writers use such systematic revision, the process moves much more quickly than if they had saved all revision for the end, and the text itself is better because the revision causes writers to pay more attention to the shape of the document as they compose it.

Some writers complain that they cannot revise as they go along because they fear writer's block. Once they begin, they must put everything down on paper in a hurry in order to keep up with their muse and finish composing before writer's block sets in. If that is the case, they are doing a disservice to their prose and to themselves: Their total writing time will take much longer than the writing time for those who revise along the way. They also run a greater risk of resisting revision totally because they complete their prose before they hold it up for inspection. It is a lot harder to revise a finished product than it is to tinker with it during assembly.

One important benefit of frequent revision is that it allows you to monitor how well your prose is sticking to the point. Before actually beginning to write, you spent some time narrowing your topic to a clearly defined idea worth writing about. Although that idea may have been phrased well, it is easy to lose sight of it in the heat of composing. As you revise sections of your prose, make sure these "chunks" are serving their intended purpose and are keeping on track. Without occasional monitoring, your prose may go off on a tangent that is fascinating but quite beside the point.

Finally, revising as you write gives you better opportunity to maintain a consistent voice and style. While you struggle to express your ideas logically, often the voice you have created begins to shift and change character. At the end of each segment, read over the text and listen to the voice. Is it the same as in the other sections? Is the style consistent, or have you suddenly become wordy or overly succinct? Being conscious of your language in each of the revising breaks allows you to spot shifts quickly and take steps to correct the problem.

A note of caution may be in order here. Some writers are obsessive about revising and cannot continue writing until each subsection is perfect. These same people often worry so much about each sentence that they have difficulty completing paragraphs. If that is a problem for you, keep in mind that these revisions within the composing process are only the first pass. After the first draft is finished, you still have a chance to look over the completed text and smooth out the rough spots. Realizing that these mini-revisions are not the final ones may relieve the pressure and allow you to move more quickly through the writing.

In short, it pays to revise as you go along, and ultimately this practice saves you time. Get in the habit of dividing your text into revisable sections prior to writing, and discipline yourself to edit each section as you finish it. The following tips may help in the revising process:

- Develop an outline to divide your text into sections before you write. (See chapter 5 for tips on outlining.)
- Stop after every subsection and revise it.
- Make sure your prose is keeping on track and not straying onto any tangents.
- Maintain consistent voice and style.
- Do not go overboard at this stage; remember there is the final revision for fine-tuning.

Revising the Completed First Draft

No matter how thoroughly you integrate revision into the composing process, a careful review of the whole text when you have finished the draft is essential. Saving a few minutes for a quick rereading is not enough time; a comprehensive review is required at this stage.

A comprehensive review assumes a greater risk than simple proofreading. At this point you have enough perspective on the piece to consider all of its parts at once; you may decide to redirect the piece, or to shift parts from one place to another, or even to scrap the material altogether and begin fresh. It takes courage to be open to these possibilities after you have spent so much time laboring over the text to arrive at this stage. In fact, fear of discovering flaws in the prose is one reason so many writers dread revising or skip it altogether.

To revise thoroughly, you should be aware of the types of revision and the importance of involving other people in the review process. An understanding of the various kinds and levels of revision will enable you to review your work more effectively and more efficiently.

Kinds of Revision

According to the current research on how writers actually revise their texts, all types of revision fall into one of three categories: rule-based revisions, cohesion-based revisions, and experience-based revisions. The tasks in the first two categories are the quickest and easiest to perform, whereas the last one involves the most complex processes. Keep in mind that writers do not perform these different kinds of revisions in any particular order; all can occur at any time during the revising process.

Rule-Based Revision

The most simple of the three, this category includes any changes you make that depend on specific grammar, punctuation, or spelling rules. Choosing among *to, too,* and *two* is a good example, or deciding whether to put the apostrophe before or after the *s* when making *Jones* possessive. These changes usually are restricted to the sentence level and are absolute changes: In other words, you have no choice in these matters if you want your prose to be correct.

Cohesion-Based Revision

The changes that fall into this category are changes in the prose's cohesion, meaning that the writer focuses on more than sentence-level revisions. Many, but not all, of these changes are governed by rules as well. You may have a wide choice about how to fix any cohesion problem you detect. For example, if you decide that a piece of writing does not hold together well, you may fix it by realigning its parallel structure (a rule-governed change), by shifting its emphasis from one idea to another (a non-rule-governed change), or by crafting better transitions within and between paragraphs. Problems with context belong in this category, too. Adding or deleting information to make the context clearer to the readers is a form of cohesion-based revision because such changes directly affect the overall coherence of the piece.

Cohesion-based revision is more complex than rule-based revision because it involves more choice and more actual text, and its focus is on the many elements contributing to the prose's cohesion rather than on the mechanics of a single sentence.

Experience-Based Revision

In this revision category, there is no absolute rule or given strategy for solving the problem you diagnose. In fact, there are no guidelines to help you with your diagnosis. The writer's experience or attitude toward the text influences the changes that occur in this category. For instance, you may decide to alter the entire thrust of your prose, not because the original was incorrect but because you think the new version will work better for the audience. Or you may want to violate a rule because the prose has more impact if the rule is broken. Perhaps a new arrangement or an alternative phrasing captures the main idea a bit better than the old version. These changes are the hardest to describe and are based on largely undefinable strategies. Possibly the best way to describe them is to say that they depend on an understanding of the spirit of language—an intangible instinct that prompts you to exchange a perfectly good word for an excellent word. As you may suspect, this type of revising requires not only sufficient practice but also a measure of talent, and it is the most difficult for beginning writers.

Effective revision involves all three of these categories and takes time as well as talent. Gifted writers who rush through the revising process may produce prose that sounds hackneyed and mundane, whereas more average writers can turn mediocre work into first-rate copy by taking the time to revise thoroughly. It may take you at least three passes through the prose if you feel the need to separate the revising tasks. Most writers perform the three revising tasks simultaneously and then return to the beginning to check the text again. It ultimately does not matter which process you use—choose the one that is most comfortable for you—but it does matter that you review your prose in all three ways. Otherwise, the quality of your writing may be as one-dimensional as your revising strategies.

A good way to see these revising strategies in action is to follow an actual article through its many drafts to the final version. The article was written for a computer magazine sold on newsstands across the country. The reporter was assigned to write a story on a new computer product from Tandy Corporation. Note how the author's changes fall into the three revision categories and how the final product would have suffered if the author had stopped revising before looking at the piece through each of these lenses:

Version 1

Tandy knows exactly how big the home and small business market is. They have to, it's their bread and butter. They also know what an opportunity there is, not just to sell hardware, but to sell software.

The DeskMate interface was never intended to be a competiter to products like Windows and Presentation Manager. It's an interface for low-end DOS machines. "An evolving market that most everyone else has ignored," says Howard Elias, a Tandy vice president.

The development of DeskMate grew out of Tandy's need to provide a standard demonstration tool for all its Radio Shack stores and Computer Centers. One allowing salespeople to easily introduce new users to the functionality of their computers. That was about four years ago.

"You don't have an interface that already has 20 programs, 200 developers looking at it, and 100 licensee sites all in a year's time," says Elias enthusiastically.

Some confusion comes into play because to Tandy Deskmate is a product but to third party developers it's an interface. Some developers complained that potential customers were calling them up and asking if you had to boot DeskMate to run their program. The answer is no. The programs use a run time of the interface, providing the same look and feel of DeskMate but without any of its utilities, like the calandar or calculator.

The developers all have confidence in Tandy's long term presence in the personal computer field and share the vision that there are a large number of users who can't run Windows but want more access to their computers.

DeskMate will run on any IBM PC-compatible machine with at least 348K of memory and either Hercules, CGA, EGA, or VGA graphics capabilities.

Tandy opinions, and opinions correctly, that the people who are spending thousands or tens of thousands of dollars for a high-end computer need ease of use and consistency a lot less than the poor guy at home running his own business with an XT compatible.

If the reporter had concentrated only on rule-governed revising strategies, the final piece might look something like this (the changes are italicized)—scarcely improved over the first version but grammatically correct:

Version 2

Tandy knows exactly how big the home and small business market is. They have to; it's their bread and butter. They also know what an opportunity there is, not just to sell hardware, but to sell software.

The DeskMate interface was never intended to be a *competitor* to products like Windows and Presentation Manager. It's an interface for low-end DOS machines. "*It's an evolving* market that most everyone else has ignored," says Howard Elias, Tandy's vice president of UK.

The development of DeskMate grew out of Tandy's need to provide a standard demonstration tool for all its Radio Shack stores and Computer Centers, *one* allowing salespeople to easily introduce new users to the functionality of their computers. That was about four years ago.

"You don't have an interface that already has 20 programs, 200 developers looking at it, and 100 licensee sites all in a year's time," says Elias enthusiastically.

Some confusion comes into play *because Tandy considers DeskMate a product, but third party developers think of it as an interface*. Some developers complained that potential customers were calling them up and asking if *they* had to boot DeskMate to run their program. The answer is no. The programs use a run time of the interface, providing the same look and feel of DeskMate but without any of its utilities—*like the calendar or calculator*.

The developers all have confidence in Tandy's long term presence in the personal computer field and share the vision that there are a large number of users who can't run Windows but want more access to their computers.

DeskMate will run on any IBM PC-compatible machine with at least 348K of memory and either Hercules, CGA, EGA, or VGA graphics capabilities.

Tandy *opines*, and *opines* correctly, that the people who are spending thousands or tens of thousands of dollars for a high-end computer need ease of use and consistency a lot less than the poor guy at home running his own business with an XT compatible.

Turning his attention to the other kinds of revision, the reporter made much more dramatic and important changes to the text. The following two versions illustrate his progress from a rough draft that has no polish and does not really provide the right focus for the readers, to a finished piece that aims directly at the target audience, coheres well, and reads with a verve that keeps readers interested. In version 3, he adds information, rearranges the text to focus the article differently, and overhauls the language to make it more vivid and fresh. It is typical that the most significant revisions appear in the third version, because it is then that the author is working more on shaping the prose for the audience than on focusing his own thoughts. By version 4, the revisions are on a much smaller scale.

Change in opener changes article's emphasis.

Version 3

Microsoft Windows and Tandy's DeskMate are clean graphical user interfaces. They shield users from the A> prompt and let them use a consistent set of commands to run various applications. Both environments sell for $99.

That's where the comparisons end.

While Microsoft sells Windows for use on 286 and 386 PCs, Tandy aims its interface at less glamorous 8088 and 8086 machines. DeskMate and most of its applications run on an IBM PC or compatible with as little as 384K of memory and a Hercules graphics card. It also runs with CGA, EGA, and VGA.

Spec give t piece gre author

The September DeskMate upgrade is a demonstrably better product and has the support of several big-name packages.

Tandy's focus has always been the low-end market, and it's no wonder: there are an estimated 13 million 8088 and 8086 PCs, about 50% of all PCs in operation. Software developers, too, are keenly aware of the older machines' staying power. In the year since DeskMate's release, 30 software makers have ported programs to the environment and another 200 are considering similar moves.

Adding Macintosh evidence supports article's assertion.

The appeal of common user interface is evident in the success of Apple's Macintosh. The Mac is easy to use because the applications packages that run on it use the same set of commands. The same is true of DeskMate. The print command for Q&A Write is the same one used for Quicken, First Publisher, or any other package that runs under DeskMate.

this was t closing i in Vers It's stro Placed because i up a g metaphor beeps, interest know out

Tandy's strategy is an abrupt departure from the IBM world's insistence that users working on $7,000 machines are the ones who need interfaces. Tandy shrewdly believes the opposite: users who run their businesses with XT compatibles need ease of use and consistency across applications much more than those running the fastlane models.

More specifics add authority.

What's more, the Tandy view is attracting an impressive list of converts. The 30 programs running under DeskMate include Symantec's Q&A Write, Intuit's Quicken, Software Publishing Corporation's PFS: First Publisher, Broderbunds Memory Mate, Electronic Art's Instant Pages, and six assorted Byte Size titles from Publishing International. Tandy promises that more are to come.

Tandy has put its marketing muscle behind DeskMate to make it the low-end environment standard. It advertises heavily and bundles DeskMate applications with its best-selling computers. In fact, most new software titles will not receive broad distribution in the 7,000 Tandy and Radio Shack stores unless they run under DeskMate.

Diction improv "marke muscle "bun

The gamble pays off.

DeskMate sales bear out the wisdom of Tandy's strategy: the company says it has sold more than 1 million copies of DeskMate since its 1988 introduction. By contrast, it took Windows 3 years to gain even modest acceptance.

Tandy—and more software developers—support the idea that users at all levels deserve a common interface. And for that position, says Brad Fregger, president of Publishing International, "they deserve the cheers of the populace."

[handwritten: Strong quotation used at end.]

Many writers would stop at this point, thinking they had done their job well enough and had improved the original version. But one more revision upgrades the piece from an adequate story to a polished, professional article.

Version 4

[handwritten: another [...]ge in [...]esis. [...]dy is raised as more [...]ectable [...]mpany.]

While graphical user interfaces like Microsoft Windows and Quarterdeck Desqview grab the headlines in business and trade magazines, Tandy's venerable DeskMate is quietly and steadily gaining momentum in the market it hopes one day to own.

[handwritten: Stronger diction: "grab", "venerable" "GUI giants".]

The GUI giants need the power of a 286 or 386 for adequate performance. But DeskMate is aimed squarely at less glamorous 8088 and 8086 machines, with the intention of making those entry-level home office and small business computers easy to use. DeskMate and most of its applications run in as little as 384K of memory and look fine on a Hercules graphics card, although they also can take advantage of more robust hardware.

Tandy's strategy is an abrupt departure from the IBM world's insistence that users working on $7,000 machines are the ones who use interfaces. Tandy shrewdly believes the opposite: users who run their businesses with XT compatibles need ease of use and consistency across applications much more than those running fastlane models.

[handwritten: The gamble is moved up even further—it is now the central metaphor.]

DeskMate, introduced in 1984 and significantly improved in a September 1988 release, is clearly making strides into the low-end of computing, a market estimated at 13 million 8088 and 8086 PCs, or about 50% of all PCs in operation. Tandy has shipped more than a million copies of DeskMate.

[handwritten: "Making strides" picks up initial analogy of Tandy quietly gaining momentum.]

That momentum has gotten the attention of software developers who are now busy adapting their applications to the Tandy environment. In the year since Tandy began a DeskMate licensing program, 30 software makers have ported programs to DeskMate, and another 200 are considering similar moves. Among the programs running under DeskMate are Symantec's Q&A Write, Intuit's Quicken, Software Publishing Corporation's PFS: First Publisher, Broderbund's Memory Mate, Electronic Art's Instant Pages, and six assorted Byte Size titles from Publishing International.

But Tandy's most impressive catch clearly is Lotus, which will ship Lotus Spreadsheet for DeskMate later this year. The Lotus product, which will sell for $219.95 (a far cry from the $495 Lotus charges for 1-2-3 Release 2.2), maintains the file compatibility of 1-2-3, but none of the macro, add-in or EMS capabilities.

[handwritten: Lotus replaces Apple Macintosh as the better support for the article's assertion.]

The pay-off.

"If a software company wants to go after the home market in a big way, you do it with Tandy," Lotus chief Jim Manzi said in announcing the DeskMate product. It's a statement that presages the arrival of even more name-brand software packages on the DeskMate scene.

Better quotatio

Tandy has put its marketing muscle behind DeskMate to make it the low-end environment standard, and it says more announcements can be expected before the year is out. It advertises heavily and bundles DeskMate applications with its best selling computers. In fact, most new software titles will not receive broad distribution in the 7,000 Tandy and Radio Shack stores unless they run under DeskMate.

This paragr paragr is later the piec than it w befor

Tandy—and more software developers—support the idea that users at all levels deserve a common interface. And for that position, says Brad Fregger, president of Publishing International, "they deserve the cheers of the populace."

—*PC/Computing, Ziff-Davis Publishing Company.*
Used with permission.

Checklists for Effective Revising

To make your revising tasks easier, and to spark your own thinking about revision, the following checklists outline basic elements in each revising category. These lists are by no means complete, but they will give you a sense of what to look for as you approach the deep revision job. Use the items you need, and feel free to add your own elements to each list.

Rule-Based Revisions

- Are the sentences grammatically correct?
- Do you overuse the passive voice?
- Are there unnecessary nominalizations?
- Are there any misspelled words?
- Have you followed the recommended style guide? (*MLA Style Guide, Chicago Manual of Style, APA Style Guide,* and so on)
- Is the text punctuated properly?

Cohesion-Based Revisions

- Are the paragraphs too long or too short?
- Does each paragraph emphasize only one point?
- Is there enough variety in the sentences and the paragraphs?
- Are the transitions between paragraphs logical and easy to follow?

- Is the information presented in parallel structure? (See Appendix I, page 230 for a full discussion of parallel structure.)

- Do the sentences within each paragraph link together smoothly?

- Is the main point presented in a step-by-step fashion or in some other way? Are you consistent in the method of presentation?

- Is there enough context for the intended readers? Do you need to add information so that the text makes better sense to your audience?

Experience-Based Revisions

- Does the prose meet the needs of the audience?

- Is the prose up to your professional standards? Is it as good as other things you have written? Why or why not?

- Is the length appropriate?

- In editing for efficiency, have you reduced the prose to a level too spare to be interesting?

- Is the language vivid and fresh enough?

- Is the overall order of the piece the best organization?

- What do your instincts tell you about your prose? Are there trouble spots?

- Can you revise anything to better capture the audience's attention and respect?

PRACTICE EXERCISE 8.1

The following rough draft is the introduction to a discussion of Irish migration in the nineteenth century. Revise the passage using each kind of revision: rule-based, cohesion-based, and experience-based. On a separate sheet of paper, list all of the changes you made and identify what kind of revision each one is.

Migration optimally is a mechanism of adjustment which functions to reduce inequalities between two areas. The subject of this study is the extent to which this may have been so for Irish persons who were migrating between Ireland and England during the first half of the nineteenth century. This study proceeds from the assumption that by following a regular pattern of temporary migration between the two communities, the mostly agricultural people of Ireland were, at least temporarily, able to preserve valued aspects of their existing social system. The monetary returns from migration enabled them to maximize the desired benefits and minimize losses of valued social institutions which would have been necessary if they had broken the links with Ireland permanently.

Essential to the argument presented in this discussion is that these people were not hapless peasants fleeing to Britain out of dire necessity. Evidence would confirm that most migrants were well aware of the range of choices available to them, and that they chose from among the range of possibilities those which produced the greatest possible number of desired benefits. Chief among such benefits was the ability to continue to live on the land; to maintain valued ties of kinship and community; and to continue to exercise autonomy with respect to decisions affecting their welfare.

The decision to migrate was to a very great extent however thrust upon many of the Irish by the decline of options and opportunities available at home. Events had caught up with Ireland, and that country was beginning a slide into an economic slump, a situation which reached its nadir by the 1840s, culminating in the Great Famine. A decade later, the outcome of the Famine transformed expectations so drastically that what had been primarily temporary migration for most persons was now more likely to be a permanent leave-taking. By the end of the nineteenth century Ireland was a demographic abnormality, and a country in which the most enterprising and energetic young persons were reared with the knowledge that in order to survive they must leave Ireland permanently. Temporary migration no longer operated to adjust economic inequalities between the two areas. There were still a few seasonal migrants, but most persons left permanently; what had been temporary became a hemorrhage of movement, with the result that every census but one between 1841 and 1961 recorded a decreasing population.

Why did this happen, and what did it mean is the subject of this discussion which will demonstrate that the nature of the migration before the 1840s was temporary and transitory. Some of the issues addressed are: historical antecedents of migration from Ireland; regions from which the migrants came; reasons which motivated them to leave; individual characteristics of the migrant population, including their adaptation to the process of migration within Ireland; and finally, the consequences of migration, both for the migrants and for Ireland.

Editing for Voice

The last revision is an edit for stylistic issues. It does not have to occur separately from your large-scale revising, but it requires a different sort of skill. In fact, this edit really requires more of an "ear" than an eye for the text. *Read your prose aloud*. Read it aloud during the revising you do during the composing process, and read it aloud at the end when you are doing the final edit. Such oral renditions of your writing allow you to hear what the words sound like and to feel the rhythm of your prose. It is amazing how a simple technique can uncover so many problems. Are there sentences that are too big of a mouthful? Simplify them. Do some sentences seem to march in a quick step down the page? Combine some of them. Are you being too strident or demanding? Soften the prose. Reading your work out loud can highlight these problems and give you the opportunity to hear them before the reader does.

Combating Fatigue

Every writer suffers from "battle fatigue" at some point during the writing process, but it is especially prevalent at the revising stage. You have been working with this material for so long and have finished an entire draft—why not let it alone and send it off "as is"? That thought has tempted every writer at some time or another.

Exhaustion gives rise to these thoughts, and they are seductively attractive ideas. But a worse problem is the feeling writers have later when they have launched their unpolished prose into the public eye and it has provided embarrassment and—sometimes—serious trouble. A weak engineering memorandum, for example, can communicate the wrong information and can mean the difference between completing a job or extending it over budget until the damage is corrected. An attorney's trial brief may lose the case before the oral argument stage because it has negatively affected the judge. Or a student's paper reaches the instructor's desk only to be returned for a complete rewrite—or worse, with a poor grade attached and no chance for revision.

It is better to fend off exhaustion before it seduces you into yielding to it. One way to accomplish this is to plan ahead so that you do not end up writing your prose at the last minute with no time or energy left for revising. Many people purposefully put off writing until the last minute because they think they work better under pressure. But most eleventh-hour writers are completely spent by the time they reach the end of their last page. If writing under pressure appeals to you, at least plan enough time to revise your first draft and edit for voice; your prose will be better for it.

Other writers who proceed at a less frantic pace can build in stopping points along the way. A coffee break or a brisk walk may do wonders for your attitude and make it possible for you to return to your writing refreshed and with renewed energy.

Another technique is to schedule a set amount of writing time per day. Some writers work the same hours each day, using the time period rather than a page quota as their guide. Working in this fashion creates a steadiness to the prose and permits writers to return each day with new energy and a clear head. But many cannot afford the luxury of writing on such a schedule. For these people, the best advice is to concentrate more heavily on revising during the composing process. Working in that way cuts down on the amount of time it takes to complete the document, and because revising requires a different sort of skill than writing does, the variety of work helps to preserve energy.

The best way to combat writer's fatigue is to expect it. If you know it will happen, you are more likely to prepare ways to handle it. If it takes you by surprise, you are vulnerable.

Word Processing and Revision

Writing with a word processor is a powerful defense against fatigue, especially the fatigue that accompanies revising long portions of text. In the past, writers had no choice but to retype the complete text to accommodate even minor revisions. With the advent of word processors, changing the text is as easy as pressing a few keys.

The time-saving element of word processing means that you can devote more energy to thinking through the revisions than to typing the final copy. Moving blocks of prose is no problem; changing sentences, deleting paragraphs, and reformatting pages no longer consume the large amount of time they once did—the software handles these tasks in seconds. Once you think the text is ready to print, the machine takes care of that, too. For these reasons alone, word processing is becoming an essential tool for writers.

But there are liabilities to revising with a word processor, and you should be aware of the potential problems as well as the benefits. One problem occurs because the computer shows only part of your document at a time. As you revise, you are limited to working with the material that fits on one screen. When you wish to move forward or backward in the text, you lose sight of the rest of the document and thereby lose valuable perspective on the specific section you are viewing. You must rely on memory to help you make decisions that will affect the whole document. For this reason, although word processors are especially effective for the revisions done during the composing process, for the final revision writers usually work best with a printed copy.

Some writers have trouble editing anything on screen. Because they first learned to write and revise on paper, they are more comfortable with this habit. As a result, the process takes much longer than necessary, but they feel more confident about the finished product. A more efficient procedure is to revise on screen as you compose the document and then print a copy to work with as you do the final revision. Take notes on the pages, allowing you to make the changes easily when you return to the screen.

At the end of each writing session, print a copy of the day's work. This habit not only ensures that you have a copy in case of computer malfunction, it also gives you the satisfaction of seeing your work on the printed page.

Peer Review

By this time, you may have looked at your work so often that you no longer have a sense of objectivity about it. Even professional writers who work by the clock can become so immersed in their writing that they lose all critical perspective and need another person's opinion about the text. Although it is a risk to ask others to review your work—there's always the chance they may not like it—it is a risk worth taking.

Regardless of the kind of writing they do, most writers depend on other people to look at the text and offer constructive criticism. Walter Lippmann justifies this dependence on criticism in his essay, "The Indispensable Opposition":

> The opposition is indispensable. A good statesman, like any other sensible human being, always learns more from his opponents than from his fervent supporters. For his supporters will push him to disaster unless his opponents show him where the dangers are. So if he is wise he will often pray to be delivered from his friends, because they will ruin him. But, though it hurts, he ought also to pray never to be left without opponents; for they keep him on the path of reason and good sense.

Common sense dictates that it is more productive to seek feedback on the prose before it goes to the final audience. Consequently, it is important to establish a review system that includes at least one outside opinion on your written draft—and more if possible. It helps if there are guidelines for the peer review. In order for this system to work well, both the writer and the reviewer should understand the "rules" of this process. If they do not, the experience can create unnecessary animosity and hurt feelings.

Peer Review Guidelines for the Writer

If you are considering giving your work to someone else to review, *hold your ego in check*. After so much hard work on the piece, you are probably sensitive to criticism and desperately want the reviewer to praise your work. Even the slightest negativity can send your ego plummeting and cause you to react with defensive anger. "Obviously," you may think, "this person doesn't understand what I was trying to do!" Perhaps that is true. Your prose may not be communicating what you mean. Give the reviewer the benefit of the doubt and reexamine the text from her point of view. Spend your energy thinking of ways to improve the text to satisfy the reviewer's questions about it, rather than on needless resistance to criticism. Remember, in most instances you have the last word on whether to implement any of the suggestions the reviewer makes. No one is forcing you to change the text—but the reviewer *is* offering you the opportunity to improve it.

When you begin the peer review process, hand your work to the reviewer without any prefatory comments other than an explanation of the necessary rhetorical situation. As your colleague reads the text, remain totally uninvolved—make no comments and ask no questions. After all, you will not be perched on the ultimate readers' shoulders to answer their questions or clarify points for them, so you should allow your prose to do all of the talking during the review as well. If possible, occupy yourself with something else while the review is underway, so that you are not tempted to interrupt.

Peer Review Guidelines for the Reviewer

If you are the reviewer, remember that the writer has spent a long time on this work and is looking to you for constructive help, not negative comments. Approach your task as though you were part of a team and with an understanding that the final product will reflect your input. In that spirit, offer suggestions about how to revise some of the awkward places, rather than merely listing them. Instead of saying "This opener doesn't work!" indicate why it doesn't work and offer possible alternatives. By so doing, you open a dialogue with the writer rather than creating a hostile situation where you are on the attack and the writer is forced into the defensive position.

It is also important that you try to read the piece from the point of view of the intended audience. Do not try to reformulate a technical report into a novel or vice versa. But if the writer's audience is not familiar to you, or if you are not familiar with certain terms in the text, there is no need to withdraw as the reviewer. Even if you are not able to understand all the terms, your comments as a lay reader may be most helpful to the writer because you are able to look at the writing without making assumptions about the content. Some readers who are experts in the field skim the prose for content only and have trouble commenting on the method of presentation.

As you read, make no comments to the author—save them for later. If you need to ask the writer for clarification of the prose, that is likely a flaw in the writing and needs to be noted for discussion after you have finished reading the entire piece.

Postreview Discussion

After the reviewer is finished reading the text and writing notes on it and the writer has had time to digest these comments, it is essential to allow time for discussion. At this point, the writer can respond fully to the critique, and the reviewer can elaborate on the textual comments. If both writer and reviewer remain positive and willing to work together to make the prose better, this discussion can be an exciting and stimulating work session. On the other hand, if either ego gets in the way, the meeting may disintegrate into a counterproductive battle of the wills.

One of the hardest tasks is staying with a piece until you get it right. Time constraints get in the way, as do boredom and irritation. Is there a point when you can become so obsessed with revising that you never feel satisfied with your work? How do you know when it is finished? Yes, there is a danger of overrevising, but peer review can help curb that impulse as can the pressure of deadlines. In answer to the final, more important question, you won't really know your writing is as good as it can be until the audience reads and understands it.

Proofreading

Proofreading is the last step. Checking the document for mechanical errors requires you to review every word to make sure it is spelled correctly, every sentence to make sure it is punctuated properly, and every page to make sure the format is consistent. Are there any typos? Do you follow the same stylistic conventions throughout? Are the page numbers placed properly and in the right order? Have you left out any words? These mechanical concerns are the sole focus of proofing the copy, and the task takes patience and care. It is a good idea to proofread your own work and then ask someone else to proof it a second time because you are so familiar with the prose that you might skim over some of the errors.

Although there are many techniques for proofreading—beginning at the end of the text and reading the words and sentences backward, dividing the discourse into small chunks and reading each at least twice, checking the whole piece once for punctuation and repeating the process for spelling and other errors, relying on computer spell-checkers—the bottom line is that you must reread the text slowly and carefully. Do not skim. And although spell-checking software is a timesaver, it can find only some of the mistakes for you. It will not diagnose misspellings such as *too* for *to*, nor will it find any words you have omitted. If you depend on spell-checkers, make sure to add your own check as well.

If you are editing someone else's work, you should use standard proofreading symbols. Once you learn them, they become second nature. This can be especially useful for future writing because these marks are used internationally to mark errors in texts. To use them, note that you need to mark the place in the actual line of text and then add the corresponding mark in the margin. That double notation alerts the reader or the typesetter to the fact that there is a correction necessary within that line.

> *Example:* The first thing to realize about what are sometimes
> callled the RULES of good english" is that there are
> almost no absolut laws, hard, fast, fixed and agreed
> upon by everone.

The usefulness of these symbols should be readily apparent. They are a shorthand way of saying "Fix this spelling," "You have a typo here," "You should not stick in this apostrophe," "You have omitted

STANDARD PROOFREADING MARKS

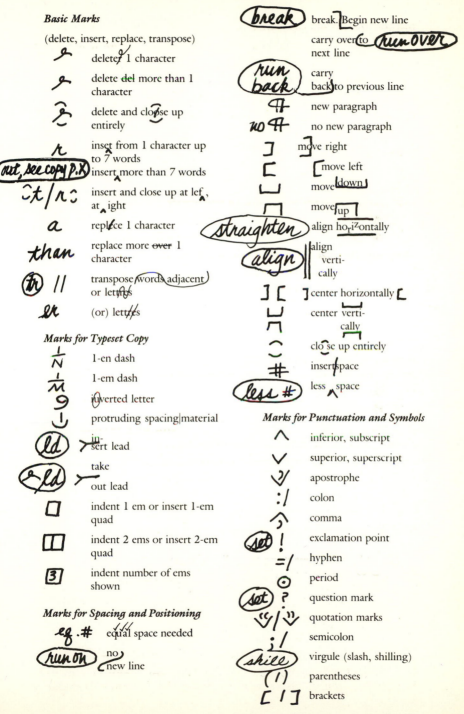

Basic Marks

(delete, insert, replace, transpose)

delete 1 character

delete del more than 1 character

delete and close up entirely

insert from 1 character up to 7 words

insert more than 7 words

insert and close up at left, at right

replace 1 character

replace more over 1 character

transpose words adjacent or letters

(or) letters

Marks for Typeset Copy

1-en dash

1-em dash

inverted letter

protruding spacing|material

insert lead

take out lead

indent 1 em or insert 1-em quad

indent 2 ems or insert 2-em quad

indent number of ems shown

Marks for Spacing and Positioning

equal space needed

no new line

break. Begin new line

carry over to next line

carry back to previous line

new paragraph

no new paragraph

move right

move left

move down

move up

align horizontally

align vertically

center horizontally

center vertically

close up entirely

insert space

less space

Marks for Punctuation and Symbols

inferior, subscript

superior, superscript

apostrophe

colon

comma

exclamation point

hyphen

period

question mark

quotation marks

semicolon

virgule (slash, shilling)

parentheses

brackets

(*continues*)

STANDARD PROOFREADING MARKS (*continued*)

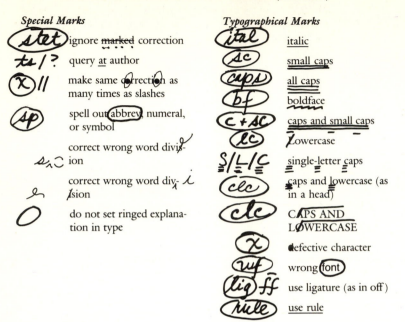

Special Marks

stet — ignore ~~marked~~ correction

* te / ?* — query at author

(x) // — make same correction as many times as slashes

sp — spell out abbrev, numeral, or symbol

— correct wrong word divi-sion

— correct wrong word divi-sion

O — do not set ringed explanation in type

Typographical Marks

ital — italic

sc — small caps

caps — all caps

bf — boldface

c + sc — caps and small caps

lc — lowercase

s/l/c — single-letter caps

clc — caps and lowercase (as in a head)

clc — CAPS AND LOWERCASE

(x) — defective character

wf — wrong font

lig ff — use ligature (as in off)

rule — use rule

a letter," "Capitalize this word," all of which are involved in the first stage of proofreading.

These proofreading symbols take a while to learn, but learning them should take the pressure off writing the initial draft. Everything does not have to be perfect in the first draft. If you know ahead of time that you can use the revising stage to fine-tune your prose, your initial panic may lessen. Revision is an integral part of the writing process because knowing that you can revise gives you a safety net. If you are willing to use it, it will be there at the end of the writing process.

PRACTICE EXERCISE 8.2

Proofread this letter to a Boston *Globe* sportswriter using the standard proofreading symbols:

Dear _____:

My name is Tom and I am 17 year old deticated Red Sox fan who loves Wade Boggs and Roger Clemenss becaus they are my favorit baseball players in the major legues. I red what you said about Wade Boggs in a March 28 sundays globe and I think you are about the ugliest man I ever seen. Anyways, this is not fare what you are saying about wade becauz you dont remember he said he was sorry an made mistake. He did and you just cant except that you just keep ranking on him and you better hope wade dont see you on the same street some day becauz hell kill you and if it was me Iwould have killed ya two. Ithink you better think hardabout get nother job becauz thats all writers write is crap and you cant do it anyways. I think Ispeek for a lot of people that would lie you to rite something nice about someone for a change. That's all I have to say rite now about you chastizing wade in a discusting article.

Revising prose is time consuming and fatiguing. Nonetheless, revising is necessary, even for writers whose prose looks effortless. It appears effortless precisely because of all the effort that went into it before publication. Taking the time to do it right is worth the trouble.

How much revising is necessary? Hemingway gave the best answer to that question:

Interviewer: "How much rewriting do you do?"

Hemingway: "It depends. I rewrote the ending of *A Farewell to Arms,* the last page of it, thirty-nine times before I was satisfied."

Interviewer: "Was there some technical problem there? What was it that had you stumped?"

Hemingway: "Getting the words right."
—Paris Review *Interview*

FOCUS ON

Your Writing Project

As a practice exercise, exaggerate the revision process in the following way. Take the first draft of a paper you have written (choose something at least three pages long) and perform these steps:

Step 1 Read the entire piece without making any marks on it or changing it in any way. (Make sure you use a printed copy and are not editing on screen.)

Step 2 Go back to the beginning and read the prose critically for rule-based revisions. Use the checklist above if necessary. Make no other kinds of revisions. Use a colored pen.

Step 3 Now read the text for cohesion-based revisions. Again, make no other kinds of changes. Use a different colored pen from the one you used in step 2.

Step 4 Finally, with yet another colored pen, revise the text from the experience-based point of view.

Step 5 Write a summary analysis of your revision process, answering questions such as: Which revision seemed easiest to do? In which category were most of your errors? What are your weak points? What are your writing strengths?

The Writing Group

If you are in a classroom situation, try this large-scale method of peer review. Divide into groups of four to five writers. Each writer should provide a copy of a rough draft to be placed in the group's folder. Determine in advance where the folder will be on file for at least one week—perhaps at the reserve desk of the library or in a faculty office where students can have easy access to it. During that time, each student in the group is responsible for reviewing and commenting on all the papers in the folder except his own. Write directly on the text, initialing all comments you make. At the end of each paper, write a summary comment listing the paper's strengths and weaknesses, and give any other insight you think may help the author. Sign your comment. All students must write comments on the papers, even if they are the last to review the work.

At the end of a week, when each student gets back a fully critiqued paper, allow time in class for discussion among the group members. You may want to keep the same groups for a few weeks during the class and then switch so that everyone has a fresh perspective, or you may want to keep the same groups for the whole time period. You will quickly find that this review process makes you much more conscious of your own prose and improves the work of others, too.

Chapter 9

Argument

The term *argument* means different things to different people. For some, argument is a means of expressing and supporting beliefs, whereas for others argument is a form of verbal combat. In this book, the term *argument* assumes that the writer wants to express a controversial point of view in a way that will convince readers of its validity. Written arguments include newspaper editorials, legal briefs, critical essays, proposals, justifications, and similar rhetorical compositions. Writers of argument have to make their cases for audiences who may well be aware of other opinions about the issue and who may even prefer the opposing views.

To write a convincing argument, then, you must have a logical position from which to argue, and you must handle the opposition skillfully. This chapter presents strategies for doing these things.

Defining the Conflict

Before planning an argument, the first thing writers must do is to understand the point of controversy. In many instances, this masquerades as an easy task because the conflict seems so apparent: pro-life versus pro-choice, capitalism versus communism, Candidate Jones versus Candidate Smith, and so on. But one of the main reasons arguments fail is that writers fail to look beneath the surface to find the real conflicts and the many subtle opinions lurking there. Arguments are rarely one-dimensional.

Take the standard conflict over capital punishment as an example (an issue mercifully omitted as a writing exercise in this book). On the surface, the conflict seems to be about whether or not states have the right to execute capital offenders, but the pro and con positions are far from absolute. Is it solely a moral question about our right to take a life, or is it more an issue of execution as a deterrent to crime? What about the problem of the criminal's mental capacity? Should we execute a murderer who has clearly committed the crime but has the mental state of a six year old? Are some of those who are for capital punishment extremist in other views; are some of those against it extremely liberal? Are the taxpayers willing to support criminals serving life sentences? Is racism or sexism involved? Are executions appropriate when they bring out sadistic onlookers wearing "Burn, baby, burn" t-shirts and lighting firecrackers when the switch is pulled? What relationship does execution have to abortion? Are they similar issues? A writer who frames an argument about capital punishment without considering these subtexts leaves the door wide open for failure.

To avoid the problems of superficiality and hastily made, perhaps unsupportable, judgments, you must analyze the conflict from as many perspectives as possible and as thoroughly as possible. That is often hard to do when you are emotionally invested in one side or another, but it is nevertheless necessary. Defining the conflict as specifically as you can means you must step outside of your emotional involvement and view the problem objectively. The following list may serve as a catalyst for your own analytical process. Each question is worth considering as you attempt to understand the full nature of the controversy prior to formulating an argument about it.

What are the logical positions of all sides? What are the bases for the logic?
Determine the rationale behind each point of view. Make sure you look only at the reasoning, not at the emotional overtones or biases. Then, consider the roots of such logic. Where does it come from and why do the proponents of each side find it valid?

What are the emotional positions of all sides? What are the bases for these emotions?

Repeat the same process as in the previous section: Find the emotional elements of the various positions and try to determine their causes.

Are there any areas of possible agreement?
As you look back over the material you have discovered so far, you may find that the opponents are not very far apart on some issues. Note them.

What are the areas of hopeless disagreement?
Similarly, you may discover that certain views are diametrically opposed with little possibility of compromise. Note these, too.

Are there any "red flag" ideas or words?
Pay attention to any language or concepts that generate immediate hostility. List these so that you can avoid them in the argument.

What are the possible alterations of each position?
Think about ways each side may be able to change without feeling overly compromised. You may want to predict how each view may shift during the argument.

Are there any related issues?
Do the questions relevant to this argument apply to any other issue? Do they overlap even slightly with other conflicts?

Can you state the opposing view fairly and objectively?
After analyzing the opponent's position, you should be able to state it in such a way that the opponent would deem fair. Make your statement brief and "operational." That means it should contain action, not just abstract concepts (that is, "By maintaining capital punishment, we send the strongest possible message to potential criminals," not "We should maintain capital punishment").

Can you state your view fairly and objectively?
Now state your own view as objectively as you stated the opponent's. Make this statement operational as well (that is, "By condoning capital punishment, we damage ourselves as surely as we punish the criminal").

The process of collecting this information is as important as the actual material you discover because it forces you to be as objective as possible and to see the situation from many perspectives. You may find that your own view shifts a bit as you perform this analysis, but that simply indicates that your original argument was not as carefully considered as it should have been; the new version will be much stronger. At the end of this process, you will have two clearly focused position statements, a wealth of background information, and all the tools you need to frame a convincing argument.

PRACTICE EXERCISE 9.1

1. Find two or more examples of arguments (newspaper editorials, political speeches, and so on), and write operational position statements for each one. If you have trouble finding the operational position in the piece, what does that say about the argument? (Make sure you have success with at least two.)

2. Complete the checklist process for an argument you have to write. You may discover that all the questions do not apply exactly, but modify the checklist to match your particular situation.

Organizing the Argument

Once you have a clear and complete idea of the issue you plan to argue, the next step is to decide how to organize your argument. As discussed in Chapter 5, organization plays a major role in the effect your prose has on the reader. This is especially true when you are writing to an audience who may not be receptive to your point of view. To present your ideas in the best possible light, you need to consider carefully the order in which you present the material, making sure that your logic appears unshakeable and that you do not create any unnecessary hostility along the way.

Logic can take many forms, but four constructions underpin most successful arguments: syllogism, enthymeme, example, and Toulmin logic. Most arguments use at least one of these techniques, and some use a combination. You should be aware of these constructions so that you can use them as part of your own persuasive strategies and also recognize them in other people's prose. Although a full discussion of each of these is material enough for several more books, a brief explanation will familiarize you with the basic concepts.

Syllogism

A syllogism resembles a mathematical proof. When all of its parts are present and correct, the syllogism is absolutely logical, offering no possibility for rational disagreement. Writers use the syllogism to appeal directly to their audience's sense of reason. Syllogisms work by presenting two propositions or "premises" and one conclusion; each of the premises must be true in order for the conclusion to be true. The famous example is as follows:

Major premise: All men are mortal beings.
Minor premise: Socrates is a man.
Conclusion: Therefore, Socrates is mortal.

To be valid, a syllogism's premises must be absolutely accurate and precisely ordered so that the parts within each section make logical sense when presented together. An invalid syllogism may contain some truth, but either its faulty premises or its imprecise order creates inferences that do not stand to reason. For example, "All those who eat sushi risk death. Sara does not eat sushi; therefore, she does not risk death." The questionable truth of this argument's major premise is one problem, and the conclusion is the other: Sara may not eat sushi, but she may risk death by not wearing a seat belt or by smoking in bed. Even though the minor premise is true, the rest of the syllogism is false. Here is another example of an invalid syllogism. Analyze it to determine why the logic is faulty:

All cats are animals.
All dogs are animals.
All cats are dogs.

In this example, the form of the syllogism creates the problem. Although the major and minor premises are totally accurate, the conclusion makes an illogical leap to suggest that the word *animals* includes only one species, and therefore felines and canines are one in the same. Discovering that one primary word has not been adequately defined is the most common way to disprove a syllogism. In this case, the definition of *animals* is much too narrow, causing a flaw in the argument.

As you can see, this technique is undeniable when it is valid, but many people use it carelessly, giving the impression of a valid argument while really combining the syllogism's parts in illogical ways. Nonetheless, when written correctly the syllogism is the basic unit of reasoning. If an argument can be expressed in a valid syllogism, it is not an argument at all; it is fact. On the other hand, most arguments depend on other techniques to convince the audience of probable truths—techniques that appeal to readers' emotional and ethical sensibilities, as well as to their sense of reason.

Enthymeme

The enthymeme is a prime example of such a strategy. Unlike the syllogism, the enthymeme is a construction based on a shared assumption of truth, not on unquestionable logic, and it can point only to probable truths. Whereas the syllogism leads to a necessary conclusion, the enthymeme leads to a tentative one; the writer still must convince the audience of its validity. Here is a simple enthymeme:

> He must be a Democrat because he advocates civil rights for minority groups.

The assumption here is the premise that "all Democrats advocate civil rights for minority groups." Because such an opinion is unprovable, the writer has not stated it directly; but if the audience shares that assumption, the enthymeme will work because it taps the audience's ingrained opinions, thereby drawing them into agreement. In fact, no enthymeme will succeed without the audience filling in the implied premise—and believing that it is accurate. This technique naturally appeals to the audience's emotional and ethical sensibilities more strongly than it does to their reason. Because of this, it is a primary tool in the art of persuasion, especially in persuasive arguments that must rely on more than logic to make their points.

In actual use, enthymemes work best in situations where the writer is trying to persuade the audience of something that is not a black-and-white issue. The following passages show enthymemes in operation. Each one has an underlying premise that is not stated directly. If the audience agrees with this unstated assumption, the argument works; if the audience does not agree, the argument fails.

> Animals are of course used as substitutes for humans in research regarding the diagnosis, treatment and prevention of disease. Virtually every major advance in medical science has been based on knowledge gained through such research. A good case in point is the development of insulin for the treatment of diabetes. There are in America alone some 11 million diabetics, most of whom live normal lives with the aid of insulin injections. Previous treatment for diabetes consisted of a starvation diet to delay, however briefly, inevitable death. Equally good examples are the development of

polio vaccine, improved treatment for heart attacks and high blood pressure, the development of transplant procedures, kidney dialysis and vaccines against numerous diseases.
　—*L. Morrison and G. Levey, "Lab Animals' Use"*

[Assumption: Medical advances are more important than animal rights.]

Rock is the trigger and substance of the nostalgia of people who came of age with it. And this nostalgia is narcissism, fascination with episodes (songs, bands, "Woodstock Nation") important only because those people and those episodes were contemporaries. The thinker was right who said that such nostalgia is modern man's worship of himself through veneration of things associated with his development.
　—*George F. Will, "Men of Wealth—and Taste?""*

[Assumption: Rock music is a negative influence.]

Regulations of the Environmental Protection Agency are being watered down because of the tremendous pressure that is exerted on government by industry. Industry makes hundreds of new chemicals every year. Very few are tested for their potential as causes of cancer. They are just dumped into the environment, as they were in Love Canal, Niagara Falls, New York, and in many other places around the country, where they become concentrated in the food chains, in our air, in our water, in our soil. Our whole world is rapidly becoming polluted with substances we haven't even looked at from the medical point of view. All to make money, to produce useless objects like plastic bottles that we throw away.
　—*Helen Caldicott, "What You Must Know About Radiation"*

[Assumption: Industry has no conscience.]

Because enthymeme deals with assumptions and probabilities rather than with absolutes, it can be easily misused to slant the audience's view of the truth. In the wrong hands, this technique can be dangerous. Understanding it allows you to look more carefully at arguments to discover the unspoken premises at the base. If you recognize these assumptions and still agree with them, then the argument is appropriate. If not, you can easily point to the invalid premise and pull the rug from under the whole structure. In your own attempts to use enthymeme correctly, consider four things:

1. Base the argument primarily on logic, not emotions. For the enthymeme to work best, it should not serve as a tool to make

a falsehood seem true. This is no way to build a strong argument. Instead, use the enthymeme only when you really support the claim you are making with it.

2. Look to the audience's ethics and emotions to discover their probable preconceptions. Although most of us try to base our thinking on logic, ethics and emotions often influence our final decisions. You should be aware of how these elements affect the audience and how they affect you, so that you can control them. Keep in mind that ethics and emotions are ways to strengthen logic, not replace it.

3. Analyze the audience's preconceptions and desire to believe in certain ways. By invoking these shared premises, you include the audience in the deliberation process, even though you invoke them only by implication.

4. Avoid making the truth claim until you can reasonably assume that the audience has already drawn similar conclusions from the evidence you present. It is much harder for an audience to disagree with a claim they have shared in developing than it is for them to disagree with a claim you present fully formed.

As examples of how enthymeme functions in actual prose, the following statements illustrate arguments that appeal to the assumptions of their readers. Each is logical to a great extent, but the persuasive hook is the unprovable premise that is assumed, not stated:

> Still, after all is said, the problem of homelessness remains largely invisible. While it is relatively easy for [the state] to present (and dispute) numbers, it is more difficult to convey the hardship that results when a fundamental human necessity disappears. Ultimately, that is the most uncountable matter of all.
> —*NY Department of Social Services*

[This argument assumes that the state is responsible for the homeless and is in part to blame for the problem.]

> But today the problem of human identity has changed. For the work that defined man's place in society and his sense of himself has also changed man's world. Work, and the advance of knowledge, has lessened man's dependence on his environment; his biology and the work he must do for biological survival are no longer sufficient to define his identity. This can be most clearly seen in our own abundant society; men no longer need to work all day to eat. They have an unprecedented freedom to choose the kind of work they

will do; they also have an unprecedented amount of time apart from the hours and days that must actually be spent in making a living. And suddenly one realizes the significance of today's identity crisis—for women, and increasingly, for men. One sees the human significance of work—not merely as the means of biological survival, but as the giver of self and the transcender of self, as the creator of human identity and human evolution.
—*Betty Friedan, "The Importance of Work"*

[This argument assumes that "work" means a job other than nurturing a family.]

Aristotle considered enthymeme the fundamental unit of all persuasive discourse because we argue only about things that no other means can establish as true. Any argument not based on absolute truth must operate at some level by means of assumption. Using enthymeme well means you must do thorough audience analysis—as discussed in the first section of this chapter—and you must design your argument to appeal directly to the audience's beliefs. If you argue in good faith, enthymeme allows you to connect with readers quickly and easily. If you use it in bad faith—slanting language and arguing what you know to be untrue—the prose tips into propaganda, and the search for probable truth becomes an exercise in underhanded manipulation.

Example

Arguing chiefly by means of example is another common method of persuasion, one often used in academic essays and other writing situations where writers make direct claims that need support. When writers use this technique, they provide evidence that suggests the validity of their view. Readers find it difficult to disagree with opinions backed by sufficient evidence, and an example is one of the most persuasive forms of evidence. "I believe X is true," you may say, and you provide two or three instances where that claim is valid, leading the audience to infer its widespread applicability. Here are a few passages that make effective use of examples to persuade readers that the assertions are valid:

The English language is suffering from a word shortage. This is because the world changes so fast nowadays that word makers cannot produce new words fast enough to keep up with all the new things that are happening.

For example, the Volkswagen has been with us for twenty years, but we still do not always have a good word to describe the peculiar state of mind which the Volkswagen induces in its driver. Without such a word, other drivers have no effective way of dealing with the Volkswagen driver as he weaves in and out of heavy traffic, feeling dangerously like a broken-field runner on an asphalt gridiron. . . .

We also need a word for the modern crime of robbery by machine. In the typical mechanized robbery, the victim puts fifteen cents into a soda-pop vending machine. The machine seizes the money, drops it into a metal loot box, and refuses to come across with the soda pop.

—*Russell Baker, "Juglipidly"*

A newly invented metaphor assists thought by evoking a visual image, while on the other hand a metaphor which is technically "dead" (e.g. *iron resolution*) has in effect reverted to being an ordinary word and can generally be used without loss of vividness. But in between these two classes there is a huge dump of worn-out metaphors which have lost all evocative power and are merely used because they save people the trouble of inventing phrases for themselves. Examples are: *Ring the changes on, take up the cudgels for, toe the line, ride roughshod over, stand shoulder to shoulder with, play into the hands of, no axe to grind, grist to the mill, fishing in troubled waters, on the order of the day, Achilles' heel, swan song, hotbed.* Many of these are used without knowledge of their meaning (what is a "rift," for instance), and incompatible metaphors are frequently mixed, a sure sign that the writer is not interested in what he is saying.

—*George Orwell, "Politics and the English Language"*

The first and most important consideration is whether the individual thinks he controls the risk. Many recreational activities are quite dangerous. Skydiving, skiing, and skateboarding are obvious examples. And it is far more dangerous to ride a bicycle around the block once a week than it is to live next to a nuclear power plant. As anyone who has ever had an automobile accident knows, the driver does not control the risk—or he would not be in the accident. But this risk is denied by the person who anticipates driving a car or skiing down a slope because he thinks he does control his risk. The same illusion often protects the cigarette smoker from fear. He has been manipulated by peer and commercial pressures and by the pharmacology of nicotine addiction, but he thinks he can stop or cut down if he needs to. Therefore, he is not fearful. This particular factor—the location of control of the risk—is exaggerated further for some people when "they" who control the risk are big, impersonal, and often mistrusted institutions. Thus, fear of nuclear power is exaggerated in part because the risk is perceived to be controlled by "big utilities" and by "remote bureaucracies" such as the Nuclear Regulatory Commission.

—*Robert L. DuPont, "The Nuclear Power Phobia"*

In each of these passages, the writer has stated an opinion that he cannot prove as undeniable fact. Yet the examples that buttress these assertions lead most readers to agree with the author. Even the last paragraph about nuclear power—certainly the most controversial example here—makes logical sense as DuPont discusses the many familiar instances when we are afraid because we are not in control. Although you may disagree with his ultimate point—that nuclear power is relatively safe—you at least will listen to what he has to say because he has caught your attention with his examples.

From the reader's point of view, examples work well if given in sufficient number and with sufficient breadth. Few would believe an argument suggesting that all of Shakespeare's women were brutally ambitious based only on the example of Lady Macbeth. Effective arguments need a broad base of supportive examples that will stand up to any charge of insufficient evidence.

Toulmin Logic

Toulmin logic, named after its major proponent Stephen Toulmin, is not so much a new form of logic as it is a method of combining enthymeme and example into a strategy for argument. This technique provides three useful terms: claim, support, and warrant. The *claim* is the basic point the writer is trying to prove; the *support* is the evidence and other appeals to the audience; and the *warrant* is the assumption underlying the entire structure. In other words, according to Toulmin logic, all argument works via assumptions, and all writers appeal to the audience's emotional and ethical sensibilities in an attempt to persuade.

A simple example will serve here. Countless mothers have told their children, "Eat your vegetables so that you will grow big and strong." Separated into its components, the argument becomes:

Claim: Vegetables are good for you.

Support: They make you grow big and strong (an appeal to emotions).

Warrant: Vegetables produce height and muscles.

Based on the shared assumption (what one student has called the "Popeye assumption") that vegetables have such power, the argument works for most kids. When it does not, parents usually add other means of emotional appeal—the starving children in other countries, the threat of no dessert, no TV, and so on.

More sophisticated arguments work in much the same way. For instance, this passage from an argument against pornography illustrates the three components of Toulmin logic:

> The basic psychological fact about pornography and obscenity is that it appeals to and revokes a kind of sexual regression. The sexual pleasure one gets from pornography and obscenity is autoerotic and infantile; to put it bluntly, it is a masturbatory exercise of the imagination, when it is not masturbation pure and simple.
> —*Irving Kristol, "Pornography and Censorship"*

Claim: Pornography is wrong.

Support: The sexual pleasure pornography creates is as infantile as masturbation.

Warrant: Masturbation is unhealthy and infantile.

As the audience for this argument, you will either agree or disagree with the author depending on your feelings about the warrant underlying the claim and the support. If the author has misread the audience's value systems and discovers too late that they do not consider masturbation unhealthy, his entire argument collapses. On the other hand, if the audience agrees with this view, the argument works well. You can certainly see from this example how important audience analysis is in planning an effective strategy for argument.

Toulmin logic, then, is a combination of example and enthymeme and is a method that allows you to create better strategies for your own arguments. If you break down your argument into its three components, you can identify the warrants you are using and see if they are appropriate for your intended audience. Such a technique guards against constructing an argument based on assumptions that are either faulty or ill-suited to the readers. It takes only a few minutes to check your argument against this method, and such a check could point out some faulty assumptions you had not recognized.

PRACTICE EXERCISE 9.2

Read the following passages and determine what logical constructions the authors are using: syllogism, enthymeme, example, or Toulmin logic. (Some of them may overlap, and authors may use several in one passage.) Write down the technique, briefly explain why you have identified it as such, and then discuss how well you think it works.

It may be a terrible mistake to take *Deep Throat* and its success seriously. These things may just happen. Their success may not mean a thing. The publicity machine marches on, and all that. But I can't help thinking that pornography that has this sort of impact must have some significance. I have seen a lot of stag films in my life—well, that's not true; I've seen about five or six—and although most of them were raunchy, a few were actually sweet and innocent and actually erotic. *Deep Throat,* on the other hand, is one of the most unpleasant, disturbing films I have ever seen—it is not just anti-female but anti-sexual as well. I walked into the World Theater feeling thoroughly unshockable . . . and I came out of the theater a quivering fanatic. Give me the goriest Peckinpah any day. There is a scene in *Deep Throat,* for example, where a man inserts a hollow glass dildo inside Miss Lovelace, fills it with Coca-Cola, and drinks it with a surgical straw—the audience was bursting with nervous laughter, while I sat through it literally faint. All I could think about was what would happen if the glass broke. I always cringe when I read reviews of this sort—crazy feminists carrying on, criticizing nonpolitical films in political terms—but as I sat through the film I was swept away in a bromide wave of movement rhetoric. "Demeaning to women," I wailed as we walked away from the theater. "Degrading to women." . . . The men I was with pretended they did not know me, and then, when I persisted in addressing my mutterings to them, they assured me that I was overreacting, that it was just a movie and that they hadn't even been turned on by it. But I refused to calm down. "Look, Nora," said one of them, playing what I suppose he thought was his trump card by appealing to my sense of humor, "there's one thing you have to admit. The scene with the Coca-Cola was hilarious."

—*Nora Ephron, "Deep Throat"*

I have been thinking a good deal about plays lately, and I have been wondering why I dislike the clear and logical construction which seems to be necessary if one is to succeed on the Modern Stage. It came into my head the other day that this construction, which all the world has learned from France, has everything of high literature except the emotion of multitude. The Greek drama has got the emotion of multitude from its chorus, which called up famous sorrows, long-leaguered Troy, much-enduring Odysseus, and all the gods and heroes to witness, as it were, some well-ordered fable, some action separated but for this from all but itself. The French play delights in well-ordered fable, but by leaving out the chorus it has created an art where poetry and imagination, always the children of far-off multitudinous things, must of necessity grow less important than the mere will. This is why, I said to myself, French dramatic poetry is so often a little rhetorical, for rhetoric is the will trying to do the work of the imagination. The Shakespearian Drama gets the emotion of multitude out of the subplot which copies the main plot, much as a shadow upon the wall copies one's body in the firelight. We think of *King Lear* less as the history of one man and his sorrows than as the history of a whole evil time. Lear's shadow is in Gloster, who also has ungrateful children, and the mind goes on imagining other shadows, shadow beyond shadow till it has pictured the world. In *Hamlet,* one hardly notices, so subtly is the web woven, that the murder of Hamlet's father and the sorrow of Hamlet are shadowed in the lives of Fortinbras and Ophelia and Laertes, whose fathers, too, have been killed. It is so in all the plays, or in all but all, and very commonly the subplot is the main plot working itself out in more ordinary men and women, and so doubly calling up before us the image of multitude. Ibsen and Maeterlinck have on the other hand created a new form, for they get multitude from the Wild Duck in the Attic, or from the Crown at the bottom of the Fountain, vague symbols that set the mind wandering from idea to idea, emotion to emotion. Indeed all the great Masters have understood that there cannot be great art without the little limited life of fable, which is always the better the simpler it is, and the rich, far-wandering, many-imaged life of the self-seen world beyond it. There are some who understand that the simple unmysterious things living as in a clear noonlight are of the nature of the sun, and that vague, many-imaged things have in them the strength of the moon. Did not the Egyptian carve it on emerald that all living things have the sun for father and the moon for mother, and has it not been said that a man of genius takes the most after his mother?

—*William Butler Yeats, "Emotion of Multitude" from* Essays and Introduction, *New York, Macmillan, 1961. Reprinted with permission.*

When in the course of human events, it becomes necessary for one people to dissolve the political bonds which have connected them with another, and to assume among the Powers of the earth, the separate and equal station to which the Laws of Nature and Nature's God entitle them, a decent respect to the opinions of mankind requires that they should declare the causes which impel them to separation.

We hold these truths to be self-evident, that all men are created equal, that they are endowed by their Creator with certain unalienable Rights, that among these are Life, Liberty, and the pursuit of Happiness.

That to secure these rights Governments are instituted among Men, deriving their just powers from the consent of the governed.

That whenever any Form of Government becomes destructive of these ends, it is the Right of the People to alter or abolish it, and to institute a new Government laying its foundation on such principles and organizing its powers in such form, as to them shall seem most likely to effect their Safety and Happiness. Prudence, indeed, will dictate that Governments long established should not be changed for light and transient causes; and accordingly all experience hath shown that mankind are more disposed to suffer, while evils are sufferable, than to right themselves by abolishing the forms to which they are accustomed. But when a long train of abuses and usurpations pursuing invariably the same Object evinces a design to reduce them under absolute Despotism, it is their right, it is their duty, to throw off such government, and to provide new Guards for their future security.

Such has been the patient suffering of these Colonies; and such is now the necessity which constrains them to alter their former Systems of Government. The History of the Present King of Great Britain is a history of repeated injuries and usurpations, all having in direct object the establishment of an absolute Tyranny over these States. To prove this, let the facts be submitted to a candid world.

He has refused his Assent to laws, the most wholesome and necessary for the public good.

He has forbidden the Governors to pass Laws of immediate and pressing importance, unless suspended in their operation till his Assent should be obtained; and when so suspended, he has utterly neglected to attend to them.

He has refused to pass other Laws for the accommodation of large districts of people, unless those people would relinquish the right of Representation in the Legislature, a right inestimable to them and formidable to tyrants only.

He has called together legislative bodies at places unusual, uncomfortable, and distant from the depository of their Public Records, for the sole purpose of fatiguing them into compliance with his measures.

He has dissolved Representative Houses repeatedly, for opposing with manly firmness his invasions on the rights of the people.

He has refused for a long time, after such dissolutions, to cause others to be elected; whereby the Legislative Powers, incapable of Annihilation, have returned to the People at large for their exercise; the State remaining in the mean time exposed to all the danger of invasion from without, and convulsions within.

He has endeavored to prevent the population of these States; for that purpose obstructing the Laws of Naturalization of Foreigners; refusing to pass others to encourage their migration hither, and raising conditions of new Appropriations of Lands.

He has obstructed the Administration of Justice, by refusing his Assent to Laws for establishing Judiciary Powers.

He has made Judges dependent on his Will alone, for the tenure of their offices, and the amount and payment of their salaries.

He has erected a multitude of New Offices, and sent hither swarms of Officers to harass our People, and eat out their substance.

He has kept among us, in time of peace, Standing Armies without the consent of our Legislature.

He has affected to render the Military independent of and superior to the Civil Power.

He has combined with others to subject us to jurisdictions foreign to our constitution, and unacknowledged by our laws; giving his Assent to their acts of pretended Legislation:

For quartering large bodies of armed troops among us:

For protecting them, by a mock Trial, from Punishment for any Murders which they should commit on the Inhabitants of these States:

For cutting off our Trade with all parts of the world:

For imposing Taxes on us without our Consent:

For depriving us in many cases, of the benefits of Trial by Jury:

For transporting us beyond Seas to be tried for pretended offenses:

For abolishing the free System of English Laws in a Neighboring Province, establishing therein an Arbitrary government, and enlarging its boundaries so as to render it at once an example and fit instrument for introducing the same absolute rule into these Colonies:

For taking away our Charters, abolishing our most valuable Laws, and altering fundamentally the Forms of our Governments:

For suspending our own legislatures, and declaring themselves invested with Power to legislate for us in all cases whatsoever.

He has abdicated Government here, by declaring us out of his Protection and waging War against us.

He has plundered our seas, ravaged our Coasts, burnt our towns and destroyed the Lives of our people.

He is at this time transporting large Armies of foreign Mercenaries to compleat the works of death, desolation and tyranny, already begun with circumstances of Cruelty and perfidy scarcely paralleled in the most barbarous ages, and totally unworthy of the Head of a civilized nation.

He has constrained our fellow Citizens taken Captive on the high Seas to bear Arms against their Country, to become the executioners of their friends and Brethren, or to fall themselves by their Hands.

He has excited domestic insurrections amongst us, and has endeavored to bring on the inhabitants of our frontiers, the merciless Indian Savages, whose known rule of warfare is an undistinguished destruction of all ages, sexes, and conditions.

In every stage of these Oppressions We Have Petitioned for Redress in the most humble terms. Our repeated petitions have been answered only by repeated injury. A Prince, whose character is thus marked by every act which may define a Tyrant, is unfit to be the ruler of a free People.

Nor have We been wanting in attention to our British brethren. We have warned them from time to time of attempts by their legislature to extend an unwarrantable jurisdiction over us. We have reminded them of the circumstances of our emigration and settlement here. We have appealed to their native justice and magnanimity and we have conjured them by the ties of our common kindred to disavow these usurpations, which would inevitably interrupt our connections and correspondence. They too have been deaf to the voice of justice and consanguinity. We must, therefore, acquiesce in the necessity, which denounces our Separation, and hold them, as we hold the rest of mankind, Enemies in War, in Peace Friends.

We, therefore, the Representatives of the United States of America, in General Congress, Assembled, appealing to the Supreme Judge of the world for the rectitude of our intentions, do, in the Name, and by Authority of the good People of these Colonies, solemnly publish and declare, That these United Colonies are, and of Right ought to be, Free and Independent States; that they are Absolved from all Allegiance to the British Crown, and that all political connection between them and the States of Great Britain, is and ought to be totally dissolved; and that as Free and Independent States, they have full power to levy War, conclude Peace, contract Alliances, establish Commerce, and to do all other Acts and Things which Independent States may of right do. And for support of this Declaration, with a firm reliance on the protection of Divine Providence, we mutually pledge to each other our lives, our Fortunes and our sacred Honor.

—*Thomas Jefferson, "The Declaration of Independence"*

Syllogism, enthymeme, example, and Toulmin logic are the persuasive tools writers can use in building arguments. In most situations, writers use them to present their own case favorably while refuting the opponent's view. Now that you have seen how these elements work, you should be able to understand how they function to strengthen the argument when you sit down to write a persuasive piece, or when you read someone else's. But even these tools of logic will not work effectively if they are not used to construct a well-organized argument. Putting together persuasive discourse requires not only the right tools but also a carefully considered blueprint for a structure that will hold up under scrutiny and possible attacks from those holding opposing views. In general, the strategies for organizing an effective argument can be best represented by four models, each appropriate in a variety of instances. Keep in mind that these are models only, not strict formulas for all argumentation. Use them to stimulate your own thinking about how to arrange your prose.

The Classical Model

Most of the early rhetoricians used discourse only for argumentation. Aristotle, Cicero, and other classical speakers used their speeches for matters of state and for philosophical debates, to convince audiences of certain points of view and move them to specific action. For these speakers, rhetoric was synonymous with persuasion.

To capture the audience's attention and eventually their assent, the classical rhetoricians developed a five-part model for argument: exordium, narratio, confirmatio, refutatio, and peroratio—or, to translate to English: introduction, statement of fact, proof, refutation, and conclusion. It is a tribute to the strength of this model that even after centuries of continued use, it is still the most common form of argument because it forces the writer (or speaker) to structure the prose in a logical, well-supported format that takes into consideration all the questions the audience may have. A brief look at the five parts shows why this is true.

The *introduction* has three major functions: to get the audience's attention, to gain their confidence, and to set the stage for the rest of the argument. After reading the introduction, the audience should understand the point you are arguing and be ready to follow you as you give further explanation.

> The testimony of at least two eyewitnesses and unquestionable forensic evidence show that Maxwell Edison is guilty of bludgeoning three people to death within the space of one week.

The *statement of fact* sets down the important background information necessary for understanding the argument. It includes only factual material, not appeals for or against any point of view. From this section, the audience should receive a clear picture of what happened or of the components that make up the issue to be argued.

> Joan Quizzical, a physical science major at State University, was found dead by the door of her apartment on Tuesday, March 21.

Professor Ellen Rigby, a faculty member at the same university, died of severe head injuries inflicted after hours in her classroom on Wednesday, March 22. Judge I. M. Walrus was beaten to death in his courtroom on Friday, March 24. Maxwell Edison was present in each instant, and evidence strongly suggests he is the perpetrator of these crimes.

In the *proof* section, you present the evidence that supports your contention. Included here are examples and other supportive material that lend credence to the opinion presented. It is helpful to think back on what convinced you of the argument's validity and try to reproduce that material for the audience. If you can be convinced, so can your audience.

Ms. Quizzical's friends have testified that she was planning a date with Mr. Edison that evening and may have let him in the door. His fingerprints on the doorknob and on the wall near the body corroborate this view. Professor Rigby had asked Mr. Edison to stay after class the day of the murder, and several students have stated that he was alone with her in the classroom at the time in question. Again, fingerprints corroborate his presence at the scene, and the bloody chalkdust on the body matches the dust found on Edison's clothes. Finally, an entire courtroom full of people saw a figure strongly resembling Edison rise from behind the bench and pound on Judge Walrus's skull with a large silver hammer.

Arguments work best when the audience is permitted to see both sides of the question before making up their own minds about which view is correct. If you include the opposition within your argument, you give the impression of fair play and unbiased judgment. The *refutation* section presents the opposing view but does so only to explain why it is incorrect. By discussing the opposition and refuting it, you take some of the "punch" out of the opposing argument.

Two women sitting in the gallery during the arraignment—Rose Smith and Valerie Hall—argued strenuously that Maxwell should go free. They base their opinions on previous relationships with Edison, and they claim there is strong evidence of a police cover-up in P.C. 31, the precinct where Edison was taken immediately after his apprehension.

The *conclusion* summarizes the argument and makes the final plea to the audience.

But the many eyewitnesses to the Walrus killing, the irrefutable physical evidence—blood matches, fingerprints, and chalkdust—

d the ultimate discovery of a large silver hammer in Edison's
rtment prove beyond reasonable doubt that Maxwell Edison is
guilty and should be punished to the full extent of the law. To do
less would be a travesty.

This model works well in many situations, but it is especially suited
to arguments that need to illustrate the thoroughness of the investigation behind the opinion presented. Academic papers and legal arguments are two such instances where writers must show that they
have exhausted all possible avenues before choosing to defend a particular view. In fact, the text of most legal documents and some academic papers features the headings *Introduction, Statement of Fact,
Proof, Refutation,* and *Conclusion.* Even papers and documents without such explicit headings divide naturally into these segments, although the divisions are not labeled.

The Rogerian Model

Carl Rogers, noted psychotherapist, suggests that many traditional
forms of argument are self-defeating because they engender hostility
rather than encourage agreement.

Try this test. The next time you are in a group of people, express
an opinion about a popular film (or book, or restaurant . . . whatever) most of the group is familiar with. The conversation will probably go something like this:

You: "I really think *Batman* is one of the worst movies
I've seen."

Bob: "Really? I loved it!"

Susan: "I agree with Joe; it was awful."

Carol: "You can't appreciate a movie like that unless you
understand it as a genre film. It's based on a comic
book, you know."

Few, if any, of the people present will ask you why you disliked
the movie. Instead, they will immediately offer their opinions and
the group will square off for debate on the qualities of the film. According to Rogers, this is our natural response in all situations where
any opinion is expressed. Rather than listening and trying to understand someone else's idea, people find it more important to turn the

spotlight on themselves and not be satisfied until they have won the argument. In the conversation above, for example, nobody noticed that you did not ask for their opinions—you wanted to express yours. It is rare in that situation for anyone to respond, "That's interesting. Why do you feel that way?"

Traditional argument so concentrates on winning that we often lose sight of the real goal of many debates: to find the truth. In situations where various groups come together to solve a problem, traditional argument does not work because it entrenches people more firmly in their own combative stances. School board meetings, for example, or business meetings—any situation where cooperation is necessary—benefit from the Rogerian model of argument. Rogerian argument's goal is not to win but rather is to encourage compromise and find a workable solution that the majority find satisfactory. It differs, too, from traditional argument in that it turns the focus from the individuals and puts it on the problem to be solved. Effective Rogerian argument forces the people involved to listen to each other and explore carefully all the options. It also downplays emotional appeals and concentrates instead on objective representations of the various points of view.

In brief, the Rogerian model includes five steps:

1. *Statement of the Problem:* Define the conflict that has created the problem. What is at issue?

2. *Opponent's Position:* State the opponent's point of view in such a way that he or she would agree with your representation.

3. *Your Position:* Give a brief statement of your viewpoint, making sure to present it as objectively as possible.

4. *Areas of Agreement:* List the areas where the two views are similar or could benefit from adopting elements of the other position.

5. *Resolution:* Based on the information discovered in the previous steps, propose a solution that encourages cooperation and compromise between both views.

As you can see, this model works well when the point of the argument is to find a mutually satisfactory solution to a problem. For example, this model is appropriate for academic inquiry or for situations that require negotiation. But in situations where the goal is more to convince than to cooperate, Rogerian argument is inappropriate.

The Exploratory Model

If you think the audience may be hostile to your opinions, or if you prefer not to state your view right away for some other reason, you may consider using the exploratory model. In this strategy, you explore a problem with the readers, coming to a mutual understanding by the end of the discourse, rather than confronting them immediately with an assertion and spending the rest of the time defending it. This model depends on two things: (1) the readers must understand from the outset that the assertion is withheld, and (2) they must be willing to stick with you all the way through to the end to discover the important conclusions.

Here is an example of a circumstance where the exploratory model would be the best option. If you heard someone say, "All stray dogs should be shot!" you would probably resist that argument altogether. But if the person said "My two-year-old neighbor was mauled this morning by a pack of stray dogs terrorizing the neighborhood. We need to find a solution to this problem before others are hurt. I've done some research and have several suggestions about how to handle this situation," you may have been pulled into the discussion more readily. Notice that no ultimate opinion is given, but you and other readers are invited along to explore the various alternatives. By the time you reach the end, the author will have led you through the options, and you will probably find mutual agreement on the best solution: "The humane society should work with the animal control officer to corral these dogs and either find appropriate homes for them or, in cases where the dogs are vicious, to put them down humanely."

Writers using the exploratory model take their readers through the discovery process, alluding to the final point but not asserting it until the end when the reader has come to the same conclusion or is at least prepared to understand it. This works especially well in writing situations where the audience is resistant to the assertion or cannot fully grasp the writer's view until they have been exposed to enough background information.

The Editorial Model

The editorial model is really the inverse of exploratory argument. Instead of withholding the opinion until the end and inviting the readers to discover the best solution, this deductive argument begins with a bold assertion, followed by further claims and support for that view. It is the most blatant of the argument models and works only in circumstances that require strong persuasive techniques in a short space of time.

Usually, the editorial model does not incorporate an extensive discussion of the opposing views or give a lengthy statement of the facts. It has a powerful effect on the audience precisely because it is so direct and so concise. The combination creates hard-hitting prose that stuns the audience with its self-assured punch. If the argument goes on too long, the prose would lose that stunning effect and the audience would begin to demand more information, more support, and more attention to the other views.

Newspaper editorials and similar short pieces are perfect examples of this form of argument. Their goal is to make a strong impression in as few words as possible and to stir readers to find out more about the subject and perhaps act on it. An example from the editorial page of the newspaper illustrates the technique:

Saving the Tuna

Someone is killing the great fish of the ocean. East Coast swordfish stocks are estimated to have fallen 60 percent from 1978 to 1987. The average size fell from 100 pounds in 1980 to 85 pounds in 1986. Nearly half the fish are under 75 pounds, too young to spawn. Blue Fin tuna are going the same route.

The issue is that the long lines used to catch tuna are killing other large ocean fish—marlin, swordfish, shark, wahoo, and dolphin. About 12,000 marlin and sailfish are killed each year as a "by-catch" of the yellow fin tuna fishery in the Gulf of Mexico.

The National Coalition for Marine Conservation believes that bringing tuna under the provisions of the US fisheries-management law is essential to saving tuna and other fish, including marlin.

Because of modern fishing methods—drift-netting and long-lining—the exception made for tuna when the law was enacted in 1976 is having disastrous consequences. Drift-netting was pioneered in the Pacific by boats from Japan, South Korea and Taiwan. Huge nets, up to 30 miles long, are dropped like curtains, snaring all large species indiscriminately. More than a dozen drift-net boats have begun to work out of New Bedford, Gloucester and Point Judith, RI.

Long-liners are also deadly. Lines up to 70 miles long are set from buoys, with baited hooks spaced at intervals and at varying depths. The hooks are small enough to catch swordfish as small as 25 pounds. To kill the young is to threaten the species.

The system does not work. What would work is the closing of certain areas to fishing when species needing protection are in those

waters. This cannot be done so long as tuna are exempt from US regulations. It is up to Congress to act.
—*Courtesy of* The Boston Globe, *August 24, 1989*

These models and the techniques of logic discussed earlier should provide you with enough information so that you can create effective argument strategies on your own. Most arguments parallel one of these models totally or are some combination with one pattern more dominant than the others. At first, it might be a good idea to follow these models carefully, before branching off to develop a strategy that combines these approaches. No matter how you choose to construct your argument, remember that it will work only to the extent that it convinces an audience, so your primary concern should be to plan a strategy with that specific audience in mind. Use the proper tools for the job at hand.

PRACTICE EXERCISE 9.3

Look at the following opening paragraphs of several arguments and make an educated guess about which argument model each represents. Explain your reasoning.

The School System has much to say these days of the virtue of reading widely, and not enough about the virtues of reading less but in depth. There are any number of reading lists for poetry, but there is not enough talk about individual poems. Poetry, finally, is one poem at a time. To read any one poem carefully is the ideal preparation for reading another. Only a poem can illustrate how poetry works.

   Above, therefore, is a poem ["Stopping by Woods on a Snowy Evening"]—one of the master lyrics of the English language, and almost certainly the best-known poem by an American poet. What happens in it?—which is to say, not *what* does it mean, but *how* does it mean? How does it go about being a human reenactment of a human experience? The author— perhaps the thousandth reader would need to be told—is Robert Frost.
—*John Ciardi, "Robert Frost: The Way to the Poem"*

Woodstock's naive, apolitical innocence has come to signify nearly everything it set out to remedy. What is represented as culture was a generation's self-identity; what it represented as music was a coming of age.

   But what was once culturally significant has now become just another commercial fact of life, another commodity to be bought and sold. The event bespeaks both today's arena-rock standards and the increasing distance between artists and their audience. Acts like Janis Joplin, Jimi Hendrix, and the Who, which had made Monterey debuts two years before, reappeared at Woodstock as professional titans of rock theatrics.

As captured on record and film, the August 1969 event bridges rock utopianism and capitalist opportunism. Record executives mingled backstage with dollar signs in their eyes, ogling a crowd that wasn't chanting "Revolution." If you watched a recent MTV broadcast broken up with beer ads and an MTV logo blazoned across idyllic shots of skinny-dipping hippies, you might have begun to realize just how skillfully corporate interests have exploited the event that momentarily charmed commercialism into trippy submission.

—*Tim Riley, "A Nation Once Again"* The Boston Phoenix, *August 18, 1989*

"Beasts abstract not," announced John Locke, expressing mankind's prevailing opinion throughout recorded history: Bishop Berkeley had, however, a sardonic rejoinder: "If the fact that brutes abstract not be made the distinguishing property of that sort of animal, I fear a great many of those that pass for men must be reckoned into their numbers." Abstract thought, at least in its more subtle varieties, is not an invariable accompaniment of everyday life for the average man. Could abstract thought be a matter not of kind but of degree? Could other animals be capable of abstract thought but more rarely and less deeply than humans?

—*Carl Sagan, "The Abstractions of Beasts"*

The distinction between active and passive euthanasia is thought to be crucial for medical ethics. The idea is that it is permissible, at least in some cases, to withhold treatment and allow a patient to die, but it is never permissible to take any direct action designed to kill the patient. This doctrine seems to be accepted by most doctors, and it is endorsed in a statement adopted by the House of Delegates of the American Medical Association on December 4, 1973:

> The intentional termination of the life of one human being by another—mercy killing—is contrary to that for which the medical profession stands and is contrary to the policy of the American Medical Association.
>
> The cessation of the employment of extraordinary means to prolong the life of the body when there is irrefutable evidence that biological death is imminent is the decision of the patient and/or his immediate family. The advice and judgment of the physician should be freely available to the patient and/or his immediate family.

However, a strong case can be made against this doctrine. In what follows I will set out some of the relevant arguments, and urge doctors to reconsider their views on this matter.

—*James Rachels, "Active and Passive Euthanasia"*

PRACTICE EXERCISE 9.4

Take some time to decide on a topic you would like to argue. Once you have determined a topic you really care about, write two different openings for it, following two different models. Then, write a brief explanation of when you might use each opening and why. What are the different effects each produces? How would the audience likely respond?

Handling the Opposition

One of the keys to arguing effectively is to include the opponent's view. By doing so, you anticipate the counterarguments and can go a long way toward defusing them before they are actually made. One word of caution: Even though you should include the opponent's argument, do not spend the majority of your time rebutting or degrading it. To do so is to feature that view instead of your own. But there are some strategies for dealing with the opposing view that will strengthen your own stance without degrading the other point of view.

You must include the opposing argument in order to present the entire story. Many writing experts suggest that including the opponent's view within your argument effectively balances your opinion and takes care of your duty to recognize the other side. But merely paying lip service to the other side does no service to your view and probably appears little more than dutiful. You must use the counterargument effectively to enhance your own position.

How do you do this? A two-part technique answers this question. First, order the material to place your argument in the stronger position. Although some rhetoricians will tell you to put your point last because the final spot has greater impact, that technique means you are always featuring the opponent's argument by putting it first. The best strategy is to begin by (1) stating your view concisely, (2) giving the opposing argument *briefly,* and (3) expanding on your view in the final position. By doing so you allow your argument to surround the counterview, literally fencing it in. It also gives you the final word. This position allows you to refer to the preceding view, giving you the leverage of comparison, and it also places your opinion last, making it the final idea the reader carries away from the discussion.

Second, when you include the counterargument, write it in clear, direct language. When you phrase it, ask yourself whether your op-

ponent would agree that your statement is fair. Forcing yourself to
state the opposing viewpoint in an unbiased manner allows you to
really understand that view—as the Rogerian model discussed in the
previous section suggests. If you are going to argue against something, it is essential that you understand it. It is surprising how many
writers never actually consider the other argument's merits in their
urgency to do battle. The best writers realize that to resolve any conflict, you must understand all of its parts. For example, consider the
following two versions of an attorney's argument. Note that the first
passage does not present both sides of the problem and therefore is
not nearly as persuasive as the revised version that follows it.

Version 1

Ms. Wharton had actual knowledge of the open and dangerous hole
but failed in her clear duty to safeguard her visitors and to issue
proper warnings. Not only did she fail to warn her unsuspecting
guests, she actually gave an open invitation to disaster by asking
them to "Feel free to look around." Mr. Revere was clearly victimized
by that invitation and Wharton's carelessness in taking appropriate
safety precautions when he fell into the 10-foot hole, sustaining
severe personal injury.

This passage is one-sided and seems slanted toward plaintiff Revere's position. If the lawyer revises the argument to begin with
Wharton's point of view, and then logically explains why that view is
unreasonable, the prose will be more trustworthy and more persuasive. In the following version, note how concisely the opposing
argument is stated—the writer wastes little time discussing it:

Version 2

Defendant Wharton should not win summary judgment on the
basis that she did not know about the dangers at the construction
site. A major thesis of Wharton's plea for summary judgment is
that she lacked actual knowledge of the unlocked foyer door and
the dangerous hole beyond it in the renovation area. However,
Wharton knew of the extensive damage to the floor, and she knew
for several weeks that the contractor planned to remove the rotten
floorboards in the renovation area near the foyer. A jury might
reasonably infer that Wharton thereby had actual knowledge of the
hole. Once she had actual knowledge of the defects, she had a clear
duty to safeguard them or to issue proper warnings, both of which
she failed to do.

Even if Wharton did not have actual knowledge of the open door
and dangerous hole, a jury could find that she had sufficient time
during her three hours at the premises before the guests arrived to
fulfill her duty to inspect and safeguard the area, especially in light

of the known renovations and anticipated floor repairs. A jury could also find that Wharton failed in her duty to warn unsuspecting guests such as Revere about the dangerous ongoing renovations on the first floor. Not only did she fail to warn, she actually issued an open invitation to disaster when she invited her guests to "Feel free to look around"—a suggestion that victimized Revere when he fell into the 10-foot hole, sustaining severe personal injury.

By clearly stating your opinion, then the opponent's, and by placing your argument in the stronger final position, you gain control over the reader's intellectual and emotional view of the problem. And because you have given a fair statement of the opponent's argument, you have probably also gained the reader's trust. You seem confident and logical—both essential ingredients for persuasive appeal.

When you include the counterargument, however, it is important to realize that your goal is to set the stage for explaining why your view is more sound. Your job is to express your logical stance strongly, not to waste time tearing down the opposition. Effective arguing keeps the focus on your view, not the opponent's. No argument will appear persuasive if you spend more time on attacking the other side than on constructing a solid logical framework for your side. Check your primary focus to make sure you include the opposition, but do not make it the center of attention. If it is central, then you probably are doing a good public relations job for the opponent. Remember, your argument—not the opposing one—needs the reader's attention.

Using Persuasive Versus Slanted Language

Many people believe that persuasion means manipulating words to suit their own ends and never telling the straight story. Part of the reason for this impression is that writers often do not recognize the difference between subjective and objective prose, nor do they understand when each is appropriate. Novice writers, especially, have difficulty avoiding the urge to use dramatic language when they argue, not realizing that effective persuasion stems from a logical base, not an emotional one. Good persuasive writing gains the audience's trust by presenting both sides of the argument in a fashion that seems well considered and reasonable. Writing persuasively means knowing how to argue your position strongly while sounding objective.

For some writers, prose is either totally objective or totally subjective—aimed directly at the audience's emotions. When these people write, they are tempted to produce melodrama rather than clear argument. They load the language with emotional appeals instead of empirical logic. The following letter to the editor illustrates what happens when a writer allows emotions to run rampant through the prose:

Dear Editor:

Congressman John Smith represents the morally bankrupt segment of our society. Neither his intellect nor his glibness can hide what is at the core of this sick individual.

A Concerned Citizen

In his anger, this writer has confused biased language with logical argument. Although exaggerated language may sometimes work when you argue orally, it rarely works in written form. When a person argues out loud, the entire physical personality comes into play: the voice inflections, the facial expressions, the gestures, and the sheer physical presence of the arguer. These physical elements of drama are not available on the page. For most readers, consciously emotive writing seems ludicrous—even in passages such as the following one where the writer tips just barely into melodrama:

The global environment is in peril. Forests are being stripped, stressed, and burned. Lands once arable are yielding to desert. The atmosphere is under assault. Wetlands are vanishing. The oceans are being choked with pollution and fished beyond sustainable levels. We are disturbing the climate and decimating the species.

If the writer had revised this paragraph by removing "stressed and burned," "choked," and "decimating the species," his opinion would seem more reasonable and more trustworthy. But as it stands, the combined effect of so many emotional words undercuts the seriousness of the author's point.

It is also true that when readers become aware that you are intentionally appealing to emotion, they wonder why you need to do it. They want to know why you don't let your argument stand on its own logic. In cases where your emotional prose replaces logic, or even where it overshadows it, you have reached the limits of emotional appeal. Keep in mind that these limits are easy to reach. It is usually better to keep your dramatic language in check rather than give it free rein.

This is not to say that emotions should play no part in persuasive writing. On the contrary, skillful use of emotional appeal in language can create a highly effective argument. To master this technique, you must maintain the audience's trust throughout the argument. The first step toward gaining this trust is to indicate that you have faith in the audience. If your argument is well reasoned, intelligent readers will see the logic. But if you rely on slanted emotional language, the readers may realize the ploy and feel insulted that you would try such propaganda on them. That realization is fatal to persuasive argument.

Try this test yourself. Read the following sentence and monitor your reactions:

> Congressman Johnson slithered off to retirement in the ooze of Louisiana—a slimy politician returning to the state that spawned him.

How do you feel about the soundness of that statement? Do you naturally rise to Johnson's defense? Would you trust the author to present a carefully reasoned point of view? When confronted with such obviously slanted language, most readers feel the need to argue the opposite side of the issue simply because they sense that the writer is being unfair.

Given these cautions about the dangers of slanted language, how can writers use language to persuade fairly?

Put yourself in the reader's place. If you read a one-sided argument, you are naturally going to mistrust it. But if all the facts and all sides are clearly represented—even if one side is advocated—you are more likely to believe the argument because you think the writer has nothing to hide. For example, consider this preliminary paragraph from a study of intelligent computers:

> Many people share the belief that computers are inherently stupid, and that even a suggestion that computers might be made smarter is ridiculous. This belief is so widespread that most people—scientists as well as laymen—never even consider the many ways in which smarter computers might help them. Misconceptions about a computer's limitations seem to be based upon two widely accepted but basically untrue premises. Let us examine these myths in turn. By pointing out some of their fallacies, perhaps I can open your mind to the fascinating prospects for smarter computers.
> —*Bertram Raphael,* The Thinking Computer

Because Raphael's language appears straightforwardly objective, and because he clearly states his preferences, you are probably more inclined to trust his argument than you would the author of the Congressman Johnson sentence. Raphael seems confident that his ideas will stand the test of audience scrutiny, even when they are placed next to other opinions. By presenting them with such apparent confidence and honesty, he has made it much more likely that readers will agree with him.

On the other hand, heavy-handed persuasion signals weak logic that needs such disguise to be convincing. Check the balance between persuasive words and straightforward logic in your own work. You should acknowledge the reader's talent for knowing when you are using manipulative diction instead of allowing the argument's own merits to do the convincing. In almost every instance, it is clear when the writer lacks confidence in the material because the argument seems rigged and the manipulative techniques are paramount.

In the following two versions of the same set of facts, note how the writers skillfully appeal to readers' emotions without resorting to melodrama or blatantly manipulative prose. As you read, see if you can determine which passage was written by Revere's attorney and which by the opponent.

Passage 1

While looking for available apartments, as a result of the landlord's express invitation, Mr. Revere went through an open door at the rear of the first floor foyer, which, he believed, led to common passageways and other apartments available for rent. Unknown to him, there was a large unguarded and unlighted hole in the floor near the open door. Mr. Revere took several cautious steps in search of a light switch. Immediately beyond a partially finished wall, Mr. Revere fell into the unguarded hole, sustaining serious disabling leg injuries.

Passage 2

At the rear of the foyer, an unfinished plywood door normally kept padlocked by the contractor during nonworking hours led to the first floor space that was still under renovation for commercial use. On the night of the plaintiff's accident, he left the second floor party and groped into an unlighted area beyond the plywood door, allegedly in search of an "available" apartment. After proceeding several steps in the dark, Revere came to an unfinished stud wall through which he stepped. After a few more steps into the darkness, Revere fell into an unguarded opening in the floor. Revere sustained personal injuries in the fall.

Obviously, word choice plays an immense role in how the audience perceives the situation. In the first version, the plaintiff's account, Revere takes cautious steps to find the light switch, implying a very short distance traveled and a sensible action. In the defendant's version, Revere gropes through obviously unfinished walls and continues irrationally through the darkness until he falls into the hole. Each writer has taken the facts and has featured elements differently to create a more positive view of the client. Note the words and phrases that elicit emotional responses from the readers: *grope,* for instance, reflects negatively on Revere, whereas *took cautious steps* is a positive statement. In the first passage the plaintiff is addressed as "Mr." Revere; in the second, he is called simply "Revere." But in neither version are the facts so slanted or the emotions so overbearing that the reader cannot understand the actual happenings or make intelligent decisions.

Rather than relying on propaganda, the effective writer emphasizes the argument's positive themes by subtly weaving them through the text in convincing designs. Even sentence structure contributes to the subtle persuasiveness. In the first passage above, the initial sentence begins with phrases that establish a justifiable context for Revere's actions. "While looking for available apartments, as a result of the landlord's express invitation" subtly wins the reader's sympathy for the information presented in the final part of the sentence, "Mr. Revere went through an open door." The writer uses the same technique again in the following sentence when he says, "Unknown to him" before describing the dangerous hole. By beginning with phrases favorable to the client, the writer leads the audience to view the action described at the end as justifiable and to sympathize with Revere's plight. These same techniques appear in the second passage as well, but turn the audience's sympathies away from Revere. "At the rear of the foyer, an unfinished plywood door normally kept padlocked" sets a different context for the plaintiff's actions. A reasonable man would not have stepped through a "stud wall" and, "after proceeding several steps in the dark" fall into a hole. In this version, Revere seems to have acted foolishly.

These examples illustrate how writers can use individual words and sentence structures to persuade the reader. Beyond the sentence-level techniques are other opportunities to carry subtle emotional appeal throughout the prose: the use of persuasive themes and equivalence chains.

Persuasive Themes and Equivalence Chains

A writer of prose can learn something from the Beethovens of this world. Think of your prose as a musical composition in which several melodic lines repeat, eliciting an emotional response from the listener. The more complicated the composition, the more the composer depends on the repeating themes to tie the piece together. Maybe you won't equal the great Fifth Symphony, but as a writer you can define these themes and weave them into your argument.

The first step is to understand the relationship between thesis and theme. The *thesis* is the main point you are trying to argue: for instance, that abortion is every woman's right or that housing discrimination is wrong. The *theme,* on the other hand, is a motif established by orchestrated connotative language that reinforces the thesis. Theme differs from thesis in that theme relies on inference and suggested meaning rather than on direct statement. For example, a thesis might be that nuclear power serves the interests of the industrialists rather than the people. Throughout the argument expressing this idea, the writer uses words and phrases that paint a picture of greedy, power-mongering industrialists controlling the country from behind the scenes. In the following example, the words that create this theme are highlighted:

> Why is there such a strong bias in favor of nuclear power in certain industries and in the Federal Government despite the grave dangers it entails? The **great oil companies now control** the mining and processing of uranium, the source of nuclear power, and expect to **profit** from it long after the oil is gone. General Electric, Westinghouse and two other companies make practically all the nuclear power plant equipment, and hope to **make a good thing** of it. Many utility companies have planned to make an **ever-increasing portion** of their **profits** from nuclear power. The utilities in turn are **largely owned and controlled** by the **most powerful** banks in the country. So there is **strong industrial and financial pressure** for nuclear power. And since our Presidents, governors and legislators **depend mainly on industry** for their campaign funds, they are **obligated** to listen to industry's wishes.
> —Benjamin Spock, *"A Statement of Nuclear Energy"*

As this example shows, the theme is created by the aggregate effect of so many connotative words. This technique can go a step further if writers set up a chain of synonyms for a word that reinforces the thesis. By repeating these synonymous (or "equivalent") words at strategic locations throughout the argument, you both continually emphasize your main point and create a sense of coherence to the discourse that it otherwise would not have. These "equivalence chains" rivet the prose together while subtly creating persuasive contexts for your ideas.

Here is another example. Note how the writer uses a collection of similar words to create an equivalence chain that links the prose implicitly to the central idea. The important words are highlighted:

> The late 1920s were an age of coteries. They were a time when many of the larger social groups, especially those based on residence in a good suburb or membership in a country club, were losing their cohesiveness. Always at dances there were smaller groups that gathered with a confidential air—"Let's get together after the crowd goes home," one heard them say. Prosperous Americans, especially the younger married people, but some of the older ones too, had begun to form cliques or sets that disregarded the conventions. Each of the little sets had its gin parties and private jokes, each had its illusion of being free, sophisticated and set apart from the mass that believed in Rotarian ideals—till slowly each group discovered that it had dozens of counterparts in every big American city. In those days, almost everyone seemed to be looking for an island, and escape from the mass was becoming a mass movement.
> —*Malcolm Cowley,* Exile's Return

To develop effective equivalence chains, you should begin by writing down your thesis in a concise sentence. Then, list a series of possible themes that might serve to persuade the readers that your thesis is correct. Under each theme, think of synonyms that carry the thematic message, and use these words liberally in your argument. Be careful not to use the same word excessively—remember that subtlety is key to this technique's success.

Here is an example of the process:

Thesis:	Abortion is an undeniable right for all women.
Possible Theme:	Abortion laws deny our religious freedom.
Equivalence Chain:	coerce, restrict, freedom, force, violate rights, and so on.

Now look at the equivalence chain at work in an actual argument:

> Those opposed to abortion seek to ban it for everyone in society. Their position is thus coercive in that it would restrict the religious freedom of others and their right to make a free moral choice. In contrast, the legalized abortion viewpoint is non-coercive. No one would think of forcing anyone to undergo an abortion or forcing doctors to perform the procedure when it violates their consciences. Where abortion is legal, everyone is free to live by her or his religious and moral principles.
> —*John D. Rockefeller, "No Retreat on Abortion"*

Remember, the whole idea of persuasion is to influence the audience without seeming to try hard to do it. Once readers become aware of your attempts to manipulate their thinking, your task of persuading becomes twice as hard. If overdone, persuasive language can turn from a strength into a weakness. Once again, the appeal must be to thought—to rational strength—not to unthinking, emotional response.

PRACTICE EXERCISE 9.5

Circle the thematic words in the following passages and determine if they are used appropriately or if they are overdone. There may be more than one theme present in one passage.

> "Refrigerators are just boxes with motors," said General Motors boss Billy Durant in 1918, justifying his decision to plunge the car maker into the appliance business, "and that's what we already make." No wonder, then, that Frigidaires soon looked like cars: swollen bulks of sheet metal appliqued with strips and bulges of chrome, and equipped with control panels that looked like dashboards. Designer Henry Dreyfuss spoke of kitchen appliances that "give you the feeling you could climb in and drive away." To keep up, General Electric was even forced to encase its beloved Monitor Top refrigerator—the Model T of the industry—in a streamlined body.
> —*Phil Patton, "Are My Appliances Showing?" Esquire, July 1989*

> Most people who bother with the matter at all would admit that the English language is in a bad way, but it is generally assumed that we cannot by conscious action do anything about it. Our civilization is decadent and our language—so the argument runs—must inevitably share in the general collapse. It follows that any struggle against the abuse of language is a sentimental archaism, like preferring candles to electric light or hansom cabs to aeroplanes. Underneath this lies the half-conscious belief that language is a natural outgrowth and not an instrument which we shape for our own purposes.
> —*George Orwell, "Politics and the English Language"*

> Despite the fact that the case against cigarette smoking has by no means been proven, the tobacco industry has in recent years suffered a notable degree of harassment: It has stopped advertising cigarettes on television. It has had to print on its packs the flat assertion that smoking "is dangerous" to one's health. We have seen effective and often very creative antismoking ads. Some magazines won't accept cigarette advertising. Some periodicals

won't publish articles which tend to exonerate tobacco. Aboard commercial airlines and on interstate trains and buses, it is not only permissible to segregate smokers; it is federally mandated. (Smokers usually have to sit in the back of the plane where there is more engine noise and more chance of being served a cold meal.) Recent law suits have sought to ban smoking in the New Orleans Superdome and to limit it in federal office buildings. And sales and excise taxes, particularly at state and local levels, have climbed to the sumptuary point in many places.
—*James Council, "The Case for Tobacco"*

When we say that all human beings, whatever their race, creed or sex, are equal, what is it we are asserting? Those who wish to defend a hierarchical inegalitarian society have often pointed out that by whatever test we choose, it simply is not true that all humans are equal. Like it or not, we must face the fact that humans come in different shapes and sizes; they come with differing moral capacities, differing intellectual abilities, differing amounts of benevolent feeling and sensitivity to the needs of others, differing abilities to communicate effectively, and differing capacities to experience pleasure or pain. In short, if the demand for equality were based on the actual equality of all human beings, we would have to stop demanding equality. It would be an unjustifiable demand.
—*Peter Singer, "All Animals are Equal"*

Re-vision—the act of looking back, of seeing with fresh eyes, of entering an old text from a new critical direction—is for us more than a chapter in cultural history: it is an act of survival. Until we can understand the assumptions in which we are drenched we cannot know ourselves. And this drive to self-knowledge, for woman, is more than a search for identity: it is part of her refusal of the destructiveness of male-dominated society. A radical critique of literature, feminist in its impulse would take the work first of all as a clue to how we live, how we have been living, how we have been led to imagine ourselves, how our language has trapped as well as liberated us; and how we can begin to see— and therefore live—afresh. A change in the concept of sexual identity is essential if we are not going to see the old political order reassert itself in every new revolution. We need to know the writing of the past, and know it differently than we have ever known it; not to pass on tradition but to break its hold over us.
—*Adrienne Rich, "When We Dead Awaken: Writing as Re-Vision"*

Democracy requires critical thinking. Almost everyone agrees that the ability to read and write should be a fundamental human right extended to everyone. We understand that a person who cannot read is in thrall to those who can. You cannot enter the developed world as a full human subject unless you can break and master the code of the word. Today, literacy doesn't stop with words and numbers. To enter social and political debates as a full participant one must also break the thrall of the magic box and master its secrets. If we fail to adopt media literacy—a basic knowledge of how and why media images are chosen—as an essential goal of public cultural policy, we doom ourselves to be forever in the grip of the powerful interests who own and control the mass media.

> —*Don Adams, Arlene Goldbard, "Steal This TV: How Media Literacy Can Change the World"*

Aristotle once said that rhetoric is the art of finding all available means of persuasion. For writers who want to argue well, Aristotle's words ring especially true: Finding available *means* of persuasion suggests that there are techniques at work behind every well-formulated argument and that a familiarity with these available methods can give writers an edge when they need their own prose to be convincing. Understanding how to persuade is really an understanding of the many possible approaches to argument and knowing when to use them.

FOCUS ON

Your Writing Project

1. Write a letter on behalf of a specific group. The letter should advocate the group's rights or make some sort of special plea for them. The audience may be a person, an agency, a company, or another group that is in a position to act on the matter.

2. Write a paper in which you argue a specific side of an issue that you have strong feelings about. Attach a cover sheet to the front of the paper, objectively stating both your point of view and that of the opposition. Make sure these views are stated fairly enough that your opponents would agree with your statement of their position.

The Writing Group

This exercise requires a classroom environment with an even number of writing groups.

Step 1:   Choose one or more issues of immediate interest to the participants.

Step 2:   Assign one side of an issue to one group and the opposite side to another. If you have more than two groups, use different issues for each pair of groups.

Step 3:   Allow enough time for the groups to research the topic and write a group paper arguing their side of the issue. This may mean several group meetings outside of class, and the members will have to write the paper jointly. You may want to use storyboarding techniques and other group methods given in the previous chapters to help with this collaborative effort.

Step 4:   Distribute copies of the finished papers to the whole class.

Step 5:   Have each group present its case orally in a fifteen-minute panel presentation. (Adjust the time to fit your situation.)

Step 6:   Based on the papers and the presentations, the class members outside of either group decide which side is more persuasive. If you have only two groups, try to find an impartial observer to make the final decision.

Appendix I

Common Grammar and Punctuation Problems

Twenty-five years ago, a struggling British graduate student in a Harris tweed sports jacket, I came to a great university on the American Middle West, to teach a course called freshman composition. I soon found that the healthy corn-fed products of American education in my classes had emerged from high school short of basic language skills, in vocabulary, expression, grammar and syntax. . . .

Happily, American know-how had already found the way out of this linguistic poverty trap. Cunning educators had devised the Six Gross Illiteracies—six fundamental grammatical misdemeanors that earned an automatic "F" on any student theme. I recall them well. There was the Violation of Fundamental Concord or Agreement ("Many a successful corporation president owes their success to our efforts.") and the Mixed Construction ("Longfellow's poetry is different from Tennyson."). There was the Fused Sentence ("The train was late, he missed his plane."). And the Comma Splice ("He told me about it, I did not believe him."). There was also the Unjustifiable Sentence Fragment ("He was the only one present who did not drink. Being the son of a minister.") and there was the Incredible Dangling Modifier ("If thoroughly stewed, the patients will enjoy our prunes.").

We young instructors enforced this basic grammatical rule book with unflinching severity—to the dismay of the football coach, I recall.

—*Malcolm Bradbury, "Speaking the Prince's English"*

Long past freshman composition, even the best writers find themselves occasionally tangled in unforgivable grammatical constructions. Although Bradbury's list is rudimentary, what follows is a collection of common problems that plague writers long after they have mastered the basic writing tools. You may find this quick reference list of the more "advanced" syntax and punctuation trouble spots helpful as you untangle contorted sentences in the writing and revising process.

Problems with Phrases and Clauses

Misplaced modifiers and dangling phrases (number 6 on Bradbury's list) become a problem when you are trying to fit a lot of information into one sentence. As you squeeze more material into each of your sentences by compacting it into phrases, you run the risk of separating that material from what it is supposed to modify. The result is often contrary to your intended meaning. For example, a well-meaning writer once wrote, "Being in a crib, my family and I traveled the West." What he meant, of course, was that *he* was in the crib, not his entire family. But the resulting sentence suggests an overcrowded, tiny bed motoring through Wyoming and Colorado.

A modifying element, whether it is a phrase or a single word, always refers to what is closest to it. The phrase "being in a crib" describes the noun that appears right after the comma: "my family." If the writer had said, "Being in a crib, I traveled the West with my family" the reference would be more clear. An even better way to avoid this problem is to change the dangling phrase into a subordinate clause by inserting the noun: "When I was still in a crib, my family and I traveled the West."

A similar difficulty occurs with misplaced adverbs. If the adverb comes next to the wrong word, the meaning of the sentence changes: "The police nearly questioned everyone" or "The police questioned nearly everyone"—which is the correct version? Simply by moving the word *nearly* one word over, the writer has created a completely new idea.

It is easy to see these errors in isolated textbook exercises. But in the heat of composing your own prose, dangling phrases and misplaced modifiers often escape notice—as this sentence illustrates. According to the preceding sentence, the phrases and modifiers are responsible for composing your prose; you are not. A revised version might read, "In the heat of composing your own prose, you often fail to notice dangling phrases and modifiers." That puts the appropriate reference closest to the modifying phrase, correcting the error.

> *Rule:* Modifying elements refer to the word closest to them. To avoid ambiguity, make sure the referent is appropriate and clear.

PRACTICE EXERCISE A.1

Revise the dangling phrases and misplaced modifiers in these sentences.

1. After determining the location, dimensions, and orientation of the tank, the concrete pavement above it was marked, cut, and removed.

2. We will analyze samples provided by you with a Photovac 10s series gas chromatograph to determine precision, accuracy, and method detection limits for the compounds of interest.

3. Based on my recent visit in April, it is my understanding that initially the health assessment work will be awarded in the form of Cooperative Agreements.

4. The computers we use in the transfer of massive amounts of information daily saves the company at least five hours of work time.

5. As a minor water power project, there is a minimum consultation period of thirty days for the Seabass Dam engineering group.

6. I only edited this essay superficially.

7. The device can be used to either add, subtract, or divide.

8. The scarf I keep around my neck, which is tied in a loose knot, is the height of fashion.

9. When considering the rhetorical function of style, it is imperative to understand the correlation between form and substance.

10. Speaking as an English teacher, it pains me to hear you dangle your participles.

Parallel Structure

One way to make your writing easier to read is to craft sentences whose parts are balanced and whose form reflects their content. If you compose each sentence so that two or more elements sharing coordinate relationships are structured the same way, your prose will be much easier to read. Caesar's words were "Veni, vidi, vici" (I came, I saw, I conquered"), not "I came, I saw, I was a conqueror." In keeping the coordinate elements of the sentence parallel in structure, he achieved a balance that increased the power and clarity of his words. When you write, you may be faced with more information than fits comfortably in such short sentences. The longer the sentence, the more important it is to keep the components parallel so that the reader does not get lost in your prose's shifting directions. For example, this sentence contains a lot of information presented in a confusing fashion:

> Would the defendant's frequent communications with Rayman, that she gave specific directions to hire and fire, the fact that she controlled the renovation work and the material used allow a jury to conclude that Nelson Rayman was her employee?

When placed in parallel structure, the sentence reads much more clearly:

> Would the defendant's frequent communications with Rayman, her specific directions to hire and fire, her control of the renovations, and her provision of the work materials allow a jury to conclude that Nelson Rayman was her employee?

> *Rule:* Sentence elements that share coordinate relationships should share the same grammatical structure.

PRACTICE EXERCISE A.2

Each of the following passages contains information that can be better presented in parallel form. Reconstruct each passage accordingly, using appropriate parallelism.

1. No warning notices were posted, and the defendant also omitted adequate precautions.

2. The administration will keep a daily log showing the petty cash balance, the amounts that have been disbursed, and when a travel and expense voucher has been completed.

3. In order to meet the job requirements, it became clear that management should invest in a networked system of personal computers. Networked PCs are compact and easy to use. They can be programmed for specific tasks and can be used for a wide variety of financial applications. These networked computers are capable of connecting every employee to a central information base. Especially important is the speed with which these machines can perform.

4. Researchers have discovered that the number of deaths from heart disease is plummeting for reasons that are far from completely clear. Most responsible for the drop is the use of preventive measures. These include attention to a better diet and a decrease in cigarette smoking. Many people who would have been candidates for heart disease in the past are now seeking early treatment for high blood pressure. Adding to the health regimen is the fact that people exercise more these days than they did in the past. Other important reasons for the decreased number of deaths are medical and surgical therapies for heart patients once the disease has been discovered.

5. The modern combine is a marvel of engineering that has taken over the role of the 40-mule hitch that pulled farmers' machinery 150 years ago. It is so efficient that it reduces the number of times corn or soybeans or wheat has to be handled to get it from the fields into the silo to an all-in-one operation. In the past, every child in those immense farm families had an exhaustive and repetitive job to perform during the harvest season. The combine has eliminated the need for that. And the farm wife has gained reprieve from preparing huge meals for a crew of hungry hands, and she also no longer must haul water out to the fields during the harvesting.

6. As is evident from his books, author Thomas McGuane likes dogs and horses. In addition, his love of golf and his fondness for the road, Indians, and hawks make their way into his tales, as do his penchant for peppery food and outdoor sex. His characters are often loony old men, though he also includes many characters who are women with sharp tongues; the protagonists usually face high stakes and have dangerous male friends. The novels are set in Key West, Fla., or in Deadrock, Mont.

Consistent Verb Tenses

> I lived like the Puri Indians of whom it is said that "for yesterday, today, and tomorrow they have only one word, and they express the variety of meaning by pointing backward for yesterday, forward for tomorrow, and overhead for the passing day."
> —*Henry David Thoreau,* Walden

Even at the advanced level, writers run into difficulty with verbs, especially forms of the past tense. Time has so many dimensions that it is problematic to express exactly the right relationships when you are writing about actions that occurred at various times in the past. For example, here are two simple statements:

> I changed jobs five months ago.
> I work at Fidelity Investments now.

Suppose you want to combine these two ideas into one sentence using only one verb. How could you do it? What about, "I have worked at Fidelity Investments for five months"? The *present perfect* tense of the verb expresses exactly what you mean because it tells of an action begun in the past and continuing to the present day. But the present perfect can also indicate an action completed at some recent indefinite time: "I have finished the project." On the other hand, if a specific past time is indicated, you would use the simple *past tense,* "I finished the project yesterday," instead of the present perfect, "have finished."

In some instances, you need to deal with two or more actions that occurred in the past but at different times:

> I came to Fidelity Investments in January.
> My boss started work there the previous October.

Whenever two or more past actions are discussed together, and some of them precede the others, use the *past perfect tense* (*had* plus the past participle of the verb) to indicate the actions that came first: "I came to Fidelity Investments in January, but my boss had started work there the previous October." Or "When I arrived, my boss had been there three months."

The present tense is less problematic, although some writers can become confused in their use of the "historical present." The "historical present" refers to an action that continues to happen or always happens in specific situations. For example, "At the end of *Gone*

With the Wind, Rhett Butler turns to Scarlett O'Hara and says, 'Frankly, my dear, I don't give a damn.'" The use of *turns* and *says* instead of *turned* and *said* is appropriate because these actions happen every time the movie plays; they are not fixed actions occurring only one time in the past. The same is true for sentences such as this one: "The play *Macbeth* illustrates what happens when ambition takes over a person's life." But note that if the sentence refers to the author's action instead of the play, the past tense is more appropriate: "When he wrote *Macbeth,* Shakespeare illustrated what happens when ambition takes over a person's life."

> *Rules:* Use the present tense for actions occurring at the present moment. Use it also for actions that happen in books, movies, poems, and so on.
>
> Use the past tense for actions occurring at a definite time before the present moment.
>
> Use the future tense for action occurring at some time beyond the present moment.
>
> Use the present perfect for actions begun in the past and continuing through the present, or for actions performed in the recent indefinite past.
>
> Use the past perfect for actions beginning and ending in the past or to indicate the action that came first when two or more past actions are discussed together.
>
> Use the future perfect for action continuing to a fixed moment in the future.

PRACTICE EXERCISE A.3

In the sentences that follow, use the appropriate tense of the verbs in parentheses.

1. The H-Canyon facility at the Chico River Plant (recover) plutonium from irradiated uranium. The Chico River Laboratory (prepare) a Safety Analysis Report for the H-Canyon facility. As part of the analysis, this report (document) the results of a chemical hazard assessment we (conduct) for the cold feed chemicals used at H-Canyon. This analysis (focus) on the exposure of workers and the general public to toxic or harmful vapors that may be released during seven plausible accident scenarios and one catastrophic event.

2. A transfer error (occur) when the piping to a tank (be) not properly connected and a large volume of a chemical (release).

3. I (be) never to see a polo match. My friend, Susan, who (see) one last Saturday, (stop) not talking about how much she (enjoy) it. So I (make) up my mind to go to a match as soon as I can.

4. The Defense Department (deny) today that there (be) conclusive evidence that their testing of nuclear weapons (have) harmful effects on local residents.

5. A recent study at the University of Texas (refine) Smith's approach to textual analysis to identify one aspect of the use of "ethos" in proposal writing. The study first (expand) Smith's method of textual analysis by enlarging the sample size. Whereas Smith (work) with small samples of 100 words, this study (focus) on 1000-word samples. An "ethos" index (develop) from a comparison of requests for proposals (RFPs) on the low end of the scale, and from samples of motivational sales and positive thinking texts on the high end.

Colons and Semicolons

Colons and semicolons are not interchangeable; they have totally different functions. Whereas colons usually introduce the completion of a thought, semicolons are used primarily to indicate breaks between complete thoughts. Nonetheless, many writers confuse the two, causing reader frustration along the way.

A semicolon has two primary uses: to separate phrases in a series when the individual phrases contain commas, and to set off clauses in a compound sentence. Note how the following sentence illustrates the confusion that may result if writers ignore the first rule:

> The winners of the vintage Mustang convertibles are Thomas King, Hopewell, Pennsylvania, Kathy Harris, Springfield, Illinois, Carol Hoffmann, Red Bluff, Montana, and Scott Jackson, New York, New York.

But look at the difference semicolons make as they separate the phrases that contain so many commas:

> The winners of the vintage Mustang convertibles are Thomas King, Hopewell, Pennsylvania; Kathy Harris, Springfield, Illinois; Carol

Hoffmann, Red Bluff, Montana; and Scott Jackson, New York, New York.

In addition to serving as clear dividers for phrases containing commas, semicolons serve as a kind of fulcrum, balancing two complete thoughts on either side of it. For instance, here are two thoughts that can be written three different ways:

Power corrupts; absolute power corrupts absolutely.

Power corrupts. Absolute power corrupts absolutely.

Power corrupts, and absolute power corrupts absolutely.

The first version probably expresses the thoughts most powerfully, with the semicolon used to connect the two independent clauses while simultaneously indicating how carefully balanced they are— the one reflecting the other. Paradoxically, the semicolon in this instance is used to separate (and at the same, connect) two or more closely related thoughts when a comma or a period would weaken the effect.

A colon, on the other hand, announces that the completion of a thought is to follow. You can use a colon in two primary ways: to introduce the rest of your thought dramatically or to introduce quoted material. For instance:

All the forecasters say the same thing: We are headed for a recession. [It is optional to capitalize the first word after a colon when a complete sentence follows.]

I can think of only one word for him: *idiot*.

The job requires the following tools: screwdriver, hammer, electric drill.

The sign posted by the construction site said: "DANGER! No Trespassing!"

One word of caution: Don't use a colon after a verb to introduce items in a list. Write "The necessary tools are screwdriver, hammer, and nails" not "The necessary tools are: screwdriver, hammer, and nails." In the latter sentence, the colon unnecessarily separates the verb from its object. If you think you need a colon to emphasize a list, insert the word *following* or a similar noun, or separate the items into tabulated form:

The necessary tools are the following: screwdriver, hammer, and nails.

The necessary tools are these: screwdriver, hammer, and nails.

The necessary tools are:
- screwdriver
- hammer
- nails

[Note that punctuation between the items and at the end of the tabulated list is optional. If the items listed are in sentence form, punctuation is appropriate; otherwise, it is superfluous.]

Rules: Use semicolons:

  —to separate phrases containing commas
  —to separate related independent clauses

 Use colons:

  —to introduce a word, phrase, or clause that completes a
   thought
  —to introduce quoted material

PRACTICE EXERCISE A.4

Punctuate these sentences, using colons and semicolons correctly:

1. The following procedures are necessary

  Carefully ease the drill downward
  Remove drilled bushing from the drill fixture
  Inspect for absence of flaring

2. There was no clear answer to the question how could we compete against such state-of-the-art equipment?

3. Knowledge without commitment is wasteful commitment without knowledge is dangerous.

4. The Blue Parrot presents Sept. 28, 8:30 P.M., Ed Trickett, $6, Sept. 29–30, 8 and 10:30 P.M., Oct. 1, 8 P.M. Tony Bird and Chuck Hall, $8.50. Oct. 4, 8:30 P.M., Chris Shaw and Bridget Ball, $6, Oct. 5, 8:30 P.M., Peter Keane, $5.50.

5. The phenomenon of Man represents nothing less than a general transformation of the earth, by the establishment at its surface of a new layer, the thinking layer, more vibrant and more conducive, in a sense, than all metal, more mobile than all fluid, more expansive than all vapor.

Punctuating Quotations

Punctuation with quotation marks is difficult at best, but a few simple tips can make the task easier.

> *Rules:* Use single quotation marks to denote a quotation within a quotation.
>
> Periods and commas always go inside quotation marks.
>
> Colons and semicolons always go outside quotation marks.
>
> Question marks and exclamation points go inside or outside quotation marks, depending on their use in the sentence.

The first three rules are easy and need little explanation. In fact, a few examples will suffice:

He said, "I love the saying 'The road to Hell is paved with good intentions.'"

He loved the admonition "The road to Hell is paved with good intentions."

"The road to Hell is paved with good intentions," he loved to say.

He loved to say, "The road to Hell is paved with good intentions"; he never followed his own admonition.

Three people in the room are especially vulnerable to his admonition, "The road to Hell is paved with good intentions": Joe Elton, Ben DiAngelo, and Sherry Connors.

The more difficult rules are those for question marks and exclamation points. When you write, determine where to put the punctuation by its function in the sentence. If the material within the quotes is a question, then put the question mark inside; if the quoted material is not a question, but the entire sentence is, put the mark outside. The same principles apply to exclamation points. For example:

In a rage, he shouted, "Who is responsible for this?"
[The quotation is a question.]

Did he shout, "Who is responsible for this?"
[The quotation and the sentence are questions. One question mark inside the quotations serves both the sentence and the quote.]

Did he shout, "I'll find out who is responsible for this"?
[The sentence is a question, but the quotation is not; put the question mark outside the quotes.]

He shouted, "Who is responsible for erasing my videotape of 'I Love Lucy'?"
['I Love Lucy' is not a question, but the rest of quotation is; put the question mark between the single and the double quotation marks.]

PRACTICE EXERCISE A.5

Punctuate these sentences correctly:

1. "A nation of immigrants" "the open door policy" "my brother's keeper" "fortress America" "isolationism" "bigotry"—these are only a few of the verbal blockages to independent thought.

2. Nine members of the Kennedy Institute for the Study of Human Reproduction and Bioethics commented on your May 2 editorial, "Who Shall Make the Ultimate Decision"

3. We can visualize some of the slogans as brightly colored banners: "Dislodge Big Money" "Power of the People" "Save This Nation from Evil Forces" "The Choice Is Yours"

4. This paragraph, said James B. Minor, a lawyer who teaches courses in legal drafting, is how a Federal regulation writer would probably write, Give us our daily bread.

5. Noel Perrin, essayist and professor of English at Dartmouth College, has written, Why cross-country skiing and snowmobiling reflect class lines so perfectly is not easy to figure out. Certainly it is not a conscious act of group loyalty. No one says, Hm, I run the town dump, so I'd better get a snow machine, or Well, I was a Wellesley drop out; I need some knickers and a pair of Finnish touring skis.

These are just a few of the grammar and punctuation problems that can snag you and slow you down as you write. Most writers have personal lists of their own trouble spots—areas where they continue to run into problems or constructions that remain mysterious even after lengthy explanations. If that is true for you, make sure you are aware of these recurring problems, and check your work for them after you have completed a rough draft. Take some time to jot down the things you have trouble with. Keep the list handy when you write so that it can serve as a reminder to you to edit the text for those particular items and to have someone else who has a better eye for those problems look over the prose as well. The more you know about your weaknesses, the easier it is for you to correct them before your writing is made public.

In the end, when you are wondering if all this attention to mechanics is worth it, remember these words:

> Punctuation, to most people, is a set of arbitrary and rather silly rules you find in printer's style books and in the back pages of school grammars. Few people realize that it is the most important single device for making things easier to read.
> —*Rudolf Flesch,* The Art of Plain Talk

Appendix II

Sample Answers to Selected Practice Exercises

Practice Exercise 7.3

3. Consider the cellular car phone—an alarmingly visible symptom of the pathetic size increase in Americans' egos. It is the unabashed symbol of self importance. It rivals BMWs, Rolexes, fax machines, and the *Wall Street Journal* as the most essential item for expressing pretentious airs to the general public. Its antennae have been sprouting fast.

Practice Exercise 7.4

1. Given that the two cases are similar, we can appropriately apply a standard similar to the *Lynch* case.
4. To be sure that all employees comply with the following procedure, Accounts Payable will not process invoices without an attached purchase order.

Practice Exercise 7.5

2. After discussing it at length, we decided that this is the preferred format.
3. John S., convicted of growing marijuana in his backyard, objected that the airplane search violated his right to be free from unwarranted police searches.

Practice Exercise 7.6

3. The Department is obligated to pay the Grantee only for the expenditures and noncancellable obligations s/he has incurred before s/he receives Departmental notice of termination.

6. Because the workers in the meat wholesaler's district depend on this bank, the public interest requires that this branch remain open.

Practice Exercise 9.5

"Refrigerators are just boxes with motors," said General Motors boss Billy Durant in 1918, justifying his decision to plunge the car maker into the appliance business, "and that's what we already make." No wonder, then, that Frigidaires soon looked like cars: swollen bulks of sheet metal appliqued with strips and bulges of chrome, and equipped with control panels that looked like dashboards. Designer Henry Dreyfuss spoke of kitchen appliances that "give you the feeling you could climb in and drive away." To keep up, General Electric was even forced to encase its beloved Monitor Top refrigerator—the Model T of the industry—in a streamlined body.

Democracy requires critical thinking. Almost everyone agrees that the ability to read and write should be a fundamental human right extended to everyone. We understand that a person who cannot read is in thrall to those who can. You cannot enter the developed world as a full human subject unless you can break and master the code of the word. Today, literacy doesn't stop with words and numbers. To enter social and political debates as a full participant, one must also break the thrall of the magic box and master its secrets. If we fail to adopt media literacy—a basic knowledge of how and why media images are chosen—as an essential goal of public cultural policy, we doom ourselves to be forever in the grip of the powerful interests who own and control the mass media.

—*Don Adams, Arlene Goldbard, "Steal This TV: How Media Literacy Can Change the World"*

Practice Exercise A.1

1. After the engineers determined the location, dimensions, and orientation of the tank, they marked, cut and removed the concrete above it.

2. If you provide us with samples, we will analyze them with a Photvac 10s series gas chromatograph to determine precision, accuracy, and method detection limits for the compounds of interest.

10. Speaking as an English teacher, I am pained to hear you dangle your participles.

Practice Exercise A.2

2. The administration will keep a daily log showing the petty cash balance, the amounts that have been dispursed, and the time of completion for travel and expense vouchers.

3. It became clear that, in order to meet job requirements, the management should invest in a networked system of personal computers. Networked PCs are compact, speedy, easy to use, easy to program, useful for a wide variety of financial applications, and capable of connecting every employee to a central information base.

Practice Exercise A.3

2. A transfer error occurs when the piping to a tank is not properly connected and a large volume of a chemical is released.

5. A recent study at the University of Texas refines Smith's approach to textual analysis to identify one aspect of the use of "ethos" in proposal writing. The study first expands Smith's method of textual analysis by enlarging the sample size. Whereas Smith worked with small samples of 100 words, this study focuses on 1000-word samples. An "ethos" index develops from a comparison of requests for proposals (RFPs) on the low end of the scale, and from samples of motivational sales and positive thinking texts on the high end.

Practice Exercise A.4

1. The following procedures are necessary:

   Carefully ease the drill downward.
   Remove drilled bushing from the drill fixture.
   Inspect for absence of flaring.

   OR

   The following procedures are necessary: Carefully ease the drill downward, remove drilled bushing from the drill fixture, and inspect for absence of flaring.

5. The phenomenon of Man represents nothing less than a general transformation of the earth, by the establishment at its surface of a new layer, the thinking layer, more vibrant and more conductive, in a sense, than all metal; more mobile than all fluid; more expansive than all vapor.

Practice Exercise A.5

4. "This paragraph," said James B. Minor, a lawyer who teaches courses in legal drafting, "is how a Federal regulation writer would probably write, 'Give us our daily bread.'"

5. Noel Perrin, essayist and professor of English at Dartmouth College, has written, "Why cross-country skiing and snowmobiling reflect class lines so perfectly is not easy to figure out. Certainly it is not a conscious act of group loyalty. No one says, 'Hm, I run the town dump, so I'd better get a snow machine,' or 'Well, I was a Wellesley drop out; I need some knickers and a pair of Finnish touring skis.'"

Index